CROMWELL

Cromwell

A PROFILE

Edited by Ivan Roots

WORLD PROFILES

General Editor: Aïda DiPace Donald

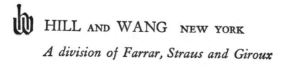 HILL AND WANG NEW YORK

A division of Farrar, Straus and Giroux

For Tegwyn
For . . . everything

The portrait of Oliver Cromwell was done in 1657 by Edward Mascall and is used by the kind permission of the Cromwell Museum, Huntingdon, England

Contents

Introduction

OLIVER CROMWELL (1599–1658) is among the best known of Englishmen as well as one of the least understood. Everything about him excites curiosity and controversy—his character, his intentions, his impact on his age—so that even after three hundred years, interpretations of him can stir up the embers of the English Civil Wars. To draw a complete profile of this extraordinary man is, in effect, to reconstruct an image of his entire era—a virtually impossible task.

We can, nevertheless, learn a great deal about Oliver Cromwell. We know more than a little of his day-to-day activities and journeyings, especially after 1642, when he began to emerge from comparative obscurity. Much of his correspondence, personal and official, survives, and there are acceptable versions of many of his public utterances and of some of his private conversations. A number of men—men who served with him or against him, in politics or in the field, who hated him or loved him—have left their impressions. Some even sought an objective assessment of him. We also have the views of poets such as Milton, Marvell, Dryden, and Waller—all of them thoughtful and intelligent observers who, like Cromwell himself, had had "somewhat to do in the world." Portraits of him exist (a few, like Robert Walker's, authentic) as well as life and death masks and what may well be his mummified, posthumously tortured head. (His remains were dug up during the Restoration, reviled, and cast into an unmarked grave at Tyburn, in a futile gesture at consigning him to oblivion.) Many anecdotes and a few songs have passed into folklore. In addition there is an enormous historical literature, much of it ephemeral, or scurrilous, but some the work of able scholars. (It is commented upon by D. H. Pennington in the essay printed below, which was written to commemorate the tercentenary in 1958 of Cromwell's death.) Yet we do not have a really satisfactory, much less a definitive, biography. The best, that of Sir Charles Firth, appeared as long ago as 1900. The most recent (1970), by Christopher Hill (a chapter of which, "Providence and Oliver Cromwell," forms part of this Profile), though brilliant and perceptive, is hardly a biography at all, but a collection of more or less discrete studies. It may be said of Oliver Cromwell: "Others abide our question; thou art free."

The formidable ambiguities and subtle ironies of Marvell's *An Horatian Ode on Cromwell's Return from Ireland* are no greater than those of the subject himself. Cromwell was inconsistent and ambivalent, diffuse and contradictory. His expression, though often direct and concrete, even epigrammatic, could be obscure and, perhaps deliberately, opaque. Obviously no man's motives can be taken at their face value. Pascal wrote, probably in Cromwell's lifetime, that the heart has its reasons which reason does not know. We can only glimpse the processes by which he settled on a particular action or withdrawal during the numerous crises of his career. Moreover, precisely what part he played in many of the episodes associated with his name cannot always be determined. There is a "cloud of detractions" lowering over his every move or moment of inertia. Even Marvell, who clearly admired him, thought that the trial and execution of the King (January 30, 1649) were the outcome of a Machiavellian plot, "twining subtile fears with hope," set off by "the wars and fortune's son." Yet the evidence we can at present assemble suggests strongly that Cromwell was in no way a party to Pride's Purge (December 12, 1648), the first step, that he was slow to back a trial and was a very late convert indeed to the notion of deposition and execution. Once resolved, however, he was vital in the action, and there is an elated almost hysterical air about his efforts to get signatures to the death warrant. So far from making bullets for other men to fire, Cromwell took them from others and then either threw them away or fired them himself. Thus he was not the initiator of Cornet Joyce's removal of the King from Holdenby House (June 3, 1647), but once it had happened he acquiesced in it and worked to exploit its possibilities; to what end is an open question.

The Barebone's Parliament six years later (June–December 1653) was not of his own devising, nor was the Instrument of Government (December 12, 1653), which established him as Lord Protector. Major General John Lambert was the true if not the only begetter of that constitution, and later betrayed in Parliament an author's sensitivity at criticism of it. The Heads of the Proposals (July 1647), the forerunner of the Instrument, had been the work not so much of Oliver as of his clearheaded son-in-law Henry Ireton, whom he obviously respected, and, again, of Lambert. The system, if it can be called that, of the major generals (May 1655–January 1657)—"a little, poor invention" was Cromwell's own phrase for it —was not conceived by the Protector but merely blessed by him. His interest in it was not passionate, and he was slow and stingy in his response to requests from individual major generals for letters of comfort or commiseration. When it failed he dropped it without a qualm. When, on February 27, 1657, a group of army officers protested to him about the introduction in the Commons of "the paper" which later became the Humble Petition and Advice (May 25, 1657), he in his turn complained that *they* had made *him* their "drudge upon all occasions." His claim that he was not a party to the drafting of the new constitution rings true enough. But the Humble Petition, which in its original form proposed the kingship which he rejected, certainly emanated from among his own entourage, from a group of men whose diversity of origin and outlook, civilian and military, points up the complexity of the Protector's own make-up. Cromwell was never an out-and-out military man, and civilian, particularly parliamentary, solutions to problems always appealed to him. This aspect of him was attractive to men of a political cast of mind, like Lord Broghill and Nathaniel Fiennes, and helps to account for their backing of him during the Protectorate. They at least could visualize him on a throne without a sword in his hand, surrounded by courtiers— kinglings, they were called—very much like themselves. For his part, Cromwell leaned toward them more and more as he grew older, more tired, and disappointed in old army associates like Lambert, whose personal ambition he also distrusted, and Harrison, whose messianic expectations Cromwell shared only fitfully and shallowly. Their suggestions failed to produce a settlement; indeed, they seemed to retard it. Not surprisingly, he turned to more practical and conservative men outside the army who showed themselves ready to be the servants of his kind of state.

H. R. Trevor-Roper, in his chapter in this Profile, says bluntly that Cromwell never initiated anything. If this is true—and there is too much to support it—then his genius must have lain elsewhere. Cromwell was surely "a man of opportunity." Such men can create opportunities for themselves or wait for them to arise, or by a touch here and there keep things ticking over until the right moment arrives, divined by themselves or advised by others. In fact, such men—like most men—are inclined to act on advice only when it coincides with their own assessment. Cromwell was certainly an opportunist, but not a simple one, rather one who worked indefatigably to hold things in train, listening carefully but without fuss to others. He would ponder, seemingly passive. He would hear the voice of God, feel the prod of Providence, and at last—sometimes almost too late it seemed to less intuitive, more impatient men—would rouse himself to action. No doubt he could have behaved in no other way, but it is difficult to imagine a more effective method of focusing attention on himself, of assuring his indispensability. It was hard-going, tense, draining, demanding, but it helped to make Cromwell a "grandee" and a great man.

Carlyle may have had Cromwell in mind when he defined genius as "a transcendent capacity of taking trouble."

Cromwell might have been, as Dryden said, "great ere fortune made him so," but he had also to achieve greatness and have it thrust upon him. Before the Civil War there was little to suggest that he would be anything more than "some village Cromwell guiltless of his country's blood." The episode in 1636 that apparently won him the soubriquet "Lord of the Fens" was well known only in a failing local community, among commoners from whom he would later enlist some of his troopers. Otherwise, during this period he was Carlyle's "most private quiet man." The collapse of "the eleven years' tyranny" was none of his doing, though he must have detested "Thorough," Laud's version more perhaps than Strafford's. His parliamentary career, begun as member for his native Huntingdon in 1628–29 and continued, for Cambridge town, in both the Short and Long Parliaments, was undistinguished before 1642. He really was then, in Trevor-Roper's disparaging phrase, "a natural back-bencher," sparkling only for a moment in November 1640 on behalf of John Lilburne, who had not yet become a Leveller. That he was close at this time to his kinsmen John Hampden and Oliver St. John and to John Pym, the leader of the onslaught on "the personal government," is not apparent. In fact, his promotion of the divisive Root-and-Branch bill in March 1641 at a time when Pym was anxiously reinforcing the fragile unity of the Commons to secure the nullification of Strafford by impeachment, suggests a remoteness from central counsels and perhaps a lack, from inexperience, of political acumen. It was the coming of war by August 1642 that gave Oliver his first real chance to shine, and that was not in Parliament. While "King Pym" laid down the foundations of an administrative and financial machine that would survive his untimely death in December 1643, Cromwell was getting on with the war as a cavalry colonel in East Anglia and, as Marvell has it, by "industrious valour" urging "his active star" "through adventure's war."

Civil wars, like family squabbles, are perplexing, at once superficial and deep-seated, hard to analyze not least by those directly involved, who can find themselves pushed into inexplicable positions. Cromwell was not the only one of the contestants to baffle friend and foe. Charles I, young Sir Harry Vane, George Monck, all are, like Napoleon III, enigmas. All, unlike Napoleon III, do seem to have had a genuine secret. Cromwell's secret was an intuitive capacity to win friends and influence people, and equally to make enemies of old friends and friends of old enemies. The twists in his relationship with John Lilburne are illuminating, pointing up his pragmatism, flexibility, and readiness to let bygones be bygones. Another quality, his capacity to compel attention without shouting at the top of his voice, was demonstrated early in the war, by his correspondence, in those sometimes long, sometimes short, but always superb letters, that can still move us today. To the Mayor and Corporation of Colchester he wrote in March 1643:

> . . . I beseech you, therefore, consider this gentleman and the soldiers; and if it be possible, make up his company a hundred-and-twenty; and send them away with what expectation is possible. It may, through God's blessing, prove very happy. One month's pay may prove all your trouble. I speak to wise men— God direct you. I rest
>
> Yours to serve you
Oliver Cromwell.

This was the man who would trust in God to keep his powder dry by seeing himself that it was kept dry. That attitude would bring him through skirmishes and pitched battles to the notorious "quarrel" with Manchester over how to wage war, from the formation of the New Model Army (another of his non-inventions) to the far-ranging Putney Debates and the restoration of army discipline, from the second Civil War to the cutting off of the King's head, through the reduction of Ireland and Scotland to the ejection of the Rump, from the euphoria of the revolution of the Saints to the weary realism of the last days of the Protectorate, ending bleakly in 1658, on September 3, his "lucky day." Through it all, his greatness, inherent and acquired, is formidably present, as is revealed directly or obliquely in the essays that have been brought together in this volume. They cover a range of vital aspects of Cromwell and his world, but, aptly, with diversity in approaches and in conclusions. Each essay sketches in or highlights a feature in the Profile.

Some additional observations may be made here. First, there is little in this volume about the younger Cromwell, before his forties and the century's forties. Some reasons for this have already been given. What little is known is not enough to produce a satisfactory article on, say, "The Conversion of Oliver Cromwell." To elucidate that episode at all, we have to speculate that it must have been something like the kind of experience described by contemporaries in their "spiritual autobiographies"—there were many of these— or retailed at second or third hand in funeral sermons, notoriously unreliable sources. Cromwell's own often-quoted letter about it (October 13, 1638) boasts how "I lived in and loved darkness, and hated light; I was a chief, the chief of sinners." That does not tell us much, and even so acute a historian as Michael Waltzer—in his *The Revolution of the Saints* (1965), where one might expect to find a great deal about this Cromwell—can make little of it. We are left guessing, too, at the disturbed man who contemplated starting off anew in the howling wildness across the Atlantic.

Second, a good deal of the comment here, particularly perhaps in the articles on industrial and foreign policies but in all of the others as well, is not centered on Cromwell himself. This confirms what I have already touched upon. Much that was labeled Cromwell's by hasty contemporaries or that still runs in his name in popular memory or imagination was not his at all. He received the blame or the credit for the work of other men, some quite unconnected with him, others spurred into action by him. Often enough, having set them off, he would leave things to them. Few of the ruins he is reported to have "knocked about a bit" have any genuine association with him. Of the countless churches in which they say he stabled his horses, hardly one was even visited by him. The history of English iconoclasm in fact owes far more to the Reformation than to the Interregnum, and in general the sixteenth century was more virulent in destruction than the seventeenth. The name Cromwell was and is still merely a convenient peg to hang a hatred or a prejudice upon, in a way a form of tribute.

There is sadly but necessarily a dearth of articles on particular aspects of Cromwell; we have many biographies but very few specialized studies. For example, I am unaware of any scholarly article that closely analyzes Cromwell's political philosophy on the lines, say, of Carl Becker's article on Thomas Jefferson's in Merrill D. Peterson's volume, *Thomas Jefferson: A Profile* (1967), in the American Profile series. The fact is that Cromwell did not have a consistent or coherent political philosophy. What he did in politics he did, and that can only be traced in the full record of his words and actions over two decades. He was not, though he was accused of being, Hobbesian or Machiavellian; he was Cromwellian. He said, and we can see that it was true, that he knew better what he did not want than what he did. So far, so good, but in practice he changed his mind about what he did not want as often as he changed his shirt. As occasion demanded, or as it seemed appropriate to him, he rose above or sank below the few simple principles he occasionally mentioned, almost *en passant,* though, like Lloyd George, no doubt "he meant them, how he meant them at the time!" At Reading, in July 1647, he said, "that which you have by force I look upon as nothing." This seems at first an odd remark from the advocate of a vigorous, even aggressive, "win-the-war" effort in both the first and the second Civil War, to say nothing of the campaigns in Ireland and Scotland. But the informed student of Cromwell, like Cromwell himself, can take it in his stride, as he can his decision in the spring of 1649 to destroy Levellerism by cutting the Levellers in pieces. Of course, it exasperated the men of tauter principles about him—the Thomas Harrisons and Edmund Ludlows. But then, they irritated him. Moreover, they were no more successful than he was.

Did Cromwell have a foreign policy? This is a question we must ask even before considering whether what went on in foreign relations in the 1650s was basically Protestant or imperialistic, Elizabethan or forward-looking. If it was all or any of these, was it Cromwell's own? How much was the effect of the enterprise of Secretary John Thurloe rather than of the intention of the Protector himself? Roger Crabtree's comprehensive article brings out many of the difficulties in the way of a clear and balanced interpretation. The questions remain, and in this area as in so many others of the 1650s, there is much for the biographer and the historian to explore. Again, did Cromwell have a plan for Ireland? "The curse of Cromwell" has hung over that "most distressful country" ever since the Drogheda massacre (September 1649), for which he was certainly responsible, though he was willing that "God alone have all the glory." But the so-called Cromwellian settlement which followed was left largely to his successors there, Ireton, Ludlow, Fleetwood, and the Protector's own son Henry, who corresponded more with Secretary Thurloe than with his father. Each of these very different men made his personal contribution within a framework of conciliar advice on the spot, of orders from England, and of an old tradition of English attitudes toward Ireland, which would survive the Protectorate, the Restoration, the Williamite settlement, and beyond. If there was a novelty in the 1650s, it was sustained military vigor, to which Cromwell, certainly as Protector, gave very little personal attention. Much the same may be said of "Cromwell and Legal Reform," "Cromwell and Social Policy," "Cromwell and Local Government," or almost any other topic that the historian cares to take up. Even "Cromwell and His Parliaments," so brilliantly explored here by H. R. Trevor-Roper, is in some ways an unproductive theme. So, too, is the feature that one might imagine to be the most emphatic of all: "Cromwell and Religion," considered over a wide spectrum in the chapter from Christopher Hill's *God's Englishman* printed below.

Was Cromwell a Calvinist? It is a convenient label but one which can be misleading, for it is capable of a fairly strict definition. "Religion," Oliver Cromwell tells us, "was not the thing at first contested for" in the Civil Wars, but "God gave it to us by way of redundancy." (It has been cogently argued that by "religion" here he probably meant "religious toleration.") Was Cromwell's own religion a redundancy? Was his stand for religious toleration—as firm, it seems, as anything in his career—an effect of deep religious feelings or of indifference? Clearly he could think it possible that he himself might be mistaken about men and their things, including their relationship with God. He was not "wedded or glued" to forms of government, whether of church or state. This rather splendid quality made him a seeker among seekers, aware at once of the individuality of others and of his own, capable of responding to men as diverse as Lilburne and Owen, Ireton and Vane. It explains why another emphatic personality, George Fox, warmed in spite of himself to the Lord Protector.

There may be a danger in probing Oliver Cromwell too far. He seems like an eye, "this sleek and seeing ball, which but a prick will make no eye at all." But what is both curious and comforting is that in fact he has survived all demonstrations of how little he really did. After about 1647, his contemporaries, friends and enemies, could not be indifferent to him. To make him a king or to assassinate him were aims which paid a realistic tribute to his unique personality, position, and achievements. His signature, always recognizable, whether firm and dashing in the 1640s or slow and shaky in the 1650s, is indelible upon those two astonishing decades. "Our chief of men," Milton called him. Where in the seventeenth century is his rival?

IVAN ROOTS

The University of Exeter
May 1973

Oliver Cromwell
1599-1658

O LIVER CROMWELL was born of a well-connected East
Anglian family at Huntingdon on April 25, 1599. He was
educated at the local grammar school and at Sidney Sussex College in Puritan Cambridge. In 1620 he married Elizabeth Bouchier,
a city merchant's daughter. The marriage, evidently a happy one,
produced nine children. Oliver sat without distinction in the Parliament of 1628–29. During the personal government of Charles I
(1629–40), he underwent the spiritual upheaval known to Puritans as "conversion." In 1640 he was elected for Cambridge borough to the Short and then to the Long Parliament. At the beginning of the Civil War in late 1642, he raised a cavalry troop and
soon acquired a reputation in East Anglia as an aggressive and
successful campaigner. By 1644 he was lieutenant general in the
Earl of Manchester's Eastern Association army. The Parliamentary

victory at Marston Moor (July 2, 1644) owed much to him and his Ironsides. He supported the formation of the New Model Army and he became second-in-command to Sir Thomas Fairfax, fighting at Naseby (June 14, 1645), which determined the outcome of the Civil War. He busied himself in parliamentary and army politics and negotiated with the King before the second Civil War in 1648, in the course of which he reduced Wales and northern England. After Pride's Purge (December 12, 1648) he came to support the trial and execution of "that man of blood, Charles Stuart." In the service of the Commonwealth he waged a ruthless campaign in Ireland (1649–50) and defeated the Scots supporting Charles II at Dunbar (September 3, 1650) and again at Worcester (September 3, 1651). In April 1653 he expelled the Rump of the Long Parliament and on December 12, on the resignation of the Barebone's Parliament, accepted office as Lord Protector of England, Scotland, and Ireland under a written constitution called the Instrument of Government. His first Parliament failed to join him in "healing and settling" and was brusquely dismissed in January 1655. In 1655 he sent an expedition to the West Indies and captured Jamaica. Soon, in alliance with France, he fought a successful war with Spain in the Netherlands (1656–58). He refused the offer of kingship from his second Parliament but accepted a more conservative constitution in the Humble Petition and Advice (May 1657). Parliament, however, proved again inimical and he dismissed it in February 1658. The last months of his life saw repression at home and victory (the battle of the Dunes, June 4, 1658) abroad. He died on September 3, 1658, having named his son Richard to be Protector. Richard resigned in May 1659 and, after a period of near-anarchy, Charles II was restored on the initiative of George Monck, Cromwell's commander in Scotland.

CROMWELL

ERNEST BARKER

The Achievement of
Oliver Cromwell

WHEN ALL IS SAID, and when all allowances have been made, it remains impossible to explain the achievement of Cromwell in any simple political terms, whether of the unification of the United Kingdom, or of colonial expansion and imperial policy, or of both. The unification and the expansion were both incidental: they were both by-products, naturally enough thrown out, of great motions of the human mind and the stirring of great events which had other intentions and purposes. Those motions, and that stirring, had produced two civil wars, which lasted from the summer of 1642 to the autumn of 1651. In the course of these civil wars two things, both unprojected and unforeseen, had happened. In the first place all the three

From Ernest Barker: *Oliver Cromwell and the English People*. Copyright 1937. Reprinted by permission of Cambridge University Press.

countries—England, Scotland, and Ireland—had been involved. The end of the struggle necessarily entailed a new settlement of their relations; and that settlement, which was not originally in debate but had been afterward drawn into debate, was necessarily made by the victor in debate; and necessarily made on the basis of a unified system, congruous with his own ecclesiastical and political ideas. It was an inevitable result; but it was as unintended as it was inevitable, and it proved to be as temporary as it was unintended. In the second place, the Civil Wars, in the course of their long duration, had raised questions of foreign policy—questions of the relations of the British Isles to other powers and the outer world. There had been threats of intervention during the wars; there was still the fear of intervention when they ended. Moreover, they had produced a military and a naval force unparalleled before in English history and unparalleled for long years afterward—a drilled and disciplined army, which numbered 60,000 foot, horse, and dragoons by the beginning of the Protectorate; and a navy vastly increased in strength and vastly improved in the quality of its officers and men. Fear was thus backed by force; and fear and force, guided by a religious crusading sentiment which was curiously mixed with a Hebraic nationalism (itself mixed, in its turn, with calculations of territorial conquest and commercial gain), issued in war with Spain. But this again was an aftermath and a by-product in the history of the Puritan Revolution and in the evolution of Oliver Cromwell. It was not an original part of the great struggle of his public life. It came at the end, in the winter of his years; and this is one of the cases in which we cannot judge by the end. We shall judge him better if we remember that at the end of the first Civil War, in the winter of 1646-47, he was seriously thinking of leaving England, with such soldiers as he could gather, to fight with the German Calvinists in the Thirty Years' War.

This brings us to the real core of Cromwell's achievement and his essential significance in the history of his country. He was the incarnation—perhaps the greatest England has had—of the genius of English Nonconformity, which is the peculiar and (it may even be said) the cardinal factor in the general development of

English politics and English national life. He was the expression of the great Free Church movement which runs through English modern history, and therefore, fundamentally—because the two things are intimately and irrevocably interconnected—he was also the expression of what I would call the great Free State movement which also runs through English history. This is a deep and solemn thesis, which demands explanation; which needs qualification; but which, in the last resort and the general account, commands its own justification.

When Cromwell appeared on the scene, at the end of 1641, the current and dominant notion in England was the notion that a single political society was, and ought to be, a single religious society. It was a notion inherited from the Middle Ages, with the one difference that, while the Middle Ages had believed that a single *universal* political society involved a single universal religious society, seventeenth-century England believed that a single *national* political society involved a single national religious society. This was, in effect, a doctrine of religious territorialism. We may also call it a doctrine of the equivalence of *populus, respublica,* and *ecclesia;* or, if we prefer the English terms used by Hooker, a doctrine of the equivalence of people, commonwealth, and Church; or, if we use German terms, a doctrine of the equivalence of *Volk, Staat,* and *Kirche.* Now in 1641 there were two schools of opinion which both accepted this doctrine, but nonetheless differed from one another. There were the Anglicans, who believed that all England should be a single Anglican Church, episcopally governed, and following a modified form of the old medieval ritual. There were the Presbyterians or Calvinists, who believed that all England should be a single Presbyterian Church, governed by presbyteries and synods of presbyteries, and following the new ritual of Geneva. These two schools, differing in spite of their common premise, not only differed on religious issues: they also differed in politics. The Anglicans, who found room for the King, in the system of episcopal government, as the supreme governor of the Church, were Royalists. The Presbyterians, who found room for a General Assembly, in the system of Presbyterian government, as the final authority of the Church, were Parliamentarians. But between them both, or over and above them both, there remained a *tertium quid*. This was the Independents; in other words, the members of the Free Churches; in other words again—to mention their two great main varieties—the Congregationalists and the Baptists. The essence of their position was that they denied what I have called the doctrine of equivalence, which was accepted by both the Anglicans and the Presbyterians. They did *not* believe that a single political society was, or ought to be, a single religious society. They did *not* profess the doctrine of religious territorialism. They were essentially and literally Nonconformists. They believed that any voluntary society of Christian men and women, in any area or neighborhood in which they were gathered together, should be free to form their own congregation and to constitute their own Free Church.

This was a cardinal tenet which lay at the heart of Cromwell's thought and vitally affected the development of England during his lifetime and for generations afterward. It had large and general consequences. One of these consequences was the idea and practice of the limited state. According to this tenet, a political society had not the right to require and impose the pattern of a single religious society, corresponding to its own image, or to demand a uniform system of ecclesiastical government and religious ritual. Liberty of conscience and liberty of worship were fundamentals; and no human authority could defeat them or abridge them. This was a great and pregnant consequence; and it might, and it ultimately did, widen out further issues—the issue, for example, of free trade, or again that of free labor, to both of which something of a religious consecration came to be attached by virtue of the original and seminal idea of the Free Church.[1] So great, and so potent, was the genius of Independent Nonconformity. But there was also another consequence of the cardinal

1. The Liberal Party, the party of free trade, was also the party of Nonconformity in its heyday; and "the Nonconformist Conscience" (a term of derision, like the term "Puritan" in its original usage, but a term of derision which turns to praise) attached a peculiar consecration to the doctrine of free trade. The Labour Party, which may be termed the party of free labor (devoted to the rights and the liberties of the trade unions), has drawn many of its leaders from the circles of the Free Churches; and the cause of the free churchman and that of the free "tradesman" (in the sense in which the term is still used colloquially in northern England) have obvious analogies and sympathies.

tenet of the Free Church. This was the idea and practice of the democratic state, dependent on the principle of free association and based on the deliberate thought of all its members, collected by due process of discussion and reduced, by that process, to the unity of a common sense. If the Independents did not desire a church after the image of the state, they came to require a state after the image of the church—that is to say, of their own Free Church. Just as the religious congregation was to be freely constituted and governed, and to wait upon God until it discovered the common "sense of the meeting" and thereby knew His way of righteousness, so the political association was also to be freely constituted and governed, and it too was to wait on the movement of the human spirit, going this way and that in discussion, until it too discovered a common sense and thereby knew the way of human justice and peace.

These were ideas which seethed in the mind of Cromwell and the minds of his brother Independents, and which they sought to realize in the hour of victory—in the years from 1653 to 1658, when both the Anglican Royalists, who stood for episcopacy and the divine right of the King, and the Presbyterian Parliamentarians, who stood for presbyteries and the sovereign right of a small and exclusive Parliament, had been defeated by the issue of the two Civil Wars. But that very phrase, "the hour of victory," reveals a great paradox in the history of the Independents, which was also the paradox of Cromwell's life and achievement. In its very nature the cause of the Free Church is not victorious, and has no hour of victory; it is a protest and a challenge to an alien majority. It is the cause of a struggling minority—protesting, challenging, resisting. It is the cause of an Antigone, face to face with Creon and his edicts. When Antigone becomes Creon— when the resister himself is armed with the powers and resources of the state—there is an inherent paradox, or rather dualism, in his position. This dualism or paradox becomes all the more evident when we reflect that the strength of Cromwell, and of his Independent adherents, lay from first to last in the army. Cromwell began his effective career as a colonel of cavalry. He became, in 1645, lieutenant general of the whole army opposed to the

King: he became, in 1650, its general. He was an army leader, carried by the army on its shoulders into control when the army became, at the end of the wars, the residuary victor in the struggle —when the King had been executed, in January 1649, and when the small and exclusive Parliament, which stood for its privilege no less stiffly than the King for his prerogative, had been evicted in April 1653. It is true that the army was a remarkable and unparalleled army; and that in two ways. Largely under the influence of Cromwell, who when he first began to raise a troop of cavalry had insisted on having around him honest godfearing men, it was an army penetrated through and through by the spirit of Independency—an army which assembled in meeting for prayer on the eve of any great issue, and would stop to sing a short psalm even in the heat and passion of battle.[2] It was also an army penetrated by a democratic spirit—an army which held itself to be a great primary assembly of the people as well as a great congregation of the faithful. It had known, in its day, what we should nowadays call soviets of soldiers (they were then called agitators or agents of the regiments): it continued to know debates, projects of constitutions, discussions of Englishmen's rights and duties. . . . But it was an army nonetheless. It gave its general a world of trouble. But he was its general; and he held it together as long as he lived.

This standing Free Church army (not all Free Church, for in its early days it had contained a number of pressed or conscripted soldiers, and in its later days it contained a number who followed the wars as an ordinary profession; but still predominantly Free Church) is a standing curiosity in English history, as its memory was a standing fear to later generations. Normally the Free Churches have stood away from the army: normally the army has stood in connection with the Crown and the Established Church, to which it then stood opposed. But these were revolutionary times; and this army was a revolutionary, and therefore abnormal, thing. It was a wedding of two different ideals—the ideal of the

2. During the battle of Dunbar, on the morning of September 3, 1650, " 'the Lord-General made a halt, and sang the Hundred-and-seventeenth Psalm.' " But he halted only till the horse could gather for the pursuit; and the Hundred-and-seventeenth Psalm is a psalm of two verses only.

voluntary life in things temporal as well as spiritual: the ideal of the life which is schooled, regimented, and drilled. The army in which these ideals were wedded believed in a free England, the home of free churchmanship and corresponding free citizenship; and yet it was constrained to hold England down by virtue of its very beliefs. After all, it was a minority. In that it was true to the general genius of its cause, which in the general run of English history has been the cause of a struggling minority. But it was a minority which for the time being held the sword, and possessed might, majesty, dominion, and power. It faced the majority boldly, but with a division in its heart, enforcing liberty, and yet disbelieving in force. The contradiction could not last; and it did not last. But there was nothing ignoble, and nothing common or mean, in all the contradiction, and all the wrestlings and strivings, which vexed in their hour of victory the general body of Independents, the Independent army which was their core, and "the great Independent," Oliver the Protector (not unfitly so called), who was summoned by a heavy and exacting destiny to reconcile the principles of the cause he led with the urgent needs of national healing and settling.

The sole and ultimate responsibility of Cromwell, and the great period of his life by which his achievement and significance must ultimately be judged, belong to the five and a half years which lie between the eviction of Parliament in April 1653 and his death in September 1658.[3] True, he had been the dynamic and driving force for at least half a dozen years earlier, in every crisis of

3. It is curious to reflect that the space of five and a half years was also the space given to Julius Caesar. Mommsen, in a famous passage of his *History of Rome* (IV, 557, in the English translation), remarks: "Caesar ruled as King of Rome for five years and a half, not half as long as Alexander; in the intervals of seven great campaigns, which allowed him to stay not more than fifteen months altogether in the capital of his empire, he regulated the destinies of the world for the present and the future. . . . Thus he worked and created, as never any mortal did before or after him; and as a worker and creator he still, after well-nigh two thousand years, lives in the memory of the nations." Cromwell's five years and a half were more pedestrian; and they were years uninterrupted by campaigns. But it would be curious to compare the fundamental significance of the five and a half years from 49 to 44 B.C. with that of the five and a half years from A.D. 1653 to 1658. Perhaps the balance would not tilt all on one side.

events. If any man won the war against the Royalists, it was he.
If any man was responsible for the execution of the King, it was
he. If any man left a mark upon Ireland—and a cruel mark at
that—it was he. But the real test came when—the war won, the
King dead, Ireland and Scotland reduced, and Parliament finally
evicted—he and his army stood, at last, face to face with the final
burden of decision. Fighting was over: the time for the short,
sharp shrift of the sword was gone: the time had come for facing
an opposition in peace, and by the methods of peace. The opposition was numerous—far more numerous than the government—
and though it was various and divided, its different sections were
gradually beginning to coalesce. On the extreme right stood the
Royalists and Anglicans: on the moderate right (but still on the
right) there were some who were Presbyterian Parliamentarians,
and some who were plain Parliamentarians, clinging to the notion of a traditional and historic constitution of which a historic
Parliament was a necessary and essential ingredient. The right in
general, which carried with it the instincts of the country, was
the side of civilianism in the face of military rule: it was the
side of traditionalism; it was also, because that was part of the
tradition, the side of religious uniformity. But there was also a
left, which went far beyond Cromwell and the main body of the
Independents. There were political Levellers, or radicals, who had
a passion for the sovereignty of the people, manhood suffrage,
the natural rights of man, and the whole of the full-fledged doctrine of revolutionary democracy which emerged in France in
1789. There were also the social Levellers—men who would be
called today Communists, but who confined their communism,
as was natural in an agrarian age, to an attack on property in
land, and to the assertion that "the Earth is the Lord's, not particular men's who claim a proper interest in it above others."
The social Levellers were few; but in raising the issue of private
property, and in pressing it against the general and captains of
the Independent army, they brought out a fact which must not be
forgotten. Cromwell and the men with whom he worked were
themselves, in many respects, innovators and radicals. But on the
point of property they too were traditional and conservative. The

doctrine of the Free Churches did not entail any social program, or any new distribution of property.

In the face of this opposition Cromwell stood, first and foremost, as he had always stood, for religious liberty. He stood for the idea and practice of the limited state, which did not enforce religious uniformity, but was bound by the "fundamental" of respecting Christian freedom of conscience and Christian freedom of worship. This meant an ensured and guaranteed toleration, obligatory on the state, and superior to the state, which thus became, under the compulsion of an overriding principle of religious liberty, the home of varied forms of belief living in a common peace and interacting on one another in a mutual influence. But the toleration which was thus to proceed from the nature of a limited state was a toleration sadly and drastically limited in its own nature. Bound by the spirit of their own belief, which would only recognize as "true religion" the Protestant form of religion, and only the more Protestant form of that form, Cromwell and his associates in the Free Churches could not tolerate Anglicanism, and far less Roman Catholicism. Both prelacy and popery lay beyond the pale. This was a large and sweeping exception to the principle of religious liberty—so large and so sweeping that it may seem, at any rate to our own age, to negate the principle. We have to remember that the initial range of the application of any principle is small, and will gradually grow with the benefit of time and the widening of men's minds. We have equally to remember that this principle, when it was enunciated, was a radical principle, and a flat contradiction of the current doctrine of the equivalence of people, commonwealth, and church. The fundamental principle, in spite of the sad and drastic exceptions to its application, is that a man may freely hold his belief, and freely celebrate his worship, according to the motion of his spirit, and that no earthly authority may interfere with that motion. Cromwell, like Luther, had a firm hold of the idea of the liberty of the Christian man in the inner springs of his life; and that idea carried him even farther than Luther, because it led him to deny, as Luther never did, the doctrine of religious territorialism—the doctrine of the equivalence of political and religious society. "Truly, these things do respect the souls of men, and the spirits, which are the men. The mind is the man." [4] He had stood for this idea in the first Civil War. "For brethren, in things of the mind," he had written to Parliament in 1645, "we look for no compulsion, but that of light and reason." He had stood for it in the second Civil War. "I desire from my heart," he wrote in 1648, "I have prayed for . . . union and right understanding between the godly people—Scots, English, Jews, Gentiles, Presbyterians, Anabaptists, and all." [5] He stood for it still in the system he created in the days of his power and Protectorate. Religious funds and endowments were used for the common benefit of the Presbyterian clergy and of the Independent clergy of the Congregationalist and Baptist varieties. By the side of the clergy paid from these funds and endowments there also existed clergy, of whatever variety or denomination, supported by the free offerings of their own voluntary congregations. The Quakers were a notable example of such voluntary congregations; but the sects were numerous in these tumultuous times. Even the Anglicans sometimes met, illegally but by connivance, for public worship; and though even

4. The passage deserves quotation in full. "The mind is the man. If that be kept pure, a man signifies somewhat; if not, I would very fain see what difference there is betwixt him and a beast. He hath only some activity to do some more mischief." (Speech of September 17, 1656.) This is like Goethe:

> Er nennt's Vernunft, und braucht's allein
> Nur tierischer als jedes Tier zu sein.

5. Quoted in C. H. Firth, *Oliver Cromwell and the Role of the Puritans in England* (London and New York, 1900), p. 205. The mention of the Jews deserves notice. Cromwell was personally favorable to the cause of the Jews, when they petitioned, in 1655, for freedom to reside for purposes of trade and to practice their religion. "The fierce multitude of the Jews" had been ordered to leave England by Edward I in 1290; and there had been no Jews in England, except by stealth, for three and a half centuries. In the time of the Commonwealth the Jews were beginning to settle again in London; the petition of 1655 was a petition for the legal recognition of such settlement. The petition was referred to a committee of the Council; the committee co-opted two judges; the two judges gave it as their opinion that there was no law forbidding the settlement of Jews. Nothing was done by the committee; but the opinion of the judges opened the way for the quiet and unmolested return of the Jews to England. (S. R. Gardiner, *History of the Commonwealth and Protectorate*, II, 101; IV, 11–15.)

that was denied to the Roman Catholics, there was no other persecution of their belief, nor were they dragooned into attendance at alien forms of worship by fine and punishment, as had been the case under the previous law of England.

In this qualified form there was, under Cromwell, a brief summer of religious liberty—not improperly so called when we remember the period of compulsory religious uniformity which preceded it, and the similar period which followed it when King and Church and Parliament were restored in 1660. This summer had abiding fruits. Thanks to Cromwell, as one of his biographers has said, "Nonconformity had time to take root and to grow so strong in England that the storm which followed the Restoration had no power to root it up." [6] English Nonconformity, with its doctrine of the limited state, and its aspiration toward a religious liberty which might become also a liberty in other spheres, continued to be a salt ingredient of English life, which maintained its peculiar savor and produced some of its most vital characteristics.

Religious liberty is a great thing; but there is also political liberty. It was said above that there were two consequences involved in the cardinal tenet of Independency. One of them was the idea and practice of the limited state—the state limited by the principle of religious liberty: the other was the idea and practice of the democratic state—the state based on the principle of free association and free discussion. It is plain that Cromwell stood for religious liberty and the limited state: can it also be said that he stood for political liberty and the democratic state? We must frankly confess that in Cromwell's view, as his biographer has justly said, "religious freedom was more important than political freedom." [7] Religion stood in the forefront of his thought. But that is not to say that he had no passion for any liberty other than religious liberty. There is one of his speeches, brief but pregnant, of April 3, 1657, which lets us into his mind. He speaks of "the two greatest concernments that God hath in the world." "The one is

6. Firth, *Cromwell*, p. 369.
7. *Ibid.*, p. 483.

that of religion, and of the just preservation of all the professors of it; to give them all due and just Liberty." This he calls "the more peculiar interest of God," or "the Interest of Christians." The other is "the Civil Liberty and Interest of the Nation." This is subordinate to "the Interest of Christians"; "yet it is the next best God hath given men in this world." It is also congruous with it: "if any think the Interest of Christians and the Interest of the Nation inconsistent, or two different things, I wish my soul may never enter into their secrets. . . ." "And upon these two interests . . . I shall live and die. . . . If I were asked, why I have engaged all along in the late war, I could give no answer that were not a wicked one if it did not comprehend these two ends."

These are words—noble words—but what did he actually do? In the first place, he clung to the idea of the sovereignty of a written constitution—the constitution contained in the Instrument of Government, which had been produced, at the end of 1653, by the officers of the army. *Prima facie,* a constitution produced by the officers of an army, though it may be called an instrument of government, can hardly appear to be an instrument of political liberty. Moreover, in a country which had just emerged from a civil war originally waged in the name of the sovereign rights of Parliament, a constitution not produced by Parliament, and overriding the rights of all subsequent Parliaments, may well seem unconstitutional. These things are true enough; and Cromwell was to experience their truth in the course of his struggles with Parliament. But there are also other things which are true. The army which produced the constitution, through the agency of its officers, held itself to be a great primary assembly of the people; and by a section of the people, though only by a section, it *was* held to be such an assembly. But much more fundamental is the fact that the constitution, however produced, was a check and a limit, not only upon any parliament which subsequently assembled, but also upon Cromwell. It was a check and a limit which he voluntarily embraced and steadily upheld. It was indeed a check and limit which stood in lieu of the consent of the people, freely given and freely renewed. That could not be had, when the bulk of the nation stood in opposition, whether to the right or the left. The written constitution was only a second best—a substitute for national consent. But at any rate it was something; and the idea struggling behind it, if not expressed in it—the idea of the sovereignty of a constitution made and accepted by the nation— was an idea in the true logic of genuine Independency.

In the second place, limited as he already was by a written constitution, Cromwell sought also to limit himself by the need of collaboration with Parliament. True, he had evicted a parliament —the old Parliament of the Civil Wars—at the beginning of the period of his own immediate rule. But the parliament which he evicted had become a narrow civilian oligarchy; and two months, after its eviction, even before the Instrument of Government had been evolved with its scheme of regular parliaments, he summoned a new parliament himself. After the adoption of the Instrument, two parliaments sat; and one of them held two sessions. They were not freely constituted parliaments: even so, they disagreed with Cromwell, and he with them; and they went their way. He was not a great Parliamentarian; but neither was he an autocrat. After all, he had been a member of Parliament himself, as the representative of Cambridge, from 1640 to 1653; and he never forgot this side of himself. He never deserted the forum entirely for the camp: he lived in both, and that was a great part of his greatness. He tried to live with Parliament, to work with Parliament, to reconcile a historic and traditional parliamentary system with the spirit of the Free Churches and the fact of a Free Church army. He did not succeed; but he did not desist from endeavor. He was at once inside and outside the main current of English history which makes for the sovereignty of Parliament— partly a soldier, and partly a civilian; partly a doctrinaire of the written constitution which aimed at setting religious liberty above the reach of Parliament, and partly a parliament man.

But there was always a deep trend of his nature which drew him to the side of liberty—civil and political as well as religious. He was a man of a natural vitality and vivacity—"of such a vivacity," says a contemporary, "as another man is when he hath drunken a cup of wine too much." He carried himself easily among his fellows: he had, says the same contemporary, "familiar rustic carriage with his soldiers in sporting." He did not speak much, it was noted, but he had a gift for making others speak.[8] These are only externals; but they are externals which suggest a free spirit, able and ready to move in free intercourse with others. The trend of his inward nature led him toward a deep feeling for the free motion of the free spirit. There was a sect of his time who were called Seekers, because they believed in the need of perpetual search for truth. He had a sympathy for them. "To be a Seeker," he once wrote, "is to be of the best sect next after a finder, and such an one shall every faithful humble Seeker be in the end." This may remind us of a saying of Jesus, in a papyrus found in Egypt: "Let not him that seeketh cease till he find, and when he findeth he shall wonder, and having wondered he shall reign, and having reigned he shall rest." [9] Seeking; finding; wondering; reigning; resting—these words are, in a sense, an epitome of Cromwell's earthly course. But it is the word "seeking" which is peculiarly characteristic. It suggests indeed one of his defects— his habit of seeking and waiting for some visible "evidence" from God, which made him an opportunist ready to identify the lead of events with the march of God's own providence. But it also suggests a great quality. He believed in the seeking mind. "The mind is the man. If that be kept pure, a man signifies somewhat." He believed that it was man's own business to keep the mind free. He held that it was "an unjust and unwise jealousy to deprive a man of his natural liberty upon a supposition he may abuse it: when he *doth* abuse it, judge." This implies, fundamentally, a grasp of the principle of what we may call *civil* liberty; and though there were civil liberties which he restricted, the restrictions grew less as he himself gained a freer hand, toward the close of his Protectorate, and was less tied by the control of the officers of his army. In the same way—and this is a still more important matter—Cromwell's belief in the seeking mind led him to grasp the principle of *political* liberty. We must all seek together: we must all bring together the results of our seeking; and

8. The contemporary is Baxter, quoted in Firth's *Cromwell*, p. 148. The man who noted Cromwell's gift for saying little, but making others talk, was Sir William Waller, quoted in Firth, *ibid.*, p. 119.

9. M. R. James, *The Apocryphal New Testament*, pp. 25–26.

then we must discuss together the results which we have found. This is a conception which he had already attained by the autumn of 1647, after the end of the first Civil War, and which he expressed in the earnest debates on the future of England which were then being held in the victorious army. Not only is he clear that any plan for the future of England must be such that "the spirits and temper of the nation are prepared to receive and go along with it"—a condition which, though he apprehended it, he failed himself in the event to satisfy—but he is also clear that any plan must be framed in the give and take of free discussion. This too was a condition which he failed in the event to satisfy. But it was nonetheless a condition which he had apprehended and never forgot. What a philosophic student of the debates of 1647 has written is fundamentally true. "What Cromwell has learned from his experience of the small democracy of the Christian congregation, is the insight into the purposes of life which the common life and discussion of a democratic society can give. . . . This is his position—toleration and recognition of differences . . . combined with insistence that individual views shall submit to the criticism of open discussion." [10]

But he was doomed to find that discussion was too difficult an art to practice, for the simple reason that toleration and recognition of differences were not present. The conflicting views conflicted too much to submit to mutual criticism or to be reconciled by the process of discussion. There is a story that Cromwell, on the night of the execution of Charles I, came to look at the face of his dead king, and as he looked sighed out the words, "Cruel Necessity." Cruel necessity was always upon him. He wrestles with this notion of necessity sadly in his speech of September 17,

10. A. D. Lindsay, *Essentials of Democracy*, pp. 19, 36. Cromwell's stipulation of 1647, that "the spirits and temper of the nation must be prepared to receive and go along with" any plan for the future of England, recurs again in his argument to the army in the midsummer of 1648. The agitators of the regiments were pressing for a hammer stroke of force. Cromwell pleaded for cooperation with the friendly elements in Parliament and an agreed solution. "What we and they gain in a free way is better than twice so much in a forced way, and will be more truly ours and our posterity's. . . . That you have by force I look upon as nothing. I do not know that force is to be used except we cannot get what is for the good of the kingdom without it." (Quoted in Firth, *Cromwell*, p. 169.)

1656. There has been, he confesses, for some time a military rule of different parts of England by major generals: there has been what he somewhat mildly terms "a keeping of some in prison"; there have been other things—*"which, we say, was Necessity."* He knows that this is a dangerous plea: "I confess, if Necessity be pretended, that is so much the more sin," but he pleads it nonetheless, as "a man of honest heart, engaged to God," who is lifted above pretension, and is only acting under dire and real compulsion. He pleads necessity the more readily because the notion of it, as a thing sent and imposed by God, is mixed in his mind with another notion—the notion of reformation, or, as he calls it, "Reformation of Manners." The people have sinned and gone astray: they must be recalled to God and the way of righteousness. Here the cause of Independency and the theory of the Free Church twists round, as it were, in the hands of its authors. It loses its edge of freedom: it begins to show a stern and sharp edge of compulsion, as of "the sword of the Lord and of Gideon." After all (we must always remember) the cause of Independency was also the cause of an army—a drilled and disciplined army, ready to impose drill and discipline on others as well as itself. This was the paradox or dualism always inherent in Independency and in the mind of "the great Independent" who led its cause. On the one hand freedom, and no compulsion in things of the mind. On the other hand an Old Testament passion for reformation, like that of the Hebrew prophets . . . and behind this passion an army.

Two notions—the notion of reformation, and the notion of necessity—thus conspired against the notion of civil and political liberty. Necessity imposed arbitrary taxes, called "decimations," on the property of Royalists. Necessity and reformation combined instituted the system of the twelve major generals, in twelve districts of England, who were charged both to repress political enemies and to suppress immorality. Civil liberty was restricted by the restriction of alehouses and race meetings. Political liberty was equally restricted by the same restrictions. Alehouses and race meetings were dangerous because the disaffected, and especially the Royalists, might meet there to discuss their grievances and to ventilate their criticisms. The political philosophy of Cromwell thus yielded to political exigency. He who had insisted, in the army debates of the autumn of 1647, "that individual views shall submit to the criticism of open discussion" was within a decade stifling criticism and preventing open discussion. He did not suppress the central parliament; but there was a period—the period of these major generals, who lasted from the autumn of 1655 to the spring of 1657—during which he suppressed the local discussion that sustains and underlies an effective central parliament. It was a period during which, on one occasion, he even "swore roundly" at Magna Charta itself—the traditional palladium of English liberties, in the name of which Parliament had originally resisted Charles I. The best that can be said for Cromwell is that the period was transitory. It ended with the abolition of the major generals in the spring of 1657. The last year and a half of Cromwell's life, from the spring of 1657 to the autumn of 1658, was a period of the decline of military power; of return to the civilian tradition of English life; of closer, if still imperfect, collaboration with Parliament; of less of the twin causes of necessity and reformation, and more of the cause of the civil liberty and "Interest of the Nation." We do not know what this period would have been if it had lasted. It did not last. Cromwell died.

H. W. KOCH

Cromwell's Genius

CROMWELL'S ROLE as a politician was resoundingly negative, yet his role as an outstanding military leader seems beyond dispute. In the final analysis he was the most successful military commander on either side during the Civil War. Indeed, his
military ability may well explain his failure as a politician, since
it is very rare for a man to combine brilliance in the profession of
arms with the ability, the feeling, and the knowledge of how to
manipulate politics in such a way as to obtain harmony and permanent results.

Before the wars, Cromwell was a gentleman farmer, descended
from the nephew of Thomas Cromwell, the minister of Henry
VIII. Few men realized the potential of the somewhat notorious
Member for Cambridge in the Short Parliament, known as much
for his political and religious radicalism as for his slovenly appear-

ance. But it was John Hampden who remarked "that though sloven, if we should ever come to break with the King (which God forbid) in such a case he will be one of the greatest men of England."

Though apparently devoid of any previous training and experience, Cromwell was commissioned captain in the cavalry of the Parliamentary army, commanding over sixty horsemen and noncommissioned officers. Even at this early stage Cromwell displayed the possession of those rare qualities of command and resolution which no training and grand exercises can impart. However, of more immediate and practical advantage was that he could gather around him a military clan such as his son Henry; Henry Ireton, his future son-in-law; John Hampden, his cousin; Valentine Walton, his brother-in-law; Edward Whalley, another cousin; and Lord Mandeville, later Earl of Manchester.

At the time of his appointment Cromwell was forty-three— hardly an auspicious age at which to enter upon a military career. It speaks much for Cromwell's convictions of the righteousness and belief in divine sanction for his decisions, convictions which inclined him toward sectarian Independency and determined his political and military career. Carlyle's words that "a man's religion is the chief fact with regard to him" is especially true of Cromwell, the product of an age in which religion still dominated the intellectual and social fabric of society. While one may doubt Cromwell's awareness of the complex foundations of the beliefs he held, there is little doubt that they gave him the moral strength which was his greatest asset as a military commander, as well as his ability to infuse first the men directly under his command and finally an entire army with a similar spirit.

It seems certain that out of the family clan under Cromwell's direct influence emerged the idea of a military association, and that because of this Parliament, on October 22, 1642—the day before the Battle of Edgehill—approved the formation of county defense unions. From these in turn emerged the Eastern Association of Norfolk, Suffolk, Essex, Hertfordshire, Huntingdon, and Lincolnshire centered on Cambridge, Oliver Cromwell's constituency. This rendered the eastern counties the most powerful bulwark of the Parliamentary army.

These counties provided England's first standing army. At the beginning of the Civil War no standing army existed, except in Ireland; armies were raised when the occasion arose, as for instance against the Scots. English leaders and troops participated in the Thirty Years' War on the European mainland in Dutch, French, Spanish, and German Imperial armies. Thus, despite the absence of a standing army, there were on the eve of the Civil War numerous individuals experienced in the methods of Continental warfare—particularly among the cavalry, the most important arm on the battlefield. Prince Rupert, nephew of Charles I, instilled his own experience into the Cavaliers. He taught his men to charge home at the gallop, sword in hand, and only to use their firearms once the enemy lines had been broken. Cromwell was very quick to learn from his opponent and stop the undisciplined charge and blazing away so characteristic of the early Parliamentary cavalry.

Cromwell realized instinctively the importance of morale. While the Cavaliers fought for the "King's Cause," to ask men simply to fight for Parliament and against absolutist despotism was too abstract and uninspiring. Cromwell's greatest achievement was to inspire the men under his command with his own religious convictions and to select men of his own religious persuasion for the command of his troops. Soon the latter enjoyed a high reputation for avoiding, as Baxter put it, "those disorders, mutinous plunderings and grievances of the country which debauched men in armies are commonly guilty of." The religious cause, the call for "liberty of conscience," created troops as brave, as serviceable, and as eager for victory as their opponents.

This, of course, did not manifest itself in the early engagements such as Edgehill. On the contrary, Essex's defeat by the Royalists put Parliament on the defensive and pointed to the need for thoroughgoing reform of the Parliamentary army. Although Cromwell's own role at Edgehill remains obscure, its lesson was not lost upon him. The growing prominence of the Eastern Association was a direct consequence, as was the type of officer and man in it. "You must get men of spirit," said Cromwell to Parliament according to his own testimony to Hampden, "and take it not ill what I say—I know you will not—of a spirit that is likely to go on as far

as gentlemen will go: or else you will be beaten still." In his Eastern Association he set out to create just that type of body. In the
words of an anonymous writer of a newsletter in circulation in
May 1643: "As for Colonel [which by then he had become] Cromwell, he hath 2,000 brave men, well-disciplined; no man swears but
pays his twelve pence; if he is drunk, he is set in stocks, or worse;
if one calls another roundhead he is cashiered: insomuch that the
counties where they come leap for joy of them, and come in and
join with them. How happy were it if all forces were thus disciplined."

Though evidence of this kind must be taken with a pinch of salt,
Cromwell in a series of letters during the same years emphasized,
"I beseech you to be careful what captains of Horse you choose,
what men be mounted: a few honest men are better than numbers
. . . I rather have a plain russet-coated captain of Horse that knows
what he fights for and loves what he knows, than that which you
call a gentleman, and is nothing else . . . I have a lovely company;
you would respect them. They are no Anabaptists, they are honest,
sober Christians: they expect to be used as Men!"

The first really decisive battle was fought on July 2, 1644, at
Marston Moor. It was brought to a successful conclusion for Parliament primarily because of Cromwell's skillful handling of his
cavalry, the men of the Eastern Association, whom he had trained
the previous autumn and winter. It was also the battle which raised
his name to national pre-eminence on both sides alike. Before the
battle he was relatively unknown; after it Prince Rupert commented that Cromwell "could himself evoke a more fierce and en-
during spirit from the People than even that which he here mag-
nifies. His 'Ironsides' [a name which Rupert gave to Cromwell and
which later applied to his own regiment until it was applied to his
entire army] are the most fearless and successful body of troops
on record, even in our annals: these fellows may have been and I
believe were, for the most part fanatics, but they were not all
hypocrites: Hypocrites never fought as they fought." And Sir
Philip Warwick added that "they chose rather to die than fly, and
custom removed fear of danger."

But Marston Moor also demonstrated that the reforms initiated
after Edgehill were still far from complete: the entire army needed

to be permeated, as far as possible, with the discipline and spirit
of Cromwell's "Ironsides." This reorganization of most of the army
between 1644 and 1645 was primarily Cromwell's work, a task
completed with outstanding success. He was convinced that peace
and stability could be obtained only through a crushing defeat of
the adversary. The iron discipline of Swedish officers, hired especially for the purpose, changed raw levies into steady soldiers; and
since Parliament lacked experts in engineering and artillery, Cromwell did not hesitate in using the services of French and German
officers—though in time it proved advisable to keep officers of these
respective nationalities apart to prevent Franco-German feuds.
What finally emerged was a "New Model Army," a standing force,
a highly professional army—but also an army in which Cromwell
and his Ironsides dominated. This also meant the domination of
Independent religious sectarianism over the Presbyterianism of Parliament.

The reputation Cromwell had established for himself is shown
by the impact upon the Parliamentary army of his arrival near
Naseby on June 13, 1645. Cromwell then nominally served as lieutenant general under Fairfax. The news spread like wildfire among
the army that "'Ironside' is come to head us!" The battle was
fought on the following day. Though Fairfax was in overall command of the army, Cromwell's cavalry brought victory after initial
Parliamentary setbacks. Instead of committing his forces at the
very beginning, he waited to see how the battle developed and then
struck the decisive blow at the decisive point with his cavalry. Tactics of this nature were not new; both Gustavus Adolphus and
Pappenheim had practiced them on the battlefields of Germany.
But, unlike them, Cromwell never headed the charge. He made
sure that he maintained a general oversight of the battle in order
to meet whatever emergencies might arise.

Prince Rupert, of course, also used the tactics acquired on the
Continent, but whereas his forces after a successful attack scattered
in the pursuit of the enemy (and usually allowed themselves to be
diverted by plundering his baggage train), the discipline instilled
into Cromwell's soldiers allowed their commander to rally the

forces again immediately, to follow up an attack, or to deploy them at other vital points. At Naseby, after his initial success, Cromwell ordered three regiments to pursue the enemy horse and then used the rest of his troops to attack the enemy's exposed left flank. Having beaten them, he penetrated farther and fell upon the Royalist center, which soon collapsed. Charles I had been decisively defeated, a defeat inflicted upon him mainly through the exertions and bravery of the New Model Army. Composed as it was mainly of Independents, this meant not only the triumph of Parliament but the ascendancy of the Independents over Parliament, finally culminating in the Protectorate under Cromwell.

Naseby finally established Cromwell's military reputation among friends and foes alike. Clarendon, a hostile witness, had to admit of Cromwell that "he was one of those men whom his very enemies could not condemn without commending him at the same time: for he could never have done half that mischief without great parts of courage, industry and judgment. He must have had a wonderful understanding in the natures and humours of men, and as great a dexterity in applying them . . . he attempted those things which no good man durst have ventured on; and achieved those in which none but a valiant and great man could have succeeded . . . yet wickedness as great as his could never have succeeded nor accomplished those designs, without the assistance of a great spirit, an admirable circumspection and sagacity, and a most magnanimous resolution."

At Naseby the New Model Army was still one of several armies which Parliament put into the field. In the first Civil War there were no less than twenty-one thousand Scots under Leslie. But after Naseby—apart from the Scots—the various other separate armies such as those of Nottinghamshire under Major General Poyntz, or Wiltshire and the four western counties under Major General Massey, were absorbed into the New Model Army or disappeared altogether. Within a matter of a few years Cromwell had created one highly professional standing English army, an army in which promotion frequently depended on merit, although the principle of seniority did not disappear altogether.

Cromwell's own religious attitudes and later his peculiar constitutional position were not without influence upon appointments and promotion. A contemporary of Cromwell's asserts that he weeded out "godly and upright-hearted men" to consolidate his own position and replaced them with "pittiful sottish beasts of his own alliance." This was hardly an unprejudiced view, but when commanding his own Eastern Association Cromwell did dismiss Presbyterian officers and later on also dismissed officers who were opposed to his Protectorate because of their republican inclinations.

Nevertheless, this cannot detract from Cromwell's achievement of creating an army as disciplined as it was effective—and well armed. The pike, a prominent weapon in 1643, had been virtually abandoned by 1650. The closing campaigns of the first Civil War, the second Civil War, and the subjugation of Ireland and Scotland bore witness to a growing professionalism. The Irish campaign in particular demonstrates Cromwell's art of generalship at its best. Politically he divided the Royalist Protestants from Ireland's Roman Catholic leaders; he achieved an almost perfect cooperation between the army and the fleet and thus mastered his logistic problems. He deployed his troops effectively, although the terrain was quite different from that in England.

In the subjugation of both Ireland and Scotland a series of systematically conducted sieges contrasted strongly with early campaigns. Cromwell laid great stress on the role of artillery, which increased progressively in firepower. The sieges of Pembroke Castle, Pontefract, and later Drogheda showed the devastating effect of Cromwell's siege trains. Both Wexford and Ross began to negotiate for surrender after the first day's cannonade.

The massive deployment of artillery and the concentration of massive forces on a narrow front illustrate Cromwell's philosophy of warfare: that in order to force a decision a decisive victory must be attained. He was not the man of slow mancuver and counter-maneuver. General MacArthur's maxim in the Second World War might well have been Cromwell's: "There is no substitute for victory." A war of lengthy maneuvers was bound to deplete troops and stores. Long-drawn-out sieges could involve sickness and epidemics among the siege forces. The determination that only the complete defeat of the enemy, speedily achieved, would also speedily restore peace largely explains the ferocity of Cromwell's attacks. He was no sentimentalist about war. Chivalry had no place in a religious conflict fought with the fervor of a crusade: it merely prolonged it. In Cromwell's eyes, war was a bloody and dirty business which must be got over as quickly as possible by all available means. The cost in human lives of a short but decisive assault would in the long run be lower than that involved in a long protracted siege. It would also be more economical, argued Cromwell in a letter from Ireland to Parliament in 1650. "Those towns that are to be reduced, especially one or two of them, if we should proceed by the rules of other states, would cost you more money than this army hath had since we came over, I hope, through the blessing of God, they will come cheaper to you." However, there were exceptions. At Clonmel, Cromwell's forces were bloodily repulsed and suffered about a thousand casualties.

Cromwell's power of direct command over the entire military forces increased together with the increasing professionalism of the army. During the early campaigns councils of war had played an important part; their resolutions were not simply arrived at by a general's order but "after much dispute." Councils were still held before the battle of Preston and the battle of Dunbar. However, after Fairfax had been replaced by Cromwell, the latter made sure that his influence not only was felt but that it also prevailed. He did this by first discussing the issues directly with the most important of his subordinates, such as Lambert and Monck, reaching a conclusion, and then at a full council meeting of the officers having Lambert explain why and how a battle would have to be fought.

The eve of Dunbar saw Cromwell and Lambert "coming to the Earl Roxburgh's House and observing [the enemy's] posture I [Cromwell] told him that it did us an opportunity and advantage to attempt upon the enemy, to which he immediately replied, that he had thought to have said the same thing to me. So that it pleased the Lord to set this apprehension upon both our hearts at the same instant. We called for Colonel Monk and showed him the thing: and coming to our quarters at night, and demonstrating our apprehensions to some of the Colonels, they also cheerfully concurred."

What Cromwell does not make clear is that it was Lambert who did the "demonstrating" and explaining to the colonels.

In his New Model Army, Cromwell had established a rough proportion of one horseman to every two footmen. Among the cavalry the horseman with spear and the heavily armed and therefore clumsy cuirassier gradually disappeared, making way for the harquebusier armed with carbine, pistol, and sword. The dragoons, of which the New Model Army contained one regiment, were simply mounted infantry, whose name derived from the name of the short-barreled musket they carried. Originating in France and Germany during the Thirty Years' War, in Cromwell's army they fulfilled the task of vanguards, rearguards, and reconnaissance units. Unlike the rest of the New Model cavalry, dragoons did not wear buff coats but wore red coats like the infantry, and hats instead of helmets. Tactics of infantry and cavalry alike were not new but adapted from those of the Continental armies.

Paradoxically Cromwell and his army were one another's greatest liability. For Cromwell the army was the base of his power, and ultimately his position rested upon the swords of his men. In the absence of a *political* countervailing force, his *military* force was the only pillar of support and reliance. Because of that he was not always his own free agent in his political decisions. With the army Cromwell stood: without it he would fall.

Cromwell's singular failure to put any tangible institution with clearly defined powers and limitations in place of the monarchy which he had helped to depose made him a liability to the army, because in essence he also failed to devise an acceptable constitutional framework within which a standing army would have its proper place. This placed the army in a position outside what had hitherto been regarded as constitutional in England. Consequently, by 1658, and even more so two years later, the majority of Englishmen, who desired nothing more than a return to constitutional legality, regarded Cromwell's army as the most glaring extra-constitutional institution to be done away with. Cromwell's failure as a politician ensured in Britain the unpopularity of any standing army for the next hundred and fifty-odd years.

Cromwell was brilliant as a leader of men, and brilliant in his generalship—but it was a brilliance which relied on the successful adaptation of techniques and tactics already in practice elsewhere. As his campaigns in Ireland and Scotland showed, he was as bold a strategist as he was a tactician: yet to evaluate his position in these respects in relation to his European contemporaries is virtually impossible, since he never had to face men of the caliber of Gustavus Adolphus, Wallenstein, or Tilly—the master generals of the Thirty Years' War.

PAUL H. HARDACRE

Cromwell and the Royalists

O N APRIL 20, 1653, Cromwell dissolved the remnants of the Long Parliament. No step more agreeable to all classes could have been taken, wrote Edward Conway,[1] who was probably speaking for property owners in general, while the deposed bishop of Chichester panegyrized:

> A soldier spake, a parliament was dumb.
> Silenc'd it was, brave general, by thee:
> Well may'st thou boast of Christian liberty,
> For sure Christ's power did never more increase,
> Than when He made the devils hold their peace.[2]

From *The Royalists during the Puritan Revolution.* © Martinus Nijhoff's Boekhandel en Uitgeversmaatschappij 1956.

1. *Calendar of State Papers, Domestic,* 1652–53, p. 298. (Hereafter *C.S.P., Dom.*)
2. Percy Simpson, "The Bodleian Manuscripts of Henry King," *Bodleian Quarterly Record,* V (1929), 336.

Royalists rejoiced at the prospect of an internecine struggle among the rebels. After all, whatever form the revolutionary government might take meant little to them. Since they were excluded from voting and from holding office, their primary interest lay in the degree to which they might enjoy peaceful possession of their lands. As one Roman Catholic gentleman phrased it, "If all this ado would procure us a fair pardon, we would make your Cromwell our idol." [3]

Reports of the new government's desire to conciliate the Royalists spread rapidly, and throughout them ran the theme of Cromwell's moderation. It was confidently asserted that he had quashed Major General Harrison's proposal to exterminate the King's party, and in a private interview with a Royalist in the fall of 1653 he declared that he did not advocate severity toward Charles's followers, although he was "but one man." [4] Indeed, as a newsletter shows, the delinquents' condition improved markedly. "The general is sedulous to please all parties," the report ran, "and very kind to the old malignants, who have found much more favor since the dissolution than in seven years before." [5]

In 1653 and 1654 many wrongs were rectified. Through the committee for relief on articles of war, some violations previously mentioned were redressed. Cromwell already enjoyed a reputation for fair dealing, having frequently interceded for persons denied privileges under articles of surrender. One way in which the Protectorate government demonstrated its aim of dealing equitably with old opponents was by reviewing the cases of prisoners of war still in confinement or on security. Sir William Davenant, the poet laureate, who was a militant Royalist in wartime, petitioned the Protector that although he had been exchanged for a Parliamentarian officer after his capture, he had been kept on bail to return to the Tower and was unable to leave London to recover his debts. In the meantime he had been himself arrested for debts and was thereby made "a double prisoner." The committee for relief substantiated

3. M. Blundell (ed.), *Cavalier: Letters of William Blundell 1620–98* (1933), p. 42.

4. W. C. Abbott (ed.), *Writings and Speeches of Oliver Cromwell*, 4 vols. (Cambridge, Mass., 1937–47), III, 103.

5. *Calendar of the Clarendon State Papers*, 3 vols. (Oxford, 1869–76), II, 203. (Hereafter *C.C.S.P.*)

his statements, and thereupon the Council of State ordered his release.[6] Similarly, more than half a group of forty-five political prisoners in the Tower in 1654 gained their liberty, but as they were considered dangerous to the peace of the state, bond was required of most and a few were banished.[7]

Another symptom of moderation was seen in the new attitude of the judiciary. According to Edmund Ludlow, Cromwell, "endeavoring to fix himself in his throne by all ways imaginable, gave direction to the judges, who were ready to go their several circuits, to take especial care to extend all favor and kindness to the cavalier party."[8] This type of evidence is almost impossible to confirm, but the Protector seems to have intimated that peaceable Royalists should be treated leniently. The hypothesis is further substantiated by the fact that about this time Cromwell appointed, as a justice of the common pleas, Matthew Hale, who had distinguished himself by defending several outstanding Royalist leaders. It is quite clear that under the Protectorate the delinquents were no longer wronged with impunity, as formerly they had been. In 1646 a Parliamentarian, who had killed a malignant for no other offense than jeering some soldiers preparing to resist the royal troops, drew only imprisonment for a year and a day, and one observer considered even this too heavy a penalty.[9] Under the Protectorate, however, a similar case came before Hale. An old Royalist, who was roaming the fields with a fowling piece, was killed by a soldier who was disarming him on the ground that carrying arms violated the Protector's orders. Hale found the soldier guilty of murder and ordered execution immediately so that no reprieve could be procured.[10]

Cromwell deplored the arbitrary confiscations of the commonwealth. These acts distressed him, he later told Parliament, although he and co-sympathizers could do little "except by our mournings, and giving our negatives when occasion served."[11]

6. C.S.P., Dom., 1654, pp. 106–07, 224.

7. Ibid., pp. 273–74, 353–54.

8. C. H. Firth (ed.), Memoirs of Edmund Ludlow, 2 vols. (Oxford, 1894), I, 379–80.

9. B. Nightingale, The Ejected of 1662 in Cumberland and Westmoreland, 2 vols. (Manchester, 1911), II, 894–95.

10. Gilbert Burnet, Lives, Characters, and an Address to Posterity, ed. John Jebb (New York, 1833), pp. 95–96.

11. Writings and Speeches of Oliver Cromwell, III, 453.

Early in his rule the Council of State reviewed some cases which had been most harshly judged. They halted any further sale of Craven's estate[12] and intervened on behalf of others, such as Lord Hatton, whose estate they freed from sequestration after the case against him was proved to have been based originally on insufficient evidence.[13]

From all the foregoing it is apparent that the lay Royalist's condition gradually improved after the advent of Cromwell. To generalize on the Royalist clergyman's fate under the Protectorate is, however, more difficult. It will be recalled that about 30 percent of the Anglican clergy had been ejected during the Civil War and Commonwealth, chiefly on grounds which justify their being regarded as Royalist sympathizers. Many of these continued to preach and otherwise violate the Puritan code. Fresh anticlerical measures were adopted under the Protectorate, and while the government still connived at occasional public preaching, this liberty was radically curtailed after 1655. Royalist ministers were now more than ever dependent on charity. That they were not starved into submission was due to the beneficence of other Royalists who had managed to salvage something from their wrecked fortunes, or to occasional donations from sympathetic parish officials. Entries relating to such donations are said to be numerous in the churchwardens' account book of at least one London parish.[14]

Such charity doubtless resulted from general affection for the Anglican liturgy and widespread aversion to the ecclesiastical changes of the Puritans. These sentiments were conclusively demonstrated in the frequency with which sequestered ministers were called upon to exercise their functions on the old religious holidays and at christenings, marriages, and funerals. The Puritans heatedly attacked the superstitious observance of Christmas and other holidays, and in 1647 Parliament had ordered that Christmas no longer be celebrated as a festival. Enforcement was difficult, however, and Parliament heard frequent complaints that the day was willfully and strictly observed.[15] Anglicans who were accustomed to a

12. M. A. E. Green (ed.), *Calendar of the Proceedings of the Committee for Compounding 1642–1656*, 5 vols. (1889–92). (Hereafter *C.C.C.*)
13. *Ibid.*, p. 1580.
14. *Notes and Queries*, 3rd ser., III (1863), 264.
15. *C.S.P., Dom., 1650*, pp. 484–85.

Christmas Day sermon were disappointed, however, for the churches were not permitted to open, and the holiday had to be observed at home. This was the experience of John Evelyn, at least, who also found an Anglican divine to christen his son "because the parish minister durst not have officiated according to the form and usage of the Church of England, to which I always adhered." [16]

By a law of 1653 marriages were to be solemnized by a justice of the peace, and all other forms were ruled invalid. All classes rebelled, and sequestered clergymen were consistently asked to perform Anglican marriages. Couples were frequently married by Anglican ritual and then again as prescribed by the law of 1653. But there is no doubt that they considered the former the only valid ceremony. Royalist ministers were also called to sickbeds and funerals, contrary to the Directory for Public Worship, which was explicit in forbidding ceremonies at interment. When Evelyn's mother-in-law Lady Browne died, he arranged her burial with the Church's full ceremony; and the same rites were performed for Dr. Edmund Smith, physician of the King, and for Sir John Bramston, formerly chief justice of the King's Bench.[17] Even Lady Manchester, who was reputed a rabid Puritan, summoned a "cavalier minister" on her deathbed, and requested her husband to give him £10 for his services.[18] Thus the Anglican clergy ministered to all classes in these matters closest to the heart, although not without hazard to themselves, both from the judiciary and from the more radical sectaries. Bramston relates the story of one who was conducting a burial with the Common Prayer Book in his hand: "The rabble threw him into the grave, and had buried him and the book doubtless (for they began to throw earth on him), had not some of the wiser townsmen rescued him." [19]

However popular they may have been as preachers, and however frequently they may have exercised their functions in private, Anglicans were constantly assailed by the Puritans. Whenever they

16. *Diary of John Evelyn*, Oct. 11, 1653.
17. *Diary of John Evelyn*, Sept. 22, 1652; *C.C.S.P.*, II, 317; Lord Braybrooke (ed.), *Autobiography of Sir John Bramston* (Camden Series, 1845), p. 97.
18. Historical Manuscript Commission, *5th Report*, p. 146. (Hereafter H.M.C.)
19. *Autobiography of Bramston*, p. 124.

managed to obtain a benefice, a cry of protest arose, no matter how influential the patron. Thus a "caveat" was presented against Ralph Brideoake, whom Lenthall, the Speaker, had presented to an Oxfordshire benefice, as it was maintained that he was a "cavalier and a dull preacher." [20] Delinquents (with a few important exceptions) had not been allowed to compound for their rights of ecclesiastical patronage, which had been reserved for disposal by the state. Yet there were complaints that enemies of the Commonwealth still controlled the patronage, thus hindering the advancement of well-affected clergymen. Even where the classical, or Presbyterian, system was erected, parishioners appointed elders who were in Anglican orders. Such evidence testifies to the truth of the charge voiced by a Puritan who wrote Lord Wharton about this time. "The inhabitants of our parish are yet stiff in retaining their old though groundless customs," he grumbled. "But they are not words that will persuade them, that have not either reason or wit enough to understand them. It must be authority; that only will be a convincing argument to refractory men." [21]

To forestall Anglican sabotage of the Puritan system, the Protector ordained in March 1654 that all persons presented to any cure should first be approved by a body of nominated commissioners for approbation of public preachers.[22] By a supplementary mandate sequestered priests were disqualified from admission until their conformity and submission to the government were proven.[23] At about the same time examiners were named to investigate and determine the justice of charges against ministers who led scandalous lives, blasphemed in their teaching, or were antagonistic toward the government, and to remove anyone found guilty.[24]

The Royalist clergy resisted these commissioners at every opportunity. One actively employed mode of obstruction was to lodge a multitude of lawsuits for recovering sequestered benefices and their revenues. William Kelsall, a Staffordshire vicar who had been ejected in 1645, had begun at least thirty actions for tithes by 1648;

20. *C.S.P., Dom., 1655,* pp. 6–7.
21. Nightingale, *Ejected of 1662,* II, 1082.
22. C. H. Firth and R. S. Rait (eds.), *Acts and Ordinances of the Interregnum 1642–60,* 3 vols. (1911), II, 855–58. (Hereafter *Acts and Ords.*)
23. *Ibid.,* pp. 1025–26.
24. *Ibid.,* pp. 968–90.

while John Tucker, a Somersetshire incumbent who associated with Cavaliers, pressed over two hundred legal complaints against his neighbors.[25] No doubt any minister, regardless of his politics, found tithes difficult to collect, but the frequency with which Royalist divines initiated recovery suits, coupled with other resistance to the Protectorate's ecclesiastical policy, was sufficient to cause Cromwell to publish a proclamation ordering the offenders to desist immediately, and to relinquish their places within a month or forfeit their fifths.[26] Qualified ministers were scarce, however, and what seems to have happened is that the Royalist clergymen were relegated from the more opulent benefices to the impecunious ones.[27]

In the fall of 1655 the government prohibited anyone from retaining ejected ministers or fellows as chaplains or teachers. It further prohibited those dismissed from conducting school or preaching in any capacity unless they first convinced the government of their peaceful intentions and obtained approval.[28] With a mournful spirit Evelyn attended what he called "the funeral sermon of preaching." [29] His fears were not completely realized, however. In January 1656 Ussher obtained an interview with the Protector, pleading on behalf of the silenced clergy. No promise was given then, but during the next month Cromwell told a few of the Episcopal leaders that the question of liberty of preaching would be laid before the Council if the ministers declared their intention of living quietly and refraining from inciting future disorder. Probably, says Gardiner, he kept his word, for the injunctions of 1655 appear rarely to have been enforced.[30] In the voluminous reports from the major generals which Secretary John Thurloe received there are practically no allusions to restrictions on ministers, and in

25. A. G. Matthews, *Walker Revised* (Oxford, 1948), pp. 320, 324. More than thirty of Walker's sufferers were parties, in the Court of Exchequer, to suits for tithes in which depositions were taken by commission, 1649–60 (*40th Annual Report of the Deputy Keeper of the Public Records*, Appendix I, *passim*).

26. *C.S.P., Dom., 1655*, pp. 224–25.

27. J. T. Rutt (ed.), *Diary of Thomas Burton*, 4 vols. (1828), I, ciii.

28. *C.S.P., Dom., 1655*, pp. 346–47.

29. *Diary of John Evelyn*, Dec. 25, 1655.

30. S. R. Gardiner, *History of the Commonwealth and Protectorate*, 4 vols. (1903), III, 335–36.

August 1656 Evelyn recorded an assembly in a London home at which an Anglican preached and "where we had a great meeting of zealous Christians, who were generally much more devout and religious than in our greatest prosperity." [31] Moreover, the Council often permitted clergymen who furnished evidence of loyalty to officiate publicly, and schoolmasters under the same circumstances were allowed to teach school. Worsley jailed some parsons who conducted marriage ceremonies contrary to the Commonwealth law, but even this offense was removed from the statute books in 1657, after which time marriage by a justice of the peace was permissible but not mandatory. [32]

In response to popular demand, therefore, Anglican ministers, conformist and ejected alike, continued to be active under Cromwell's rule. It is difficult to agree, however, with those who maintain that they enjoyed any substantial or general relief under the Protectorate. Anglican tradition was strong in the nation at large, and Cromwell himself favored liberty of worship for all peaceable persons. However, the Puritan minority on whose support his government rested, and from whose ranks the law-enforcing authorities were drawn, was far less tolerant than he, while the constitutions under which he governed specifically excluded prelacy (and Catholicism) from the freedom of religion guaranteed to all Christians. As the Protector had remarked in 1653 when he told a Cavalier that he was opposed to "rigour" against the Royalists, he was "but one man."

The Roman Catholics enjoyed more concrete benefits with the result that their interest in the Royalist cause was proportionately lessened. While Cromwell inclined toward a mild policy, he could not ignore the increased activities of the Roman Catholic priests and regulars. To him, also, the "Spanish interest" of the English Catholics was indisputable. Therefore, he gave orders in June 1654 that all known priests and Jesuits be seized, and in the same month Southworth, the only Catholic so punished for religious reasons during the Protectorate, was executed. The Venetian representative reported that upon being apprised of this execution Cromwell ap-

31. *Diary of John Evelyn,* Aug. 3, 1656.
32. T. Birch (ed.), *State Papers of John Thurloe,* 7 vols. (1742), IV, 523; (Hereafter Thurloe); *Acts and Ords.,* II, 1139.

peared stirred and stated that he favored toleration for all, yet made
it clear that he was obliged to enforce the law as it stood.[33] It
should be observed that Catholics who complied with the law,
however, found that the Protectorate dispensed ready justice. For,
when one confessed priest who was imprisoned finally took the
oath of abjuration, the Council liberated him immediately.[34]

About the same time this incident occurred, Cromwell under-
took a negotiation which would seem to indicate that he was considering further means of ameliorating the Roman Catholics' condition. In the spring of 1655 agents were sent to Rome. The two
persons employed were English Catholics, and although the evidence is not complete, the mission appears to have been partly to
obtain intelligence and partly to contract some form of "engage-
ment" with the Pope, by which the English Roman Catholics presumably would have profited. The scheme fell through as a result
of mismanagement by a negotiator, but at least it is evidence of a
government *volte-face*.[35]

Possibly to dispel the notion that he was trafficking with the
Pope, Cromwell issued a proclamation in April 1655 demanding
conviction of recusants and more active enforcement of the previous year's laws against Jesuits and priests.[36] No quickening of
persecution occurred, however, as is shown by the absence of indictments for recusancy in the sessions records of the time. The
principal purpose of the April proclamation was to furnish the
exchequer with Catholic names in the hope that fresh fines and
sequestrations could be levied. Justices of the peace received detailed instructions and printed forms on which to report the names
of those who when summoned refused the oath and those who

33. *Calendar of State Papers, Venetian,* XXIX, 233–34. (Hereafter *C.S.P.,
Ven.*)

34. *C.S.P., Dom., 1655,* p. 116.

35. The agents were Thomas Bayly, a recent convert to Catholicism, and
William Metham, a former student at the English College at Rome. That
the mission was at the direction of the government appears from the correspondence of Longland, Cromwell's agent at Leghorn (Thurloe, III, 635;
IV, 59, 92, 172, 200, 232–33, 310; cf. G. F. Warner [ed.], *Correspondence of
Sir Edward Nicholas,* 4 vols. [Camden Series 1886–1920], III, 52–53. [Here-
after *Nicholas Papers*]).

36. R. R. Steele (ed.), *A Bibliography of Royal Proclamations 1485–1714,*
2 vols. (Oxford, 1910), I, 3047.

failed to appear.[37] Nevertheless, new sources of revenue were not revealed, for a survey of sequestered Catholics in the fall of 1655 showed almost no change from the numbers sequestered in the same counties in 1651.[38]

On the whole, a report by the French ambassador that the Catholics fared better under the Protectorate than under any former government is substantiated, as is Cromwell's own statement to Mazarin that, while he could not grant them open toleration, there was less reason for complaint of "rigor upon men's consciences" under his government than there was under that of the Commonwealth. He went on to say that as soon as he could remove some "impediments" (presumably Presbyterian hostility), he hoped further to improve the Catholics' condition.[39] Attendance at the chapels of the Catholic ambassadors was resumed. The Venetian representative reported in October 1655 that he had six masses said every working day and ten on festivals, and that neither his spacious chapel nor the number of masses was sufficient to accommodate those seeking admittance.[40] These meetings became too flagrant, however, and in January 1656 the government arrested a large number leaving mass. Some were released on security, and recognizances were taken of about forty to appear at the next Middlesex sessions. Probably, says Gardiner, these latter escaped with a warning not to repeat their offense.[41]

Any project for outright toleration which Cromwell might have entertained was defeated on the old question of revenues. As another means of fund-raising for the Spanish war, Parliament advocated reviving the recusancy laws, and a proposed bill required suspected recusants to appear and take a new oath of abjuration or forfeit two-thirds of their estates. The prospect of the bill's passage raised a storm of protest. Cromwell attempted in vain to forestall the bill, but despite his objections and those of members who protested in the name of liberty of conscience, the bill was passed and

37. *C.S.P., Dom., 1655*, pp. 252, 286; J. C. Jeaffreson (ed.), *Middlesex County Records*, III, 238–39.

38. *C.C.C.*, I, 429, 741.

39. *Writings and Speeches of Oliver Cromwell*, IV, 368–69; Gardiner, *Commonwealth and Protectorate*, IV, 18–20.

40. *C.S.P., Ven.*, XXX, 128–29.

41. *Middlesex County Records*, III, 241–47; Gardiner, *loc. cit.*

was accepted by the Protector on June 26, 1657.[42] The new oath was modeled on both those of 1606 and 1643. By the earlier the taker had renounced the Pope's power to depose princes and absolve their subjects from civil obedience. This clause had been omitted from that of 1643 but was reinserted in the one of 1657, which also included rejecting the doctrines of transubstantiation, purgatory, the worship of consecrated hosts or images, and salvation by works—which points it had in common with the oath of 1643. The oath of 1657 contained nothing novel.

Judging from the printed sessions records, the act was ineffective in persuading Catholics to recant. In London, for example, out of seventy-six persons summoned in January 1658, only one appeared and took the oath, the rest being proclaimed papists and subject to sequestration of two-thirds of their property.[43] Cromwell probably fulfilled his assurances to the French ambassador that he would do what he could to prevent the execution of the act's severest sections. Prynne later complained that Cromwell had sheltered the Catholics, that he had been intimate with Catholic leaders like Sir Kenelm Digby, and that he had suspended the laws against priests.[44] Confirmation comes from a Catholic source, the Venetian ambassador, and it is known that French pressure obtained the release of imprisoned priests.[45]

Socially, indeed, the Protector's moderate policy contributed strongly to a substantial reconciliation with the Royalists. Most probably did as the Fanshawes, who "lived an innocent country life, minding only the country sport and the country affairs."[46] Many years later Sir John Reresby recorded his memoirs of life in London. "There was little satisfaction in that town in those days," he wrote. "There was no court made to Oliver but by his own party, and then only in case of business or by the officers of the

42. *Diary of Thomas Burton,* II, 148–55; *Acts and Ords.,* II, 1170–80; William Prynne, *A True and Perfect Narrative* (n.p., 1659), pp. 57–58.

43. H. Bowler (ed.), *London Sessions Records* (Catholic Record Society Publications, xxxiv, 1934), p. xlvi.

44. Prynne, *loc. cit.*

45. *C.S.P., Ven.,* XXXI, 124–25; C. H. Firth, *The Last Years of the Protectorate, 1656–1658* (London, 1909), II, 221–22.

46. H. C. Fanshawe (ed.), *The Memoirs of Ann Lady Fanshawe* (London, 1907), pp. 83–84.

army." [47] Nothing could be more untrue. The social influence exercised by the Protector's court, while probably not equaling that of Charles's, was certainly very considerable. What is more remarkable so far as Reresby's comment is concerned, is that Royalists followed the court's doings and even participated. Royalist ladies eagerly adopted court fashions.[48] Sir John Southcote, who had fought for the King and gone into exile after Naseby, returned to England at about the time of Cromwell's accession as Protector, when he became friendly with Lady Elizabeth Claypole, Oliver's daughter. At her request he bought damask beds and dress material in Paris, and through her influence he regained some of his son's horses, which had been confiscated by the military.[49] Frances, another of Cromwell's daughters, was also the center of much social activity, in which the Royalists took part. Her marriage in 1657 was attended by the Earl of Newport, who fought for the King and compounded heavily, and who was seen dancing with Cromwell's wife; while the Countess of Devonshire, who corresponded with Charles II's party, also attended and gave the bride a valuable gift.[50]

As Protector, Cromwell granted many honors. The members of his "Other House" were generally distinguished by the title of "Lord," and in addition he formally created two peers. Charles Howard was nominated Baron Dacres of Gilsland and Viscount Howard of Morpeth, and Edmond Dunch, Cromwell's cousin, Baron of Burnell. He also conferred baronetcies and knighthoods generously. While Restoration plays lampooned the persons thus ennobled, there is little evidence that they were ridiculed during the Commonwealth. Instead of being infuriated when Howard was elevated to the peerage, Lady Devonshire, whose Royalism was undiluted, wrote that there were rumors of creating more nobles, a step she considered long overdue.[51]

The Protector did not, however, remove one particular Royalist grievance. This was the prohibition from using titles granted by

47. Andrew Browning (ed.), *Memoirs of Sir John Reresby* (Glasgow, 1936), p. 22.
48. *English Historical Review*, XLVII (1932), 311.
49. H.M.C., *2nd Report*, p. 148.
50. H.M.C., *5th Report*, pp. 177, 183.
51. H.M.C., *15th Report*, App., pt. VII, p. 160.

the King since 1642. As noted previously, by an act of 1646 all honors and titles conferred by Charles I since the earlier year were annulled, and their use as forms of address was forbidden. This was re-enacted in 1652, those concerned were directed to deliver all such patents to the Court of Chancery to be canceled, and fines were established for violators. Whether this act was enforced to any great extent is questionable. A poet mocked the "griev'd Countesse," who sobbed as she surrendered her patent, and Sir John Reresby left Cambridge because his college refused to recognize the baronetcy bestowed on his father by Charles in May 1642. On the other hand, the Marquis of Dorchester successfully evaded the law by a judicious bribe, and while he continued to sign legal documents with his prewar title of Kingston, he signed other papers "Dorchester," the title given him in 1645.[52]

Whatever the degree of social reconciliation, and however greatly the peaceable Royalist may have profited from Cromwell's early moderation, there were still signs that Royalism burned strongly in some breasts. Abundant evidence appears in the sessions records of the period 1654–58. Men were constantly being apprehended for abusing the Protector or drinking to the King. Doubtless many of the offenders were old Royalists, but probably just as many, feeling no special affection toward the Stuarts, simply detested the military dictatorship under which they now existed. For example, William Beck, a shipwright of Stepney, was imprisoned for speaking disparagingly of Cromwell, but he contended in a petition for release he must have been mad or drunk, having always been loyal.[53]

The punishment for antagonistic expressions varied. Richard Browne, an old Royalist soldier, was fined five pounds for saying that the soldiers were all plundering rogues and cowards and that Cromwell was a murderer who deserved to be hanged or beheaded.[54] Others were forced only to give articles for good be-

52. C. H. Firth, *House of Lords during the Civil War* (1910), pp. 234–35; *Memoirs of Sir John Reresby*, p. 3; C.C.S.P., III, 412. Cf. M. A. E. Green (ed.), *Calendar of the Proceedings of the Committee for Advance of Money 1642–56*, 3 vols. (1888), I, 105.
53. C.S.P., Dom., *1655*, p. 154.
54. J. Raine (ed.), *Depositions from the Castle of York during the Seventeenth Century* (Surtees Society, XL, 1861), p. 73.

havior, while two little boys who were overheard abusing Cromwell were put in the stocks.[55]

Possibly the Protector feared that the theater would be exploited to assemble plotters. Certainly this was the reasoning behind his policy regarding sporting events. As did the previous government, Cromwell's considered these a blind for plots and treason. In Warwickshire ten thousand had gathered supposedly to watch a bearbaiting; a cockfight was held weekly in Dorset and attended by "divers unknown blades"; while just before one of the periodic risings of the time, a fox hunt which continued for several days was held near the scene of the outbreak.[56] The Protector took precautions to suppress such assemblies, and troops policed the country to prevent horse races and other sporting events which could be used as a cover for seditious activities. Racing was not entirely stamped out, however. When the Earl of Exeter asked whether the running for Lady Grantham's cup at Lincoln would be permitted, he was informed that it was not intended to deprive gentlemen of their sport so long as inimical crowds did not congregate, and a few months later nearly 150 horsemen were reported to be competing near the capital.[57]

Even more serious was the strong local influence exercised by Royalists elected to places of trust, although ordinances of 1647 prohibited delinquents from either voting or holding public office without government consent.[58] "Look on all South Wales," ran one complaint, "and you will hardly hear of a man there that serves in the House but have either been made by delinquents or have been commissioners of array or otherwise assisting the king."[59] Elections to the 1654 Parliament climaxed this movement and Royalists also penetrated lower offices, down to justices of the peace and jurymen. Then, too, they wielded a negative power, as when Ludlow was defeated in 1654 partly through Royalist influence.[60]

55. *Nicholas Papers,* II, 267.
56. *C.S.P., Dom., 1653–54,* p. 171; Thurloe, III, 122, 649.
57. Thurloe, IV, 607; V, 200.
58. *Acts and Ords.,* I, 1009.
59. C. H. Firth (ed.), *The Clarke Papers: Selections from the Papers of William Clarke 1647–60,* 4 vols. (Camden Society, 1891–1901), II, 157–60.
60. *Memoirs of Edmund Ludlow,* I, 545.

Inhabitants of Brecknock reported that undersheriffs forced them to vote for a compounded delinquent. The "well-affected" of Tiverton, Devon, made a similar report against Robert Shapcote, a field officer under Charles I, and more lately a debauchee with other Royalists. A knight elected for Somerset was accused of extolling *Eikon Basilike* in verse, and many similar charges were filed.[61]

That Cromwell feared admitting delinquents to the franchise is proved by a proclamation of 1655 ordering their continued exclusion regardless of the statute's expiration.[62] But they continued to vote and to be returned to Parliament, where they actively opposed measures prejudicial to their interests.

When insurrections did occur, old Royalists and compounders were occasionally involved, but in general they tended to refrain from plots. The average party member chose only to pursue his trade unmolested and unmolesting:

> From the first war I have not struck a stroke
> But from the camp betook me to my book.
> Though I confess I had an itching hand
> To work some feat, but I took no command.[63]

Nevertheless the zeal of some of the second generation, "new sprung up cavaliers, such as young gentlemen lately come to their lands and estates," [64] frequently reacted heavily on the more peaceable Royalists. A tavern meeting of conspirators at "the Palsgrave's Head," a packet of papers under a loose board in Coney Court, a thinly disguised letter about the good condition of the lawsuit, or two hundred horseloads of ware out of Surrey—any of these and countless other bits of evidence might trap a Villiers, a Seymour, or a Russell and expose all who had supported Charles I to sedition accusations. Thus, after the Royalist plot of 1655 exploded, the Protector condemned the whole party as "implacable in their malice

61. *C.S.P., Dom., 1654,* pp. 270–71, 279–80, 280–83.
62. Gardiner, *Commonwealth and Protectorate,* IV, 49–50. In 1657 a bill was introduced closing offices of trust to all delinquents, but it did not pass, possibly because of arguments such as that raised by the member who said that the Royalists would be happy to be spared the responsibility of office-holding (*Diary of Thomas Burton,* II, 34).
63. *The Delinquent's Passport* (n.p., n.d.).
64. Firth, *Last Years of the Protectorate,* II, 55.

and revenge, and never to be drawn from their adhering to that cursed interest." [65]

To prevent a recurrence, the Protector partitioned the country into ten (later eleven) districts, each to be policed by troops commanded by a major general. The major generals were responsible for several functions, but the one primarily concerning a general study of the Royalists is the enforcement of money-raising and security measures.

Funds to pay the troops were to be furnished by the Royalists themselves, who were divided into three classes. Those who had rebelled since the establishment of the Protectorate were to be imprisoned or banished, and their estates were to be sequestered except for an allowance of one-third to their wives and children. Others whose words or actions implied that they still adhered to the King were to be imprisoned or banished without sequestration. The third group, comprising the majority, included all who had previously fought against Parliament or had been sequestered, and they were to pay an annual tax of 10 percent on lands worth £100 a year and £10 on every £1,500 worth of personal property. However, immunity was promised any former Royalist who could honestly say that he had abandoned the King's interest, who was above suspicion of complicity in the late plot, and who could show by good works in the past or by real proof in the future a desire to live peaceably.[66]

About November 1655 the first reports from the major generals began to come to the government. Whalley requested a list of all compounders in his district. Although the sequestration committee protested against the toil involved, their records furnished the major generals with a basis for decimation. By the middle of the month Thurloe declared that the Cavaliers had quietly submitted.[67]

The Royalists' general poverty, however, hindered the major generals more than any other single factor, and certainly more than the resistance which individual delinquents could offer. An-

65. *The [Old] Parliamentary or Constitutional History of England,* 2nd ed., 24 vols. (1762–63), XX, 438. (Hereafter *Old Parl. Hist.*)

66. D. W. Rannie, "Cromwell's Major-Generals," *Eng. Hist. Rev.,* X (1895), 471–506; *Old Parl. Hist.,* XX, 435–60.

67. *C.C.C.,* I, 734; Thurloe, IV, 156, 191.

other stumbling block was legal uncertainty and confusion as to the true ownership of the land on which the Royalists were residing. Henry Slingsby's case furnishes an example. His estate, forfeited under the first act for sale in 1651, had been purchased for his use in the name of his nephew, Slingsby Bethel. On the ground that Slingsby enjoyed the acres which had formerly been his, and on the very strong presumption that they had been bought exclusively for him, Major General Lilburne began to inventory the goods and survey the land, preparatory to setting a fine.[68]

Soon after they set to work, the major generals began to realize that the tax was too incomprehensive, and that the revenue would be insufficient to support their troops unless those possessing estates yielding less than £100 a year were made subject to decimation. Moreover, the persons whom the major generals regarded as especially dangerous in 1655 were not the landed Royalists, who were less inclined to intrigue because they had more to lose, but the poorer men, with less than £100 income a year. "Most of your desperate people," wrote General Lilburne, "which are a more considerable number than those that are taxed, escape, I may say, unpunished." [69]

The anticipated revenue was further reduced by relieving persons who applied for dispensation from decimation when they stated that they had truly changed their interests and were determined to live amicably with their neighbors. Robert Abbott, scrivener of London, petitioned that he had compounded for his delinquency, lived peaceably ever since, and that he had not been implicated in the late conspiracy. He submitted favorable reports from his aldermen and showed that his livelihood depended on his credit, whereupon the Protector approved his case, like that of many others, and relieved him from decimation.[70] Warwick Lord Mohun, who had fought for the King and had been fined £2,000

68. D. Parsons (ed.), *Diary of Sir Henry Slingsby* (1836), pp. 352–54. Cf. the commissioners for Durham to the Protector, Feb. 16, 1656: "At present we have not, nor could not perfect the work, there being many men's estates here so encumbered by reason they were forfeited to the commonwealth for treason, and purchased by several persons, as we suppose, in trust for the delinquents" (Thurloe, IV, 541).
69. *Ibid.*, p. 321.
70. *C.S.P., Dom., 1655–56*, p. 316.

when he compounded, was restored to good standing when he now voluntarily offered £500 to the state and avowed his allegiance to the Protectorate government.[71] Cromwell's leniency in such cases was deplored by the military, who feared that his indulgence would discredit the major generals and encourage sedition. But such cases were exceptional, and the Protector was overoptimistic when he said that the government enjoyed "a good acceptation" with its former enemies.[72]

Some time after the establishment of the major generals, they received instructions instituting additional anti-Royalist measures. All who had borne arms against the Commonwealth were to furnish bonds for their peaceable behavior in such sums as the major generals should think fit, and all Royalist householders were to give similar security for the peaceable behavior of their servants. These sureties were levied on all delinquents regardless of income, and, unlike former means of garnering income of which the major generals disapproved, of course affected the poorer Royalists as well as the wealthy ones. General Goffe began with those who were exempted from decimation, sparing the richer classes at first, since, "to put them upon all the hard terms at once, it may be, would not go down so easily." [73] Nevertheless, these demands roused a storm of protest.

One step which Royalists took to escape the rule of the major generals was to leave their homes and go to London. Besides the obvious attractions of the metropolis, they seem to have enjoyed better treatment there than from local authorities. Devonshire's experience was probably typical. It was said that he was "most civilly used" in London, "yet the implacable officers in the country make his bailiffs pay." [74] The capital was becoming a center of potential enemies to the government, and therefore, for the first time since 1651, Royalists were banished. This decree was well enforced and well obeyed, thorough searches being made for offenders; but few were found, almost all delinquents seemingly having gone to the country. The terms of the proclamation expired in

71. *Ibid.,* p. 393; Thurloe, IV, 494.
72. *Clarke Papers,* III, 65–66.
73. Thurloe, IV, 208.
74. H.M.C., *Portland MSS.,* II, 141.

October 1655, and the Royalists began to drift back. However, their expulsion was reordered; and when one of the King's messengers tried to deliver instructions to his supporters in London, none could be found.[75] The banishment of the delinquents from the capital was not an innovation, of course, but as a security measure it was far better executed under Cromwell than under any previous government. The reason for his success in this respect was the thoroughness with which visitors to London were kept under surveillance. Exceptions were made and licenses to come to town issued, but only to those who had given security to the major generals for their peaceable behavior. On arrival they were required to make a personal appearance at the office of registry, where their names and town addresses were entered in a book.[76] They reported again on departing, at which time the major general of the county to which they were traveling was notified. The Protector's intelligence system left little to be desired.

New plots in 1657 and 1658 precipitated the usual restrictions on Royalists, but it was a sign of the times that when Ormond went to England in January 1658 to confer with party leaders he traveled with almost complete impunity.[77] Fresh instances of Anglican activities were made known to the government, and persons attending Anglican sermons on Christmas 1657 were arrested, but the tide could not be stemmed. "Christmas day was never more exactly observed by this city than the last," said a newsletter, and at York one of Thurloe's correspondents attended a service at which the preacher declared all persons schismatics who failed to observe the holiday.[78] Royalist influence in Bedfordshire in 1658 is illustrated by the petition of a Puritan minister, not episcopally ordained, whose congregation had been seduced by the Anglican party. When the widow of one old compounder died, this minister

75. C.S.P., Dom., 1656–57, p. 92.
76. Mercurius Politicus, No. 288 (Dec. 13–20, 1655), pp. 5829–30. The register of London visitors from Nov. 1655 to June 1656 is in British Museum Add. MS. 34,014. See also Alfred R. Bax, "Suspected Persons in Surrey during the Commonwealth," Surrey Archaeological Collections, XIV (1899), 164–89.
77. Edward Hyde, Earl of Clarendon, The History of the Rebellion and Civil Wars in England, ed. W. D. Macray, 6 vols. (Oxford, 1888), XV, 86.
78. Clarke Papers, III, 130; Thurloe, VI, 711. Cf. Mercurius Politicus, No. 396 (Dec. 24–31, 1657), pp. 198–99.

offered to allow the family to bury her in the churchyard with their own minister officiating. They scornfully refused his offer, called him a scoundrel and a clown, and forcibly entered the church, there reading the burial service according to the Book of Common Prayer.[79]

79. *C.S.P., Dom., 1658–59*, p. 37.

AUSTIN WOOLRYCH

Oliver Cromwell and the Rule of the Saints

REVOLUTIONS have a way of getting out of hand. Unless they are skillfully controlled by a close-knit, well-prepared power group, they are apt to go far beyond the intentions of the men who first launch them. Few who assembled in the French Estates General in 1789 would have willed the Terror; millions of Russians who rejoiced at the downfall of Tsarist autocracy became appalled at the lengths to which the events of 1917 eventually led them.

In the England of 1640, most members of the Long Parliament were much more conservative in their aims than even the mildest revolutionaries of 1789 or 1917. They represented the greater landowners who traditionally ruled the county communities, and to a lesser extent the merchant oligarchies which ruled the major towns. They were members of a well-established governing class, whose interests they meant to reaffirm and strengthen. Insofar as they had a social policy, it scarcely looked beyond the concerns of their own kind. Their prevailing political belief was in the sanctity of an ancient constitution which they imagined had existed from time immemorial; they came to reassert the fundamentals of that constitution against a court and a government which, so they thought, had sought to pervert it.

In politics that meant the pruning of the royal prerogative and the securing of the rights of Parliament and the common law, which they carried through by statute during 1641. Over religion they were more divided, but most of them wanted no more than a moderate reformation within the traditional framework of episcopacy and a Book of Common Prayer. And religion, as Cromwell said, "was not the thing at first contested for"; the majority of the politicians saw it as a secondary issue at the most.

The moderate aims of 1640–41 led not to a settlement but to civil war. Most of the Parliament men were profoundly unhappy about it, for civil war is a dangerous business for conservative men to engage in, and most of them knew it. Besides the slaughter, the destruction, the breaking of ties of kinship and neighborhood, and the awful drain of wealth, the gentry could not fight a war without arming their inferiors. And once thoughtful yeomen and husbandmen, craftsmen and artisans, were called to risk their lives and livelihoods in battle, they were bound to ask what the struggle held for them. One of the most absorbing aspects of the English Revolution is the political awakening of large classes of men who had hitherto lain outside the political nation. They would not long be content to leave politics to men of birth and property to settle, or religion to their parish ministers.

Politics and religion were closely linked in the minds of these men "of the middling sort," and their education in both proceeded apace during the war years. Congregations of Independents and sectaries sprang up in great numbers, and it is fruitless to argue whether radical religious attitudes were an expression of social and political frustration or whether the beliefs and practices of the sects themselves generated democratic political ideas. The interplay was continuous. The movement was widespread, but there were two special breeding grounds of political and religious radicalism: the city of London and the cavalry of the New Model Army.

One reason why Cromwell's troopers fought superbly was that they believed they were fighting the Lord's battles. Many of their chaplains stood on the extreme left wing of Puritanism, and instilled in them a faith that the overthrow of tyranny in church and state was only the first stage in the unfolding of God's great purpose for England. They saw themselves as the shock troops of a second chosen people, and their goal was the New Jerusalem —the progressive realization of the Kingdom of God on earth. They outraged the sober, orthodox Presbyterians with their demand for liberty of conscience, but their aspirations were not to be confined to the religious sphere. Richard Baxter went among them soon after the first Civil War and was shocked at the hold that the hotter sectaries had gained over them. Sometimes he heard them contend for "church democracy," sometimes for "state democracy." The two concepts were easily linked in their minds. At one level the old order was identified with Babylon and they with the Israelites, the servants of an avenging Jehovah. At another, scarcely distinguished, King Charles figures as the heir of William the Conqueror and they as the victims of the Norman yoke. Baxter heard them ask, "What were the Lords of England but William the Conqueror's colonels? or the barons but his majors? or the knights but his captains?" [1]

This was the language of the Levellers, who found in the Norman yoke a potent historical myth. The Leveller movement first took shape in London in the immediate aftermath of the first Civil War. It drew its strength from those orders of urban society that the Great Rebellion had awakened to political consciousness but not to political rights: the smaller traders, the shopkeepers, the master craftsmen, the journeymen, and not least the apprentices —those distant forebears of modern student protest movements. It sought, less successfully, to extend its appeal to the smaller sort of countryfolk. To all who had suffered under the dominance

1. M. Sylvester (ed.), *Reliquiae Baxterianae* (1696), Part 1, § 73.

of merchant capitalists or exploiting landlords, the Levellers offered an ideology and a program. Their demands are deservedly famous: biennial parliaments, a vast extension of the franchise, equal constituencies, radical reform of the law, popular election of magistrates, provision of free schools and hospitals, a code of indefeasible natural rights, and much else.

But a program was of little avail so long as they were up against the implacable hostility of the Parliament and the city authorities. Their only hope was to capture the allegiance of the army and use it as an instrument of revolutionary action. Their Agreement of the People was mere paper without the backing of the sword.

About the Levellers' bid to win over the army and its ultimate failure I can say no more now; the story has often been told. The point I would stress here is that the Leveller program was never the only expression that the aspirations of the politically underprivileged found during the ferment of the later 1640s. When such men, whether soldiers or citizens or both, looked ahead and asked what the overthrow of tyranny should signify for such as them, there were always *two* strains in their hopes for the future.

The Leveller program offered radical political remedies for their temporal grievances, whether political or social or economic. It held forth a kind of secular New Jerusalem. But there were always those who saw a more mystical and visionary significance in the victories with which the Lord had blessed the "people of God." The preachers of the sects and of the more extreme Independent congregations taught them that God was gathering His saints, that this was the beginning of those last times that the scriptural prophets had foretold, when the triumph of God's people would pave the way for Christ's kingdom on earth. For them, the unfolding of the millennium had begun.

For some years these two strains, the democratic and the millenarian, were not in conflict. The Levellers demanded full religious liberty as a fundamental natural right; the sectaries raised their flocks on much the same social soil as the Levellers, and felt the same urge to challenge the political ascendancy of the great ones of this earth. The chief Leveller leaders themselves had a sectarian background, and drew many sectaries into their movement. There was always a latent inconsistency between the Leveller ideal of

equal political rights for all free men and the more militant
sectaries' feeling that only the godly should bear rule in the New
Jerusalem, but there was a way around this apparent clash of principles. The Levellers, before circumstances forced them to compromise, generally held that religion and civil government occupied quite distinct spheres and should be segregated, for the civil
magistrate ministered only to the outward man and should have
no power to impose on consciences or enforce any form of national religion. That had been the view of that great sectary Roger
Williams. It was Milton's view too, and most of the sects went no
further.

But from about 1649 some ominous cracks began to appear.
By that time the Leveller movement was past its peak. Its rise and
decline were both rapid. Its first full-scale challenge developed
during the upheavals of 1647; its last serious bid for power failed
when the Leveller mutinies in the army were crushed in the
spring of 1649. It was defeated because Fairfax and Cromwell
stood foursquare with the Rump of the Long Parliament in opposing it, and because the great majority of the soldiers remained
loyal to their old commanders.

But while this military defeat was the immediate cause of the
Levellers' failure, one reason why it proved so final was that the
Leveller program was itself being called in question by people
of the same kind who had first supported it. Many of the smaller
citizens of London and some larger provincial towns, and many
soldiers too, began to ask whether a secular and democratic commonwealth *was* the kind of dispensation that the Lord had in
store for England. The contrary idea of a rule of the saints was
soon canvassed with increasing intensity. The movement for a
government by the godly in preparation for the millennium began to gather strength just when the campaign for a government
by the people on the basis of equal natural rights was being
crushed in a one-sided trial by battle. It is as if the failure to
remodel politics and society on a secular, rational basis inclined
many of these russet-coated revolutionaries to look for a more
apocalyptic kind of triumph—to translate their hopes for a more
just and equal society into an anticipation of the cosmic drama
foretold for the end of time in the cloudy pages of the Book of

Daniel and the Revelation of St. John the Divine. They read this heady stuff eagerly, with the literal minds of simple men.

Here by way of example are some propositions that a group of sectaries in Norfolk put to Fairfax and the General Council of the Army shortly after the execution of Charles I. They prayed the army not to "be instrumental for the setting up of a mere natural and worldly government, like that of heathen Rome and Athens." They asked

> Whether there is not a kingdom and dominion of the church, or of Christ and the Saints, to be expected upon earth? . . . Whether the kingdoms of the world and powers thereof, as kings, yea parliaments also, and magistrates . . . must not be put down, before this kingdom can be erected? . . .
>
> Whether this be not the time (or near upon it) of putting down that worldly government, and erecting this new kingdom? . . . How can the kingdom be the Saints' when the ungodly are electors, and elected to govern?

They proposed a government based not on the people as a whole but on the "gathered churches," that is to say those congregations which had been voluntarily formed by a company of "visible saints" coming together, testifying to each other of their experience of regeneration, and solemnly covenanting to walk together in the ways of the Lord. They envisaged a nation-wide federating of such churches and the election by them of general assemblies or "church parliaments"; "and then shall God give them authority and rule over the nations and kingdoms of the world." [2]

Now the whole history of Christian churches has been punctuated with episodes in which groups or sects have become obsessed with a conviction that the Last Times are imminent—that Christ is shortly coming again in glory, and that the Saints (meaning the faithful remnant that the Lord has saved against this day) must prepare for His reign by overturning all mere worldly principalities and powers. More than a century before the Civil War such beliefs had flared up among the Continental Anabaptists. Their violent seizure of power in Münster in 1534

2. *Certain Quaeres Humbly Presented . . . By Many Christian People* (1649); extracts printed in A. S. P. Woodhouse (ed.), *Puritanism and Liberty* (1951), pp. 241–47.

had sent a profound shock through the European nations, Catholic and Protestant alike, and had intensified a bitter persecution. Tudor England had, however, been almost immune from Anabaptism; the English Baptist churches stem from other and later sources.

Millenarianism entered very little into English Protestant experience before the social and political ferment of the 1640s created the right climate. But it caught on rapidly when the sober, orthodox divines of the central Puritan tradition found themselves challenged by firebrand sectarian prophets who fed their humbler flocks with a wilder gospel. Not that the expectation of the kingdom of Christ was confined to tub preachers and to soldiers possessed with the conviction that they fought a holy war. Some of the best-known divines preached to highly respectable audiences, including Parliament itself, that the struggle now afoot portended a working-out of God's purpose for the progressive establishment of His kingdom on earth, and that England was to be a second chosen nation. Cromwell among others was deeply imbued with the idea.

But it took on a cruder color in some of the sects, and their millenarian note changed to a harsher tone after the execution of the King and the establishment of the Commonwealth. Like the Leveller movement, it was partly an expression of frustration at the small benefit that Parliament's victory had brought to the unprivileged orders of society. A group was emerging called the Fifth Monarchy men, and their temper was militant and aggressive. Their beliefs were a mishmash of Daniel and Revelation, with dashes of Zechariah and Ezekiel and Malachi; but the core of their creed was based on Daniel's dream of the four beasts. These were interpreted as the four monarchies or empires of the ancient world. The first three were variously identified, but the fourth and most terrible beast represented the Roman Empire. Rome, however, had not perished as Babylon and Persia and Macedon had perished, for its power had been usurped and perpetuated by the Papacy, and the Papacy was equated with the Beast in Revelation and with Antichrist. There was much fascinated speculation about the ten horns of the Great Beast, and particularly about the little horn that had the eyes of a man and a mouth that spoke, and made war upon the saints; this was commonly taken to signify Charles I, until the Fifth Monarchists came to cast Cromwell for the part. But their main belief, sustained by much fantastic arithmetic, was that the day foretold for the destruction of the Beast (i.e., Antichrist) was at hand. It was for them to fulfill the prophecy that "the saints of the most High shall take the kingdom, and possess the kingdom for ever" (Daniel vii: 18), or alternatively that "they lived and reigned with Christ a thousand years" (Revelation xx: 4). Their task was to "overturn, overturn, overturn," in order to prepare the land for the Fifth Monarchy, the reign of Christ Himself.

There was nothing eccentric in the fact that men were searching the darker prophecies of the Old and New Testaments in an attempt to apply their meaning to their own revolutionary times. Virtually everyone accepted that the Scriptures were the revealed word of God, and a generation later Isaac Newton thought it worth much of his time to try to unravel their chronological riddles. What distinguished the Fifth Monarchy men was their emotional need to torture the cryptic figures in Revelation into forecasting a very imminent date for the millennium, and to read in them a divine call to violent action. This action, moreover, implied a social revolution, for the institutions that they were intent on overturning—Parliament, the common law, the Church establishment—were those that helped to sustain the political ascendancy of men of property. The cataclysmic irruption of an avenging God was to effect what the democratic program of the Levellers had failed to secure, for the saints whose arms He would strengthen to take the kingdom and possess it were sure to be found among the despised and downtrodden of mankind.

Just how widespread the Fifth Monarchy movement became is more than we know, but it developed three main areas of strength. In London there were several congregations, but the chief was at Blackfriars, where Christopher Feake fulminated to massive gatherings. In Wales the itinerant preachers Vavasor Powell and Morgan Llwyd built up a formidable network of disciples. And thirdly there was the army.

During the early years of the Commonwealth most of the army was too busy fighting to take much part in politics. But when

Ireland and Scotland were finally conquered, and when the battle of Worcester crowned its career of victory in 1651, the army soon showed the country that three more years of hardship and danger had only sharpened its revolutionary temper. A militant religious enthusiasm had taken a hold over considerable sections of the soldiery and not a few of their officers. These saints in arms found a redoubtable leader in Major General Harrison, who was converted to Fifth Monarchist beliefs not long after Worcester.

For a God-intoxicated man, as in his fashion he was, Harrison was an unexpectedly flamboyant figure, with a taste for fine scarlet coats and gold hatbands. But there was no mistaking his fierce sense of divine mission. Baxter describes him as "of a sanguine complexion, naturally of such a vivacity, hilarity and alacrity as another man hath when he hath drunken a cup too much." He had watched Harrison in action at the battle of Langport, and heard him at the moment of victory "with a loud voice break into the praises of God with fluent expressions, as if he had been in rapture." [3]

By the time that Harrison became an avowed Fifth Monarchist the army was becoming increasingly discontented with the rule of the Rump of the Long Parliament. During 1652 this remnant of a House of Commons elected a dozen years earlier was still resisting pressure to settle a more permanent constitution and make way for a more truly representative government. This is not the place to chronicle the army's various grievances, but behind them all was a feeling that these politicians were clinging to authority for the sake of the corrupt profits that power put in their grasp. The Rump, the army felt, was manifestly failing to measure up to what Cromwell called "the interest of the people of God."

A case in point was the Commission for the Propagation of the Gospel in Wales. This body had been set up in 1650, with Harrison at the head of its members, to evangelize the Welsh people, and through it Harrison had become the close associate of Vavasor Powell and other preachers of the Fifth Monarchy. But its term was for three years only, and when it expired at the end of March 1653 the Rump declined to renew it. Not unnaturally the House

3. *Reliquiae Baxterianae*, Part 1, §§ 78, 82.

distrusted these millenarian firebrands and wanted to replace them with safer and more orthodox ministers. But Cromwell at this time stood close to Harrison and regarded the renewal of the Commission as a touchstone of the Rump's integrity. When it was refused, his attitude to the Parliament hardened appreciably.

So far, Cromwell had steadily resisted the army's pressure to dissolve the Rump by force. His veneration for Parliament as an institution was sincere, and he knew how hard it would be to establish a legally constituted government after such an act of violence. But as he complained to a confidant, "he was pushed on by two parties to do that, the consideration of the issue whereof made his hair to stand on end." [4]

The two parties were rival factions within the army. One was headed by John Lambert, the popular and able young major general, and its discontents were mainly secular and practical. Lambert, as far as we know, wanted the army to set up a small Council of State to govern the country until it was settled enough to elect its own representatives once more. The other party was led by Harrison and consisted of the religious enthusiasts. Harrison believed that the time was now fully ripe for a rule of the saints, and he was said to favor the form that the Fifth Monarchist preachers Christopher Feake and John Rogers were urging: a sanhedrin of seventy godly men, after the model of Jerusalem's government in biblical times.

Although both parties were pressing Cromwell to expel the Rump he still held them back. In April 1653 the House got down at last to debating a Bill for a New Representative. But he found to his dismay that it proposed not a general election and a new Parliament but merely by-elections to the vacant seats. The Rumpers would sit on, and judge whether the new members fulfilled the qualifications that the Rumpers themselves imposed. Moreover, there were strong rumors that they intended to remove Cromwell from the generalship and install someone more submissive—Fairfax, perhaps—in his place.

Cromwell now arranged urgent conferences between leading officers and Rumpers, and put to the latter one last expedient. Let them hand over authority to a select body of "men fearing

4. C. H. Firth (ed.), *Memoirs of Edmund Ludlow* (Oxford, 1894), I, 346.

God, and of approved integrity," who would govern until the country could be trusted again to elect a properly constituted Parliament. Forty was about the number he had in mind. Clearly he was thinking in terms of a nominated assembly *before* he expelled the Rump. Late at night on April 19 he thought he had persuaded the leading members to consider this scheme before they went further. Next morning, however, they tried to rush their own bill through in his absence, and it was then that he summoned his famous file of musketeers and cleared the House.

It was a precipitate act, and he had laid no plans for what should follow. He set up a temporary Council of State, consisting at first of only ten men, with Lambert as its first president. But he referred the question of a more permanent settlement to the Council of Officers, a larger body whose membership fluctuated around thirty or forty. A military dictatorship was in his grasp, had he wanted it; but he did not.

Yet what were the alternatives? To summon a new Parliament by means of a general election, as the army had until recently urged the Rump to do, was almost out of the question. Not only had the army no shred of legal right to issue the writs, but the former members could convincingly invoke the act of 1641 whereby the Long Parliament might be dissolved only with its own consent. Moreover, the army would have been bound to resort to arbitrary means in order to exclude its bitter opponents among the Royalists, the Presbyterians, and the Rumpers. It would have been a hopelessly risky venture, and Harrison's party would have opposed it strenuously on principle.

So it made a certain sense when the Council of Officers decided upon a nominated assembly as the new "supreme authority." It was to be a body of "men fearing God and of approved integrity" such as Cromwell had lately urged upon the Rump, only larger and (within limits) more representative. The number decided upon was 140, with varying numbers of members for each English county and five or six apiece for Scotland, Ireland, and Wales.

How were they chosen? The story accepted until recently, deriving mainly from Gardiner's *History of the Commonwealth and Protectorate,* was that the Council of Officers sent circular letters to the gathered churches in each county, inviting them to recommend such godly men as they thought fit for the trust of government, and that from the lists returned the officers selected most of the members. But Gardiner for once was wrong. There was almost certainly no general invitation to the churches, though some few churches sent in lists of names unbidden, and Harrison personally worked hand in glove with the Welsh saints in picking the members for North Wales. Only fifteen of the original 140 nominees, however, are known to have been proposed by their churches, and in fact the Council of Officers picked whom it pleased. Cromwell claimed later that "not an officer of the degree of a captain but named more than he himself did." [5]

The assembly thus summoned soon gained the nickname of Barebone's Parliament, because among its members was Praise-God Barbon or Barebone, the godly leather merchant and Baptist lay preacher of Fleet Street. But it was not called a Parliament by those who summoned it; it gave itself that title after it met. Some historians have seen it as a wholehearted attempt to establish a rule of the saints, and assumed that Cromwell was converted for the time to Harrison's notions. This view needs to be qualified.

Cromwell never shared the crazier and more violent dreams of the Fifth Monarchy men. He certainly wanted a government that would promote "the interest of the people of God," but, as his opening speech was to make clear, he regarded the assembly as an interim expedient. He set a term of sixteen months to its authority. He looked to it to bring the unsettled nation back to calm and prosperity, and to teach it the benefits of a Commonwealth so that as soon as possible the people could be trusted again to elect their own representatives. In his view and that of the more moderate officers, the task called for men whose Puritan zeal was tempered by a sense of political realities, and where possible made respectable by birth and property. Harrison and his faction in the Council of Officers, which included men like Rich, Saunders, Mason, Packer, Wigan, and Chillenden, saw things differently. They were not looking for a mere caretaker government to educate the people in the benefits and responsi-

5. W. C. Abbott, *Writings and Speeches of Oliver Cromwell* (Cambridge, Mass., 1937–47), IV, 418.

bilities of a self-governing republic. They wanted a sanhedrin of
the saints, a dictatorship of the godly that would prepare for the
millennium by overturning every vestige of the old "carnal" government. It was they, we can be sure, who nominated the many
obscure zealots who were to get Barebone's Parliament such a
bad name.

Yet Cromwell evidently did not recognize the difference that
lay between him and Harrison. He could be such a victim of
rhetoric, his own as well as others', that he could not see where he
was being led. He had his own vision of the Kingdom of Christ
in England's green and pleasant land, though a less crude one
than Harrison's. Early in June, just as the Council of Officers
completed its work of selecting the forthcoming assembly's members, came news of a naval victory over the Dutch. Cromwell and
the Council of State published a declaration calling for a day of
thanksgiving. He hailed the victory—and surely the words are
his own—as marking "the day of [the Lord's] righteousness and
faithfulness . . . of His beginning to heal the Creation; the day
of gathering His people." He saw it as "an answer to the faith
and prayer of God's people, and to their hopes and expectations
from the Lord. It is a mercy minding us of, and sealing to us, all
our former mercies. A mercy at such a time as this, to say no
more; what mercies it hath in the bowels of it, time will declare:
who knows?" [6]

How like this is to the speech he made a month later when he
opened the new assembly and told its members

> Truly you are called by God to rule with Him, and for Him.
> And you are called to be faithful with the Saints, who have been
> somewhat instrumental to your call. . . . Jesus Christ is owned
> this day by your call; and you own Him by your willingness to
> appear for Him; and you manifest this, as far as poor creatures
> can, to be the day of the power of Christ. . . .
>
> And why should we be afraid to say or think, that this may
> be the door to usher in the things that God has promised; which
> have been prophesied of; which He has set the hearts of His
> people to wait for and expect? [7]

6. *A Declaration from the General and Council of State* (1653).
7. Abbott, *op. cit.*, pp. 63–64.

All too soon Cromwell was to be deeply disillusioned with this assembly. But before explaining why, we had better take a closer look at its composition. It was a widely variegated body, reflecting the diverse intentions of the officers who had chosen it. It was not for the most part the conventicle of simple, impractical enthusiasts that some textbooks still portray. Too much still lingers on of the Royalist legend, typified by Clarendon's assertion that "much the major part of them consisted of inferior persons, of no quality or name, artificers of the meanest trades, known only by their gifts in praying and preaching." [8]

This is a travesty. No fewer than 115 members were justices of the peace—the very great majority, that is, of those who sat for the English counties or for Wales. Admittedly the office of J.P. had fallen in the social scale since prewar days, but most county magistrates were still men of some substance, and so were most members of Barebone's Parliament. It boasted one rather moth-eaten peer in his own right, Lord Eure, besides Viscount Lisle, the heir of the Earl of Leicester. Four baronets and four knights answered Cromwell's summons, and a good two-thirds of the membership can be ranked among the landed gentry—though there were naturally many more of the lesser gentry than in a typical seventeenth-century Parliament. The company included Sir Anthony Ashley Cooper, the future Earl of Shaftesbury; Charles Howard, the future Earl of Carlisle; Edward Montagu, the future Earl of Sandwich; not to mention honest George Monck, the future Duke of Albermarle. Others such as Francis Lascelles, Richard Lucy, Sir Gilbert Pickering, Sir William Roberts, Walter Strickland, William Sydenham, Sir Charles Wolseley, and many more would not have been out of place in a typical elected Parliament of that age.

Only a score or so had sat in Parliament before, but that is not surprising, considering that the great majority of former M.P.s, whether Royalists, Presbyterians, or Rumpers, were now so hostile to the army that they were virtually ruled out. But fifty-five of Barebone's fellow members were to be elected to one or more subsequent Parliaments, mostly under the Protectorate; twenty-

8. *History of the Rebellion*, V, 282.

two would be called to Cromwell's new upper house in 1657; and twenty were to be back at Westminster under Charles II (fourteen in the Commons and six in the Lords). About a third of the members had been to a university, and despite the army's decision to exclude practicing lawyers, about forty had studied at one or other of the Inns of Court. Thirteen of these had been called to the bar, so the House was not so devoid of legal experience as has sometimes been said.

One surprise is the paucity of army men in it. This is because Cromwell and the Council of Officers were so anxious to avoid any semblance of a military dictatorship that they decided not to nominate serving officers. The only exceptions were four of the representatives of Ireland, seven or eight governors of towns or garrisons, the two generals at sea (Blake and Monck), and five leading officers (including Cromwell and Lambert and Harrison) whom the House itself co-opted after it had met—though of these five only Desborough seems to have taken any appreciable part in its proceedings. It is true that about sixty members were called by military titles—some regularly, some not—but most of them had laid down their commissions long ago, or held rank only in the local militia. England had its own brand of Kentucky colonels in the 1650s.

We must now return to the central question of why this assembly disappointed Cromwell's hopes—and disappointed them so utterly that he was intensely relieved when it finally resigned its power back into his hands. The basic reason lay in a rift that very soon appeared between the more moderate members and the more radical ones. These are relative terms, for the moderates were themselves mostly reformers, as their legislation shows. But they were content to exercise the traditional function of a Parliament within the general framework of the law of the land. The hard core of the radical faction, on the other hand, was intent on proclaiming new heavens and a new earth, and on sweeping away everything that might hinder the imminent triumph of the saints. The split was not only religious and political; it was (as we shall see) social as well.

Was it Cromwell's fault that these divisions occurred? H. R. Trevor-Roper has belabored him for failing to provide the kind of leadership and management that might have kept this pseudo-Parliament on the rails. Of course it *was* naïve to assemble 140 men, mostly without parliamentary experience, and expect good laws and wise policies to flow from them by the inspiration of Providence. Of course they needed a nucleus of well-briefed speakers and able tacticians to steer constructive measures through their rambling debates. Yet it is not easy to see where such a managerial core was to be found. It was certainly not found in the Council of State of thirty-one members that Cromwell left the House to elect as it pleased.

There was no unity even among Cromwell's closest associates, the men who shared with him the nominating of the assembly. Lambert and Harrison, each with a powerful following in the army, were not only at odds with each other; *both* turned against the new supreme authority that the Council of Officers had set up. Lambert withdrew from the Council of State from the day on which Barebone's Parliament first met, and he probably never took his seat in the House either. He retired first to his grand house at Wimbledon and then to his Yorkshire home. According to the French ambassador he resented the transference of power to the new assembly from the small interim Council of State in which he had held a dominant position. Harrison sat in the House and the Council of State for three weeks or so, but then withdrew in disgust with some of his radical friends. He returned only late in the assembly's brief life, and then probably sat only a few times. His motives were the opposite of Lambert's: he found that his fellow saints were not in command of the assembly as he had hoped, and that Cromwell's sympathies were falling more and more on the side of the moderate majority.

The rift between the two main groups in the House began to open in mid-July, after only ten days' sitting. The matter of debate was tithes, an old and bitter grievance of the sectaries. But whereas the moderates were prepared like Cromwell himself to consider some other mode of financial support for the parish clergy that would be fairer in incidence and less subject to religious scruples, the more radical members wanted to do away with any form of public maintenance and any kind of established parochial ministry. They wished religion to be left entirely to the gathered churches, each maintaining its own pastors by its own contributions, and all entirely independent of the state. This proved to be the rock on which Barebone's Parliament finally shipwrecked. An associated issue was the right of lay patrons to present to church livings. Naturally the radicals opposed it on principle, and they won one of their rare successes when they carried a vote to bring in a bill that would have abolished lay patronage outright.

The reform of the law was another bone of contention. Nearly all agreed that the law stood in need of considerable reform, but it was one thing to remedy the abuses of the common law while preserving its essential and venerable structure, and quite another to abrogate it lock, stock, and barrel and to substitute a simple written code "within the bigness of a pocket-book." The radicals succeeded in setting up a committee to do just that. The Court of Chancery was a similar case. Something certainly needed to be done about its tangled mysteries and ruinously expensive delays, but to vote as the radicals did for its total abolition without erecting any other institution to take over its jurisdiction filled conservative men with dismay.

There are several things worth remarking about this persistent conflict between moderates and radicals. Firstly, these were not organized parties but loose groupings, whose strength fluctuated according to the matter under debate. Secondly, the moderates could nearly always command a majority when they turned up in strength. They did so early in November when the House elected a new Council of State, and they succeeded in turning nearly all the radical councillors out. But although one cannot give anything like firm figures for the strengths of these groupings, it is possible to identify a kernel of perhaps forty members who took the radical line on most issues. On some important ones they carried a varying number of fellow travelers with them. And despite the withdrawal of Harrison and some of his friends they were mostly zealous in attendance, whereas the moderates were not. The House became very thin as the autumn wore on.

A further feature of this cleavage was the marked social distinction between the two main groups. Nearly all the men of birth and property whom I have mentioned were on the moderate side;

the radical core was with a few exceptions of lower social status. These zealots were not for the most part the "base mechanics" of Royalist legend, but they included men who had been raised from obscurity by their careers in the Civil Wars, aldermen and the like of provincial towns, squireens on the shadowy fringes of the gentry, and a few others of still more modest origin. It did not endear them to the moderates that these pretenders to divine illumination were in so many cases godly tradesmen or Bible-thumping ex-colonels.

Cromwell was probably sensitive to this social factor when he complained in August that he was "more troubled now with the fool, than before with the knave." [9] He became particularly troubled because the radicals' aims implied an increasing threat to property. Tithes were a case in point, because so large a proportion of tithes had passed into the hands of lay impropriators and constituted a definite part of the value of the estates to which they were annexed. Advowsons, or the right to present to parish livings, were also a marketable property. The common law itself, which the radicals threatened to destroy, was in large part the land law of the propertied classes. But what dismayed Cromwell most of all was the threat to do away with any kind of publicly supported parochial clergy. His main charge against Barebone's Parliament, years later, was that "the ministry and propriety [i.e., property] were like to be destroyed." [10]

The nucleus of avowed Fifth Monarchy men in the House was small. I cannot be sure of more than eleven members who confessed themselves as such, though these were just the center of a larger group of radical sectaries who followed their lead. A little caucus of these enthusiasts met regularly to concert policy at the house of one of their number called Arthur Squibb, who was a thorough-paced Fifth Monarchist. They kept close contact, too, with the great prayer meetings at Blackfriars, where Christopher Feake thundered the millenarian gospel.

This association with the most fanatical element among London's citizenry brought the Parliament into increasing disrepute. It was a nuisance to Cromwell in other ways, for the Fifth Mon-

9. Bodleian Library, Clarendon MS. 46, f. 230.
10. Abbott, *op. cit.,* p. 418.

archists were doing their utmost to frustrate his efforts to make peace with the Dutch. They were filled with crazy dreams of universal conquest. John Canne, for instance, proclaimed as a message from the Lord that "our proper work is . . . not to look after merchants, as to grow great and rich by the wealth of other nations, but to break their power and strength in pieces. . . . Speaking here I say, as it were from heaven, that it is not prizes, or the enemy's goods, our hearts or hands should desirously be upon: But to destroy Babylon, stain the Glory of Kings and Kingdoms, and lay low the high and great mountains of the earth." [11] Feake's congregation sang doggerel hymns of his own composing which breathed fire and slaughter from the Lord against the proud and wealthy cities of Holland. Harrison is said to have railed constantly against the peace with the Dutch and against Cromwell for seeking it.

By the autumn Feake and his brethren at Blackfriars were denouncing Cromwell himself as "the man of sin, the old dragon and many other scripture ill names." The attack was extended to other chief officers of the army. There was a proposal in Parliament that they should forgo a year's pay. They were aspersed in the House as janissaries and denounced from the pulpit as pensioners of Babylon. Vavasor Powell "told the sword-men in general, that the Spirit of God was departed from them; that heretofore they had been precious and excellent men, but that their parks, and new houses, and gallant wives, had choked them up." [12]

Within the House the behavior of the self-styled saints became increasingly intolerable. They claimed to enjoy "an extraordinary call from Christ." [13] They would come in from their religious exercises with their Bibles in their hands and solemnly deliver their latest promptings from the Almighty; one of them claimed for some extravagant assertion "that he spake it not, but the Lord in him." Moderate members heard themselves "unsainted and condemned into the fourth monarchy, and looked upon as ob-

11. J. Canne, *A Voice from the Temple to the Higher Powers* (1653), Conclusion.
12. *Strena Vavasoriensis* (1654), p. 19.
13. *An Answer to a Paper Entituled A True Narrative* (1654), p. 2.

structors of Reformation, and no longer fit for the work." [14]
These zealots behaved as though "actuated by a more high and
active spirit of Dreams and Phantasie, which set an end to reasoning, and led them out to a pretence of infallibility in all their
determinations." [15] According to one report, "they resolved to
divide and separate themselves from the other members, who followed them not in their excesses, and to constitute themselves
into a power distinct from them." [16] They were said to be planning to remodel the army and place its command in other hands.

No wonder Cromwell looked on these proceedings with growing exasperation. No wonder Lambert quietly returned from his
sulks in the north and began to work out a new written constitution that would set Cromwell at the head of the state, with a
system of checks and balances to ensure there would be no more
such excesses in the future. But Cromwell was not prepared to
dissolve another Parliament by force, and he probably had no
hand in the plot that brought this ill-starred assembly to an end.
Lambert was probably deep in it, but the canker of internal dis-
sension made the fruit ready to fall at a touch. The last and fatal
conflict came over a scheme to settle the Church and its ministry
—a scheme long considered by a well-balanced committee and
similar in principle to that which Cromwell was shortly to promul-
gate as Lord Protector. The first article was tensely debated for
six days. When it came to a division the radicals mustered their
fullest strength and probably exploited some complex cross-voting;
at any rate, the article was rejected by two votes.

That was on Saturday, December 10. On Sunday the leading
moderates caballed together and on Monday morning they came
to the House unusually early. One after another they denounced
their opponents for threatening the ministry of the Church, an-
tagonizing the army, and jeopardizing both property and the
law. Then without taking a vote they trooped out of the House
with the Speaker at their head, marched to Whitehall, and resigned their authority into Cromwell's hands. A rump of about
thirty radicals sat on until a pair of colonels arrived and civilly

14. *Ibid.*, pp. 3, 9.
15. *A True State of the Case of the Commonwealth* (1654), p. 15.
16. *Ibid.*, p. 20.

requested them to leave. Within a day or two a clear majority of
the members had signed a brief instrument of abdication.

The rest is well known. Cromwell accepted the written constitution from the hands of Lambert and half a dozen fellow officers,
and four days after Barebone's Parliament ceased to sit he was
solemnly installed as Lord Protector.

It was not the end of the Fifth Monarchy men, though from
now on they were an isolated and despised minority. Most of the
sects accepted the wide liberty of conscience that the Protectorate
extended to them. Harrison, however, broke with Cromwell completely, and on refusing to give any assurance that he would live
peaceably was stripped of his commissions and briefly imprisoned.
Feake and Rogers were also incarcerated for a time. Cromwell did
not want to persecute the Fifth Monarchy men, but their open
incitements to sedition forced him to restrain them.

In February 1654 he summoned some of their leaders before the
Council to see what persuasion could do. There he and some Independent ministers argued at length with Harrison and Rich and
two leaders of the Fifth Monarchist caucus in Barebone's Parliament, John Carew and Hugh Courtney. Secretary Thurloe reported their defiant views:

> That the present authority is not any authority, nor to be obeyed,
> and consequently arms may be taken up against it. That the
> magistrate which is carnal hath no right, nor can have; and the
> great objection which they make against this Government [the
> Protectoral constitution] was because it had a Parliament in it,
> whereby power is derived from the people, whereas all power
> belongs to Christ. . . . Mr. Carew added that my Lord Protec-
> tor, when the little Parliament was dissolved, took the crown off
> from the head of Christ, and put it upon his own.[17]

The further activities and conspiracies of the Fifth Monarchists
cannot be chronicled here. They always looked back on Barebone's Parliament as their great opportunity and their great defeat,
and in 1659, after Cromwell's death, some of them agitated afresh
for a supreme assembly elected by the gathered churches. Cromwell himself referred in retrospect to his experiment as "a story
of my own weakness and folly." It provided one of the harshest

17. C. H. Firth (ed.), *The Clarke Papers* (1891–1901), II, 244.

lessons in his political education. I do not agree with those historians who see in the Protectorate a simple process of political reaction, but insofar as it marked a return to more traditional modes of government Cromwell's experience of the militant saints probably influenced him even more than his earlier contest with the Levellers. And after the Restoration, when the Royalists looked back on all they hated most in the Great Rebellion, they were more apt to remember the extravagances of the sectaries than the challenge of the Levellers. Perhaps it was because the saints had come a shade nearer to success; perhaps because the Fifth Monarchy movement was somewhat longer a-dying. It had its last fling in the cooper Thomas Venner's crazy rising in 1661. At any rate, enthusiasm was soon to become at least as dirty a word as democracy. No doubt that was part of the climate of European thought, but in England it was surely intensified by lingering memories of the millenarians' brief attempt to set up a rule of the saints.

GEORGE D. HEATH III

Cromwell and Lambert, 1653–57

THE GENERALITY of mankind is so likely to be dazzled by
the glamorous and pompous ceremonies which surround those
who are invested with the outward insignia of political power that
sometimes even the most astute observers are deceived into mistaking the shadow of power for its substance. Because Oliver
Cromwell as Lord Protector of England received ambassadors,
opened parliaments, and lived in royal palaces, many contemporary
observers—and indeed many subsequent historians—have been inclined to ignore or to minimize the vast power wielded by Major
General John Lambert. The great Victorian historian S. R. Gardiner was the first to begin the correction of this distorted view,
but even Gardiner failed to emphasize sufficiently the importance
of Lambert's vast influence during the years 1653–57.

Major General John Lambert had gained a reputation during the Civil Wars as a soldier's soldier, whose military fame rivaled that of Cromwell himself. Moreover, he had gained enormous popularity not only on account of his warm engaging personality, his moderation, and his sense of justice but particularly on account of his keen interest in the welfare of the rank and file. Some measure of the esteem and the affection in which he was held is evidenced by the sobriquet "honest John," by which he was universally known throughout the army.[1]

Quite apart from Lambert's popularity and ability as a general, however, were other qualities, most unusual in a professional soldier: his extraordinary powers of persuasion, his ability as a negotiator, and his talent for harmonizing conflicting viewpoints. Furthermore, Lambert soon began to display a great aptitude for political and constitutional leadership. There is good evidence that Lambert had had legal training at one of the Inns of Court before the Civil War.[2] However that may be, we know that he served as spokesman for the officers in negotiations with the parliamentary commissioners in 1647, and that later in the same year he served as Ireton's collaborator in drawing up the various declarations of the army in its dispute with Parliament. But the most signal testimonial to Lambert's political leadership and to his ability as a political theoretician came in 1647, when his army colleagues entrusted him—again in collaboration with Ireton—with the task of drawing up the army's proposed written constitution for the settlement of the kingdom, known as the Heads of the Proposals. Its spirit of moderation and tolerance toward all parties would seem to indicate strongly Lambert's influence.

Shortly afterward, Lambert departed from the scene of political action, leaving Ireton to act virtually alone and unaided as the

---

1. *Dictionary of National Biography*, XXXI, 11–18; W. H. Dawson, *Cromwell's Understudy: Life and Times of General John Lambert* (London, 1938), pp. 42, 90–91, 101–03, 124–25; C. H. Firth (ed.), *Memoirs of Edmund Ludlow, Lieutenant General of the Horse in the Army of the Commonwealth of England, 1625–1672* (Oxford, 1894), I, 280–81; Clarendon, *History of the Rebellion and Civil Wars in England* (Oxford, 1840), II, 714.

2. Bulstrode Whitelocke, *Memorials of the English Affairs . . . from the Beginning of the Reign of King Charles the First to King Charles the Second* (Oxford, 1853), II, 163.

political spokesman of the Army Grandees in the debates at Putney. Lambert's absence as commander in the North also caused him to miss the great drama of Pride's Purge and the trial and execution of the King. However, his position as commander in the North was a semi-political one, and he had ample opportunity to display his statesmanlike gifts in that area; he not only transformed a sullen, near-mutinous soldiery into a contented, obedient army by the exercise of his sense of justice and moderation but also succeeded in reconciling the army with the civilian population in those parts. Later, after the defeat of the Scots at Dunbar and Worcester, he served as a commissioner over the dour Presbyterians of Scotland, who were still smarting from their defeat by the "heretical" English Independents, and by his conciliatory manner and his sense of justice won golden testimonials from the people of that proud country.[3]

With the death of Ireton in 1651, Lambert succeeded to the former's position as the chief political theoretician and idea man of the army. Lambert's new position received partial recognition by his appointment to succeed Ireton as Lord Deputy of Ireland —one of the choicest plums that an army officer could hope for. It is true, however, that several months after Lambert's appointment and after he had spent a very large sum of money in outfitting himself for that semi-regal position, Parliament suddenly abolished the lord lieutenancy, held by Cromwell, and with it Lambert's position of lord deputy lapsed automatically.[4] This affront undoubtedly caused Lambert to take great umbrage against the Rump Parliament, which was already highly unpopular with the army because of its failure to enact the latter's program of reform and especially because of its stubborn refusal to dissolve itself and pave the way for another body more amenable to the army's wishes.[5]

As a result the army brought great pressure to bear on Crom-

3. Dawson, *Cromwell's Understudy*, pp. 46–47, 57–66, 144–59.
4. Lucy Hutchinson, *Memoirs of the Life of Colonel Hutchinson*, ed. J. Hutchinson (London, 1905), pp. 360–61.
5. T. Birch (ed.), *Thurloe State Papers: A Collection of the State Papers of John Thurloe, Esq., Secretary first to the Council of State and afterwards to the Two Protectors* (London, 1742), VII, 660; Whitelocke, *Memorials*, pp. 548–51.

well to dissolve the Rump by force if need be. As he himself testified: "I am pushed on by two parties to do that, the consideration of the issue whereof makes my hair to stand on end." One of the parties, Cromwell maintained, was led by Lambert, who was motivated by a desire for revenge because Parliament had cut him out of the lord deputyship of Ireland; the other party was led by Major General Harrison, "who is an honest man and aims at good things, yet from the impatience of his spirit will not wait the Lord's leisure, but hurries me on to that which he and all honest men will have cause to repent." [6] From this statement two things are clear: first, Cromwell's extreme reluctance to dissolve the Rump; second, of the two parties mentioned, Harrison's Fifth Monarchist faction was the more determined and uncompromising.

There is a vast amount of other evidence which confirms Cromwell's extreme reluctance to dissolve the Rump. He not only failed to sign the army's celebrated petition to Parliament of August 13, 1652, but he also persuaded the officers to delete a demand for the immediate dissolution of Parliament. Somewhat later he arranged for meetings between leading members of Parliament and the officers, at which he endeavored to effect a reconciliation of the two groups.[7] These conferences were fruitless, however, and the officers held meetings at which they composed threatening addresses to Parliament and urged Cromwell to dissolve it by force. Even so, Cromwell hazarded his leadership of the army by his opposition to a forced dissolution. Thus, on March 11, 1653, the Council of Officers at St. James would have passed a resolution to "turn them out had not both the General and Colonel Desborough interceded." On April 1 it was said: "Our soldiers resolve to have speedily a new representative, and the Parliament resolve the contrary. The General sticks close to the House, which causeth him to be daily railed on by the preaching party, who say they must have both a new Parliament and General before the work be done." [8] Cromwell later in his speech to the hundred officers on

6. *Ludlow Memoirs,* I, 346.
7. C. H. Firth, *Oliver Cromwell and the Rule of the Puritans in England* (London, 1901), p. 317.
8. S. R. Gardiner, *History of the Commonwealth and Protectorate* (London, 1894), II, 171.

February 27, 1657, charged that "they had made him dissolve the Long Parliament for 'twas done against his judgment." [9]

After the dissolution two alternatives for the future government were presented. The first, sponsored by Lambert and the more moderate reformers, suggested that power be concentrated in the hands of a small council of ten or twelve, pending more permanent arrangements, which probably meant a written constitution. The second, sponsored by Harrison and his extreme Fifth Monarchist reformers, suggested that an assembly of seventy of the most virtuous and godly of the Puritan "saints," modeled after the Jewish Sanhedrin, be summoned to rule England. [10]

Following the dissolution of the Rump, Lambert became president of the Council of Officers as a result of an election. Lord Hatton, a prominent Royalist, clearly shows the reputation enjoyed by Lambert at this time:

> Lambert is esteemed the general man; his interest is more universal in the army and country and not confined to a particular party. They speak him an unfathomed person, still undeclared and consequently the more to be feared. They say he hath the ruling reason in the council and when the General is about hath still the chair. He cunningly and tacitly opposes Harrison to the general, and he knows himself enough for Harrison— some think for them both. He hath the present vogue as a person that would (or might at least) do something considerable for the dissolved Parliament, some hope for the King also. [11]

If Lambert held such a powerful position, the question naturally arises why a version of Harrison's scheme rather than Lambert's was adopted as the next experiment in government. Although there is no direct evidence on this point, it would appear that the farsighted Lambert, knowing well that it would require a lengthy period to draw up his idea of a written constitution and feeling certain that Harrison's "saints" would be almost certain to discredit themselves in the public eye by their lack of political expe-

9. W. C. Abbott, *Writings and Speeches of Oliver Cromwell* (Cambridge, Mass., 1937–47), IV, 417.
10. *Ludlow Memoirs,* I, 346–58.
11. Newsletter, May 13, 1653, *Calendar of the Clarendon Papers* (Oxford, 1869–76), No. 1153.

rience as well as by their religious fanaticism, suggested to Cromwell that Harrison's scheme be given a trial, hoping thus to give Harrison's party enough rope to hang itself. A variation of Harrison's scheme was put into operation. The Independent, or "gathered" churches, were invited to send in the names of those they considered the most virtuous and godly of their number, and from this group the officers selected 140 members, who were summoned to Westminster in Cromwell's name in his capacity as commander-in-chief of the army.[12] That the summons went out in Cromwell's name gave the impression that Cromwell had personally selected the members. This appearance of power was deceptive; in his speech to the hundred officers in 1657 Cromwell said that others, as well as he, had appointed the members of the Nominated Parliament.[13]

While a detailed analysis of the work of the Nominated Parliament is beyond the scope of this essay, it is necessary to say that the extreme zealots, led by Harrison, seized the initiative in that body and inaugurated a period of the most drastic reform, wholly without regard to the powerful vested interests of the beneficed clergy, the lawyers, the landowners, or even of the army which had summoned it. Therefore, after sitting only a few months, the Nominated Parliament had succeeded in discrediting itself with every influential element of the Puritan ruling class—as the astute Lambert had probably foreseen.[14] In the meantime, Lambert had ostentatiously disassociated himself from the Parliament and had withdrawn to his palatial home at Wimbledon, in whose elegant surroundings he addressed himself to the task of drawing up and perfecting the details of his plan of government.[15] Unfortunately, little is known of the details of the making of the Instrument of

12. Pauluzzi to Morosini, May 23/13, *Calendar of State Papers and Manuscripts Relating to English Affairs existing in the Archives and Collections of Venice and in other Libraries of Northern Italy*, ed. H. F. Brown and A. B. Hind (London, 1929–37), p. 379; Gardiner, *Commonwealth and Protectorate*, II, 231–34.

13. Abbott, *Cromwell*, IV, 418.

14. *Journals of the House of Commons, 1547–1714*, VII, 296, 351; Gardiner, *Commonwealth and Protectorate*, II, 253 n. 4, 264 n. 1; W. Godwin, *History of the Commonwealth of England from its Commencement to the Restoration of Charles the Second* (London, 1824–28), IV, 88.

15. Dawson, *Cromwell's Understudy*, pp. 172, 175.

Government, as Lambert's constitution came to be called, beyond the fact that Lambert was the chief, if not the sole author, and that he had been working on it for two months prior to the dissolution of the Nominated Parliament on December 12, 1653.[16]

On November 26, M. de Bordeaux-Neufville, the French envoy, reported that Lambert had returned to London to preside over a meeting of the Council of Officers, whose purpose was "to change the Parliament, place authority in a council of a few persons and destroy the Anabaptists."[17] Events were to confirm this prediction, for on December 12 the Nominated Parliament was induced to "abdicate" its powers and return them to Cromwell by a ruse engineered by Lambert's conservative followers—particularly Wolseley and Sydenham. Lambert himself remained in the background. The next day, however, Lambert formally presented the deed of the Nominees' "abdication" and at the same time presented his Instrument of Government, which had probably been discussed with the Council of Officers beforehand.[18] After two days of discussion, during which relatively minor alterations seem to have been made, Cromwell finally accepted it. Shortly thereafter he was inaugurated Protector on December 16, 1653, in a pompous ceremony in which Lambert played a most conspicuous part, acting as a sort of master of ceremonies.[19]

The entire episode of the destruction of the Nominees and the inauguration of the Protectorate, on the basis of the Instrument of Government, was everywhere regarded as a stunning triumph for Lambert and a corresponding defeat for Harrison and the zealots.

16. T. Burton, *Diary of Thomas Burton, Esq. Member of the Parliaments of Oliver and Richard Cromwell from 1656 to 1659 . . . with an Introduction Containing an Account of the Parliament of 1654,* ed. J. T. Rutt (London, 1828), IV, 63; *Ludlow Memoirs,* I, 369–70.

17. Bordeaux to Brienne, December 6/November 26, 1653, *French Transcripts, R.O.*

18. *Ludlow Memoirs,* I, 366; "An Exact Relation" in *Somers Tracts: A Collection of Scarce and Valuable Tracts . . . Selected from Public as well as Private Libraries, Particularly that of the Late Lord Somers,* ed. Sir Walter Scott (London, 1809–15), VI, 282–83; intercepted letter for Paris, December 14, *Thurloe State Papers,* I, 632.

19. Gardiner, *Commonwealth and Protectorate,* II, 283; intercepted letter for Paris, December 14, *op. cit.; Ludlow Memoirs,* I, 372.

In anger Harrison and his followers denounced the new regime at the cost of their commissions and their freedom.[20]

To understand the real basis of Lambert's power, however, it is necessary to analyze his Instrument of Government in some detail. It was certainly one of the most cunningly contrived constitutional documents ever drawn up because its general tenor, as derived from a casual first reading, gave the impression that Parliament was to have very considerable powers. A more careful reading and an analysis of the fine print revealed that Parliament had little power. The Instrument gave the appearance of a constitutional government by a Protector and a Parliament: the executive power vested in the former; legislative power, predominantly in the latter. Various articles, often written in an indirect and inconspicuous fashion, so narrowed and whittled down the powers of Parliament as to make it virtually the helpless tool of the executive.[21]

Even more deceptive than the apparent power of Parliament was the illusory nature of the Protector's power. Here again, great pains were taken to give the impression that the enormous powers of the executive resided solely and exclusively in the Protector, but close analysis disclosed that the Protector was an imposing front man for a powerful Council. Superficially, it must be admitted, the Protector was to be a dazzling figure. He was invested with all the panoply of power and the majestic insignia of the chief of state. He was to reside in the royal palaces, to live in quasi-regal state, to hold court, to open Parliament, to receive ambassadors, and to be the source of all magistracy and honors. But when it came to the specific enumeration and definition of the Protector's powers, it was with the proviso that most of them could be exercised only with the advice and consent of the Council. The Instrument provided that the Protector should govern and administer England,

20. Intercepted letter for Paris, December 14, *op. cit.;* intercepted letter from Thomas Crocker to Francis Edwards, December 23, *Thurloe State Papers,* I, 645; Dawson, *Cromwell's Understudy,* pp. 182–83, 185; *Ludlow Memoirs,* II, 380.

21. S. R. Gardiner (ed.), *Constitutional Documents of the Puritan Revolution, 1625–1660* (Oxford, 1906), pp. 406 ff. for Articles II, III, VI, X, XII, XIV, XV, XVII, XXI, XXIV, XXVII, XXX.

Ireland, and Scotland by "the advice of the Council"; that he should in the intervals of Parliament control the armed forces "with the advice and consent of the major part of the Council"; that he should conduct foreign affairs and possess the power to make war and peace only with "the advice and consent of the major part of the Council." The same proviso applied to several other powers: summoning special parliaments, raising revenue for the support of the administration of the government and armed forces, and making laws and ordinances which should be legally binding unless and until altered by Parliament.[22]

All these restrictions on the Protector's powers would have been meaningless if the Council had been the tool of the Protector, as the Privy Council had been under the Tudors and Stuarts. Instead of being subject to appointment and dismissal at the whim or caprice of the Protector, the members of the Council according to the provisions of the Instrument held office for life unless convicted of "miscarriage or other corruption." The Council itself seemed to have the major share in choosing any replacements of dead or convicted members. It was, therefore, a co-optative body like the governing council of many of the boroughs. Furthermore, Lambert and a number of his military and civilian allies—such as Desborough, Fleetwood, Sydenham, Pickering, and Strickland— gained membership on the Council and became a powerful faction. Because of the persuasive influence of Lambert on most issues they could usually pick up sufficient votes to form a majority. Moreover, although Cromwell was named Protector for life, the office was to be elective—not by Parliament, but by a majority of the Council. Nothing is more convincing of Lambert's dominance than the almost universal expectation during the first Protectorate that the Council would elect Lambert as Cromwell's successor.[23]

Although the total executive powers of the Protector-in-Council were far stronger than that of any English monarch, the powers

22. *Ibid.* for Articles II–V, XXII, XXV–XXVII, XXX, XXXII.
23. *Ibid.* for Articles XXV, XXVI, XXXII; R. Baillie, *Letters and Journals of Robert Baillie, Principal of the University of Glasgow, 1637–1662*, ed. D. Laing (Edinburgh, 1841–42), II, 419–20; letter from Van Sommelsdyjk to Nicholas, November 10, 1654, *Thurloe State Papers*, II, 681; *Ludlow Memoirs*, I, 400.

of the Protector *solus* were extremely limited. Indeed, he was little more than Chairman of the Board—to use an analogy from the business world—who had but one vote. That Cromwell regarded himself in this light is confirmed by his own statement: "I was a child in swaddling clothes. I cannot transgress. By the government [i.e., the Instrument] I can do nothing but in ordination with the Council." In December 1654, when he was reproached for not having abolished tithes, he replied that "for his part he could not do it for he was but one and his council allege it not fit to take them away." [24] His son, Henry Cromwell, when sent to Ireland in March 1654, explained, "You that are here may think he had power, but they made a very kickshaw of him at London." One nineteenth-century English historian attributed "the extraordinary vacillations" in foreign policy to "the difficulty—far more real than modern writers imagine—of securing the support of that majority of the councillors to whom the Instrument of Government gave the decisive voice." [25]

Whatever Cromwell's talents as a military leader, they do not seem to have extended to the political sphere. He had a peculiar ignorance and distrust, amounting almost to contempt, for political theory. He played almost no part in drawing up the various political manifestoes of the army, and in the crucial army political debates at Putney in the autumn of 1647 he sat by, almost completely inarticulate, leaving the task of defending the conservative Heads of the Proposals against the Levellers' Radical Agreement of the People almost exclusively to his son-in-law, Ireton.[26] Moreover, Cromwell was notorious for his lack of political initiative, for his long agonizing doubts, and for his hesitation about making political decisions. Instead of boldly seizing the initiative and forcing events, as Napoleon was so fond of doing, Cromwell often floun-

---

24. Abbott, *Writings and Speeches of Cromwell,* IV, 488; B. T. to (?), December 21, 1654, C. H. Firth (ed.), *Clarke Papers: Selections from the Papers of William Clarke, Secretary to the Council of the Army 1647–49 and to General Monck and the Commander of the Army in Scotland 1651–60* (Cambridge, 1891–1900), I, 49, 54, 60, 62, II, xxxvi.

25. *Ludlow Memoirs,* I, 381–82; Gardiner, *Commonwealth and Protectorate,* II, 477.

26. A. S. P. Wood, *Puritanism and Liberty: The Army Debates 1647–1649 from the Clarke MSS* (London, 1938).

dered about helplessly and aimlessly until he was literally "pushed" —a term he himself used—into a decision by an acute crisis.[27] Before the Protectorate, Cromwell played a passive role, leaving the political initiative, the chief ideas, and the planning to more imaginative, more resourceful, and more fertile political minds; he continued to play during the first Protectorate a role somewhat analogous to that of a constitutional monarch who reigns but does not govern, who usually is content to follow the ideas and advice of his ministers.

The versatile Lambert offers a brilliant contrast to the politically sluggish, irresolute Cromwell in the originality of his thinking on constitutional problems, in the resourcefulness of his political leadership, in the boldness of his administrative initiative, and in the persuasiveness and charm of his personality. The great German historian Ranke maintained: "To him is due the idea, and in great measure the establishment, of the first Protectorate; for he possessed the faculty of discovering the proper expedients in political no less than in military emergencies, and of persuading others to accept them." William Godwin, the historian of the Commonwealth, concluded: "Of all the counsellors of the Protector Lambert was held to be the man who combined the most statesmanlike qualities with the most daring spirit of enterprise." [28] Lambert appeared very prominently as a veritable master of ceremonies on all the great state occasions of the first Protectorate, often riding alone in the carriage with Cromwell while his fellow councillors walked bareheaded alongside. He lived in princely state at Wimbledon, where he collected great works of art and served as the official host for foreign diplomats.[29]

There is evidence that Lambert was certainly the first man in the army which, in the last analysis, wielded real *de facto* sovereignty. The well-informed Venetian envoy noted: "The man who is first and has most credit with the army is Major-General Lambert. They say that at heart he has no love for Cromwell,

27. Firth, *Oliver Cromwell*, p. 478.

28. L. von Ranke, *History of England principally in the Seventeenth Century* (Oxford, 1875), III, 261; Godwin, *History of the Commonwealth*, quoted in Dawson, *Cromwell's Understudy*, p. 174, n. 1.

29. Dawson, *Cromwell's Understudy*, pp. 182, 215–16, 145–49, 193.

although outwardly he professes the most complete attachment being won over by distinguished employments and immense rewards. At any rate none is better than he to make changes and form a party." [30] According to a contemporary newsletter, as fast as any officer lost his position, Lambert had "a friend of his put in his place"; a correspondent of Secretary Nicholas declared that Lambert had "made choice of all the new life guards [of Cromwell] and they are absolutely his creatures." [31]

In the opinion of some contemporary observers, Lambert as a member of the Council was equal or even superior in influence to Cromwell. The Cavalier historian the Earl of Clarendon, who had no reason to favor him, concluded that Lambert was "unquestionably the second in command of the army" and that he "was principal in raising him [Cromwell] to be Protector under the Instrument of Government." [32] Several Royalist newswriters, who had exceptionally good sources of information and who had nothing to gain by exaggerating Lambert's influence, went much further in assessing his power. One of them wrote in the spring of 1656 that "Mr. Temple tells me that Lambert hath the Protector in a string and if he pleases can depose him when he will. . . . I hear a few rising persons but are his confidants. 'Tis thought that the Council do also for the most part affect him though at present they stick close to the Protector." [33] Another Royalist writer confirmed and amplified the first: "Lambert is now remarkably the army's darling, and the only person courted. . . . It lies in his power to raise Cromwell higher or else to set up in his place." He related how a member of the Council, who upon being asked what Lambert's intentions were, declared that "Lambert would let this man [Cromwell] continue Protector, but that he would rule him as he pleased, which he may do so long as he hath the army at his devotion." [34]

30. Sagredo's Relation of England, *Calendar of State Papers: Venice,* XXX, 299.
31. Quoted in Dawson, *Cromwell's Understudy,* pp. 194, 209.
32. Clarendon, *Rebellion and Civil Wars,* II, 864.
33. *Thurloe State Papers,* IV, 676.
34. T. Carte (ed.), *Collection of Original Letters and Papers Concerning Affairs in England, 1641–60, Found among the Duke of Ormonde's Papers* (London, 1739), II, 89–90.

From such evidence one must conclude that if Cromwell's position was analogous to that of a constitutional monarch who reigns but does not rule, then Lambert's position corresponded to that of a prime minister who actually governs in his monarch's name. In several important instances where the views of Cromwell and Lambert clashed, Lambert's won out: in the abrupt dissolution of the Parliament of 1654, in the inauguration of the system of major generals, in the summoning of a special parliament in 1656, and finally in the purge of about 120 duly elected members of Parliament.

In 1654, when the first Parliament of the Protectorate not only refused to ratify Lambert's Instrument of Government but amended it so drastically as to make it unrecognizable, Cromwell dissolved the Parliament abruptly in order to save the Instrument.[35] Three years later Cromwell stated that the constitution had needed "mending" but clearly implied that the officers had compelled him to dissolve the Parliament "against his mind." [36] The evidence points unmistakably to Lambert, the leader of the officers and the author of the Instrument, as the person mainly responsible for the forced dissolution.

Practically all of his contemporaries regarded Lambert as author of the plan for placing English local government under the supervision of major generals. Both Clarendon and Lucy Hutchinson, the Puritan writer, agreed not only that Lambert originated the scheme but that he was also chiefly responsible for pushing it through the Council.[37] Later historians such as Gardiner[38] and W. H. Dawson concurred in this view. Dawson formulated a very cogent case to prove that Lambert was the author of the portion of the scheme which provided that the major generals and the local militia which they commanded should be financed by a non-parliamentary tax on the Cavaliers, known as the "decimation." [39] When Cromwell's personal friends, relatives, and followers turned against the major generals, Lambert arose to their defense in the

35. Abbott, Cromwell, III, 586; Commons Journals, VII, 415.
36. Abbott, Cromwell, IV, 418.
37. Clarendon, Rebellion and Civil Wars, II, 887; Hutchinson, Memoirs, p. 371.
38. Gardiner, Commonwealth and Protectorate, III, 179–81.
39. Dawson, Cromwell's Understudy, pp. 202–05.

Parliament of 1656.[40] Cromwell in his speech to the officers on February 27, 1657, strongly suggested that they were the authors of the plan when he said "you thought it necessary to have major-generals."[41] Later on he complained to Colonel John Hutchinson that "Lambert had put him upon all those violent actions for which he now accused him and sought his ruin."[42]

The fateful decision to call a special session of Parliament in 1656 resulted from the Council's consideration of four possible ways to raise desperately needed revenue. Francisco Giavarina, the Venetian Resident in London, wrote that in spite of Cromwell's "fixed determination . . . to try the third of the plans" the Council overruled the Protector and decided to summon Parliament.[43] Cromwell confirmed this opinion in his speech to the hundred officers: "Then you would have this Parliament called; it was against my judgment, but I could have no quietness till was done."[44]

So great was the unpopularity of the "arbitrary proceedings" of the major generals that the results of the parliamentary elections of 1656 were not altogether satisfactory to the government.[45] Consequently, the Council felt that in order to obtain a cooperative Parliament it had to exclude a large number of members who entertained opposing political views. Since the Instrument had made the Council the sole judge of elections, it justified its action by simply alleging that the excluded members were not "persons of integrity, fearing God, and of good conversation" as prescribed by Article XVII of the Instrument.[46] Since there was no provision for a supreme court to give an authoritative interpretation of the Instrument, the excluded members had no authority to whom an appeal could be taken. This arrogant, highhanded action seems to have been the work of Lambert and the military party in the Council. In his speech to the hundred officers Cromwell declared: "When they [the elected members] were chosen you garbled them,

40. Burton, *Diary*, I, 240.
41. Abbott, *Cromwell*, IV, 417.
42. Hutchinson, *Memoirs*, p. 375.
43. Giavarina to Doge, June 16/6, *Calendar of State Papers: Venice*, XXX, 230–31.
44. Abbott, *Cromwell*, IV, 417, 418.
45. Gardiner, *Commonwealth and Protectorate*, IV, 277.
46. Gardiner, *Constitutional Documents*, p. 411.

kept out and put in whom you pleased by the Instrument and I
am sworne to make good all you doe, right or wrong and because
120 are excluded I must think them malignants or scandalous
whether they are soe or not." [47]

There is considerable reason to believe that Cromwell had been
chafing under the domination of Lambert's military party for some
time.[48] Perhaps the greatest of all the various humiliations which
he suffered at the hands of Lambert's military party occurred in
the spring of 1656, when the army began to demand that the office
of General be separated from that of Protector in order that someone more closely identified with the welfare of the soldiers could
devote himself to them. Cromwell swallowed his pride as best he
could and agreed, provided the command of the army should be
given to his son-in-law Fleetwood. However, the army made it
plain that it would have none of Fleetwood; that, on the contrary,
it wanted its idol, its "darling," the man who had fought for its
interests and especially its arrears of pay. It wanted Lambert. This
last demand was too much; Cromwell refused to give up his office
of General.[49] Although the army did not press the matter further,
its demand and the growing unpopularity of the "arbitrary proceedings" probably persuaded Cromwell to seek an opportunity
to escape from the strait jacket of Lambert's Instrument of Government.

Such an opportunity was not long in forthcoming. The Parliament of 1656 had scarcely settled down when a group of conservative lawyers, erstwhile Royalists, and friends of the Protector devised a scheme for ridding England of the dominance of Lambert's military party. The Presbyterian majority, which dominated
the Parliament even after the purge, supported this plan.[50] Although the proposed new constitution was not formally introduced
until the latter part of February 1657, discussion of some of its
main features went on behind the scenes all during the autumn

47. Abbott, *Cromwell,* IV, 418.
48. Letter to Ormonde, March 3, 1656, Carte, *Original Letters,* II, 89.
49. Giavarina to Doge, June 16/6, *Calendar of State Papers: Venice,*
XXX, 230–31.
50. Baillie, *Letters and Journals,* II, 419.

of 1656.[51] The essence of the scheme, which was eventually known as the Humble Petition and Advice, was to make Cromwell king, to re-establish a second House of Parliament similar to the Lords, and to deprive the all-powerful Council of much of its power.[52] A Scottish observer, Robert Baillie, reported that it was proposed to make the crown hereditary in Cromwell's family because "all expected a more moderate and meek ruling from the Protector and his children, than from Lambert, or any of the Army." [53]

The Humble Petition and Advice could not be established without Cromwell's tacit consent. The first indication that he might be prepared to give his approval came when his friends astounded contemporary observers by opposing a bill, introduced by Lambert's military party, to establish the major generals and the "decimation" tax on a permanent basis. No sooner had the measure been introduced than the Protector's courtiers, led by his favorite son-in-law, John Claypole, Master of the Horse, argued against it to the great mortification of the military party. Combined with the Presbyterians, they succeeded in defeating it by a decisive majority. The major generals and the Instrument of Government were so closely linked together in the popular mind as products of Lambert's authority that the defeat was also considered a mortal blow to Lambert's Instrument.[54]

So delighted were the Presbyterians by the overthrow of "arbitrary sword-government" that they suddenly appropriated £400,-000, although they had been extremely slow, grudging, and niggardly about voting funds in the past. Their reaction to the turn of events strongly suggests some kind of behind-the-scenes "deal." [55]

The bargain between the Cromwellians and the Presbyterians having been sealed by the defeat of the major generals, the way was now clear for the introduction of the Humble Petition and Advice on February 23, 1657. In spite of the intense fury with which Lambert and the military party attacked it, they lacked the votes

51. Firth, "Cromwell and the Crown," *English Historical Review*, XVII (1902), 429–42.
52. Gardiner, *Constitutional Documents*, pp. 447–59.
53. Baillie, *Letters and Journals*, II, 420.
54. *Ludlow Memoirs*, II, 19; *Commons Journals*, VII, 482.
55. *Ibid.*, p. 483.

to defeat the proposed constitution.[56] Therefore, they decided to shift the focus of their attack from Parliament to Cromwell and bring sufficient pressure to compel him to repudiate it. When Lambert and the Army Grandees met on the evening of February 26 with some of the junior officers, Lambert urged joint action.[57] On the following evening a hundred officers, led by Lambert, approached Cromwell and petitioned him to reject the proposal to make him king, well-knowing that this was the very heart and core of the proposed constitution. The very size of the delegation was undoubtedly calculated to serve as a veiled threat of mutiny. However, on this occasion Lambert and his colleagues seriously misjudged their man; instead of the floundering irresolution and painful indecision to which they had grown accustomed, Cromwell surprised them by presenting the man of action, the fierce warrior, the victor of Marston Moor and Naseby. The pent-up fury and frustration of the last four years burst through the surface of his reticence and restraint. In blunt, forthright language he poured out his indignation. He gave a thumbnail sketch of the events of the past three years, beginning with the dissolution of the Rump in 1653. Throughout this entire period the officers—here he pointed to a "principal officer," probably Lambert—had made the decisions, while he, Cromwell, had simply served to execute them; he had served as their "drudge upon all occasions." He then proceeded to specify and enumerate those occasions: the dissolution of the Rump in April 1653, the summoning of the Nominated Parliament in July of the same year, the calling of the Parliament of 1654 and its abrupt dissolution before it had accomplished anything in order to save Lambert's Instrument, the inauguration of the system of the major generals in 1655, the summoning of a special session of Parliament in 1656, and the exclusion from it of one hundred and twenty members. At one point Cromwell accused the officers of amending the Instrument "when you know that I am sworne not to suffer it to be altered but by Parliament, and then you might have given me a kick on the breech and turned me going." It was now time, he said, "to come to a settlement and lay aside arbitrary

56. *Ludlow Memoirs,* II, 21–23.
57. *Clarke Papers,* III, 92.

proceedings." According to one version he added, "this Instrument of Government will not doe your worke."[58]

As a flash of lightning on a dark night serves to illuminate the salient features of a landscape for a few moments with startling clarity, so Cromwell's angry, hard-hitting speech served to reveal the real reasons for important political developments during the first Protectorate. Not one of the hundred or so auditors of his speech ever denied the truth of Cromwell's assertions. The speech was a veritable declaration of independence, a defiance of Lambert and his military party, who had controlled political affairs. Lambert's movement collapsed under Cromwell's attack. After that, the best his party could do was wage a forlorn rearguard action. The victorious Presbyterians enacted the constitution proposed by the Humble Petition and Advice. Section by section they stripped the omnipotent Council of much of its power—especially of the power of judging elections and of excluding members—added new members to the Council to dilute the influence of Lambert's party, and seriously weakened the army's cherished principle of religious toleration. When the vital section which requested Cromwell to assume the crown came up for debate, the Presbyterians overcame the last ditch efforts of the military faction and enacted it into law.[59]

The question now remained whether Cromwell would accept the crown, for unless he did, it was expressly provided that none of the Petition and Advice would go into effect.[60] Although Cromwell undoubtedly wanted to accept, so many complex factors were involved that he underwent an agonizing period of six weeks of his customary hesitation and doubt. Finally, he allowed himself to be persuaded, but just before making a formal announcement to that effect, he was deterred by the announcement of Lambert, Desborough, and Fleetwood that they would resign their commands if he did so. According to Ludlow, Lambert told Cromwell that if he should accept the crown he "could not assure the army

58. Abbott, *Cromwell*, IV, 417–18.
59. Gardiner, *Constitutional Documents*, pp. 449–55; *Commons Journals*, VII, 511.
60. Gardiner, *Constitutional Documents*, p. 458.

to him." This opposition apparently was decisive, for Cromwell declined the crown shortly thereafter.[61]

Thus Lambert was able to prevent a complete victory by Cromwell and the Presbyterians. However, they soon got their revenge when Parliament amended the Petition and Advice in such fashion as to allow Cromwell to accept it without the royal title; it also stipulated that the councillors had to take an oath of allegiance to the Protector, a provision which had been conspicuously absent from the Instrument of Government. Lambert opposed the adoption of this oath with all the force and eloquence at his command and refused to take it when it became law. Symbolic of his fall from power was his failure to appear for the first time at the elaborate state ceremonies, which were the occasion of Cromwell's second inauguration as Protector on June 26, 1657.[62] Deprived shortly thereafter of both his civilian and his military offices, he retired from public service for the remainder of Cromwell's life. Although he survived the Restoration, Lambert never regained the power and prestige he had held during most of the Protectorate, and died in obscurity. The nature of his end possibly explains why historians have never appreciated the vital role Lambert played during the years of Cromwell's rule.

61. *Ludlow Memoirs,* II, 23–25, 28, 29.
62. Burton, *Diary,* II, 282, 511–15; *Ludlow Memoirs,* II, 29.

H. R. TREVOR-ROPER

Oliver Cromwell and His Parliaments

OLIVER CROMWELL and his parliaments—the theme is almost a tragi-comedy. Cromwell was himself a member of Parliament; he was the appointed general of the armies of Parliament; and the Victorians, in the greatest days of parliamentary government, set up his statue outside the rebuilt Houses of Parliament. But what were Cromwell's relations with Parliament? The Long Parliament, which appointed him, he first purged by force and then violently expelled from authority. His own Parliament, the Parliament of Saints, which to a large extent was nominated by his government, was carried away by hysteria, rent by intrigue and dissolved, after six months, by an undignified act of suicide.

"Oliver Cromwell and His Parliaments," from *Religion, the Reformation and social Change,* copyright © H. R. Trevor-Roper 1956, 1959, 1960, 1963, 1964, 1967, 1972, published by The Macmillan Press Ltd. Reprinted by permission of The Macmillan Press Ltd. and of A. D. Peters and Company.

Of the parliaments of the Protectorate, elected on a new franchise and within new limits determined by the government, the first was purged by force within a week and dissolved, by a trick hardly distinguishable from fraud, before its legal term; the second was purged by fraud at the beginning and, when that fraud was reversed, became at once unmanageable and was dissolved within a fortnight. On a superficial view, Cromwell was as great an enemy of Parliament as ever Charles I or Archbishop Laud had been, the only difference being that, as an enemy, he was more successful: he scattered all his parliaments and died in his bed, while theirs deprived them of their power and brought them both ultimately to the block.

Nevertheless, between Cromwell and the Stuarts, in this matter, there was a more fundamental difference than this; for even if he could never control his parliaments in fact, Cromwell at least never rejected them in theory. This is not because he was deliberately consistent with his own parliamentary past. Cromwell was deliberately consistent in nothing. No political career is so full of undefended inconsistencies as his. But he was fundamentally and instinctively conservative, and he saw in Parliament part of the natural order of things. He did not regard it, as Archbishop Laud had regarded it, as "that hydra" or "that noise": he regarded it as the necessary legislature of England; and it was merely, in his eyes, an unfortunate and incomprehensible accident that his own particular parliaments consistently fell below the traditional standard of usefulness. Therefore again and again he summoned and faced them; again and again he wrestled with the hydra, sought to shout down the noise; and again and again, in the end, like the good man in a tragedy, caught in the trap of his own weakness, he resorted to force and fraud, to purges, expulsions, and recriminations. He descended like Moses from Sinai upon the naughty children of Israel, smashing in turn the divine constitutions he had obtained for them; and the surprised and indignant members, scattered before their time, went out from his presence overwhelmed with turbid oratory, protestations of his own virtue and their waywardness, romantic reminiscences, proprietary appeals to the Lord, and great broken gobbets from the Pentateuch and the Psalms.

Why was Oliver Cromwell so uniformly unsuccessful with his parliaments? To answer this question we must first look a little more closely at the aims and character both of Oliver Cromwell and of that opposition to the Court of Charles I of which he was first an obscure and ultimately the most powerful representative: an opposition not of practiced politicians (the practiced politicians of 1640 were dead, or had lost control, by 1644), nor of City merchants (the great London merchants were largely Royalist in 1640),[1] but of gentry: the backwoods gentry who, in 1640, sat on the back benches of Parliament, but who, as war and revolution progressed, gradually broke through the crumbling leadership which had at first contained them: the Independents.

Now these Independent gentry, it is important to emphasize, were not, as a class, revolutionary: that is, they did not hold revolutionary ideas. There were revolutionaries among the Independents, of course. There were revolutionaries in Parliament, men like "Harry Marten and his gang"—Henry Neville, Thomas Chaloner, and others: intellectual republicans who had traveled in Italy, read Machiavelli and Botero, and cultivated the doctrine of *raison d'état;* just as there were also revolutionaries outside Parliament: the Levellers and the Fifth Monarchy men. But if these men were the successive sparks which kindled the various stages of revolution, they were not the essential tinder of it. The majority of the members of Parliament, who at first accidentally launched the revolutionary movement and were afterward borne along or consumed by it, were not clearheaded men like these. They were not thinkers or even dreamers, but plain, conservative, untraveled, country gentlemen whose passion came not from radical thought or systematic doctrine but from indignation: indignation which the electioneering ability of a few great lords and the parliamentary genius of John Pym had contrived to turn into a political force, and which no later leaders were able wholly either to harness or to con-

1. Valerie Pearl, in her valuable work, *London and the Outbreak of the Puritan Revolution* (Oxford, 1961), has shown the strength of Royalism in the effective City government until the internal revolution of Dec. 1641: a revolution described by Clarendon, *History of the Rebellion* (1843), pp. 149–50, and in the anonymous *Letter from Mercurius Civicus to Mercurius Rusticus* (1643), printed in *Somers Tracts* (1811), IV, 580.

tain. These were the men who formed the solid stuff of parliamentary opposition to Charles I: men whose social views were conservative enough, but whose political passions were radical, and became more radical as they discovered depth below depth of royal duplicity. These were the men who became, in time, the Independents; and Cromwell, though he transcended them in personality and military genius, was their typical, if also their greatest, representative.

Why were these men, in 1640, so indignant? They were indignant, above all, against the Court. Curiously it was the Court of James I rather than the Court of Charles I which aroused their strongest moral feelings; but then most of them were now middle-aged and those of them who had previous parliamentary experience had necessarily acquired it before 1628—the younger men, brought up under Charles I, tended to be Royalist.[2] It was the corrupt, extravagant Court of James I and the Duke of Buckingham, whose lavish expenses, "so vast and unlimited by the old good rules of economy,"[3] first insulted their own necessarily careful estate management, and whose open, vulgar immorality further scandalized their severe Puritan spirits.[4] But James I, by combining with his faults a certain political canniness, had postponed the impact of this indignation, and the very extravagance of his court, with its sinecures and monopolies and pensions, had often bribed the potential leaders of opposition into silence. His son had corrected the moral abuses,[5] but by his political faults had nourished and increased and armed that indignation which those abuses had first engendered. Indeed, by his very parsimony Charles I hastened his own failure: for by cutting down the extravagance of the Court

2. This point—that the Royalist members were, on an average, ten years younger than the Parliamentarians in 1640—is clearly illustrated by D. Brunton and D. H. Pennington, *Members of the Long Parliament* (1954), pp. 14–20.

3. Clarendon, *History of the Rebellion,* ed. W. D. Macray, I, 12.

4. For the indignation which even courtiers, brought up at the orderly Court of Queen Elizabeth, felt at the vulgarity and immodesty of the Court of James I, see the letters of Lord Thomas Howard and Sir John Harington printed in N. E. McClure, *Letters and Epigrams of Sir John Harington* (Philadelphia, 1930), pp. 32–34, 118–21.

5. As even the Puritan Mrs. Hutchinson vividly admits. See her *Memoirs of Colonel Hutchinson* (Everyman edition), p. 67.

he had cut down the alleviating perquisites which had previously divided the opposition, and by raising the revenue from wardships he had rendered "all the rich families of England . . . exceedingly incensed and even indevoted to the Crown." [6] By 1640 political and moral indignation were combined against the House of Stuart and were together a powerful force in the hands of those practical politicians who perhaps shared it, who could certainly exploit it, and who thought (but wrongly) that they could also control it.

And what were the positive ideals of these outraged but largely unpolitical conservative gentry? Naturally, in the circumstances, they were not very constructive. These men looked back, not forward: back from the House of Stuart which had so insulted them to the House of Tudor of which their fathers had spoken; and in the reign of Elizabeth they discovered, or invented, a golden age: an age when the Court had been, as it seemed, in harmony with the country and the Crown with its parliaments; an age when a Protestant queen, governing parsimoniously at home and laying only tolerable burdens on "her faithful Commons," had nevertheless made England glorious abroad—head of "the Protestant interest" throughout the world, victor over Spain in the Indies, protector of the Netherlands in Europe. Since 1603 that glorious position had been lost. King James had alienated the gentry, abandoned Protestantism for "Arminian" policy at home and popish alliances abroad, made peace with Spain, and surrendered, with the "cautionary towns," the protectorate over the Netherlands. When the religious struggle had broken out anew in Europe, it was not the King of England who had inherited the mantle of Queen Elizabeth as defender of the Protestant faith: it was a new champion from the North, the King of Sweden. In the 1630s, when Gustavus Adolphus swept triumphantly through Germany, he became the hero of the frustrated, mutinous English gentry; and when he fell at Lützen, scarcely an English squire but wrote, in his manor house, a doggerel epitaph on the new polestar of his loyalty, "the Lion of the North."

Such were the basic political views, or prejudices, of the English back-benchers who poured into Parliament in 1640. But they had

6. Clarendon, *History of the Rebellion*, I, 199.

social views also, and these too led them back to the same golden age of the Protestant queen. First there was the desire for decentralization—the revolt of the provinces and of the provincial gentry not only against the growing, parasitic Stuart Court, but also against the growing, "dropsical" City of London; against the centralized Church, whether Anglican or "Presbyterian"; and against the expensive monopoly of higher education by the two great universities. All this was implied in the Independent program.[7] And also, what we must never forget, for it was a great element in the Protestant tradition, there was the demand for an organic society responsible for the welfare of its members. Ever since, among the first Reformers, "the Commonwealth Men," had protested against the irresponsibility, the practical inhumanity, the privileged uselessness of the pre-Reformation Church, the English Protestants had laid emphasis upon the collective nature of society and the mutual obligations of the classes which make it up.[8] Under Elizabeth, and especially in the long reign of Lord Burghley, something more than lip service had been paid to this ideal; but under the Stuarts, and particularly in the reign of James I (that formative era of English Puritanism), the ideal had again been eclipsed as Court and Church became once again openly parasitic upon society. Those were the years in which the cry for social justice had become insistent and the common law, so extolled by its most successful practitioner, Sir Edward Coke, became, in other eyes, one of the most oppressive of social burdens. When the Anglican Archbishop Laud had failed in his desperate, purblind, but in some respects heroic, efforts to reform society centrally and from above, the Puritan opposition inherited much of his program and sought to realize it in another form, as a decentralized, Independent commonwealth. The radicals would have achieved such reformation violently and devised new paper constitutions to secure and preserve

7. I have touched upon this aspect of the Independent program in my essay *The Gentry 1540–1640* (Economic History Society, 1954), p. 43.

8. I do not mean to imply that such views were not held in the Catholic Church *after* the Reformation. The revolt was European, and both Protestant and Catholic Churches inherited it, and competed with each other in formulating it. Similar "collectivist" doctrines were formulated by the Jesuits in Spain; but in England, being Protestant, it was part of the Protestant tradition.

it. The conservative Puritans, who were radical only in temper, not in their social or political doctrines, shied away from such novel remedies. Believing just as sincerely in a better, more decentralized, more responsible society, they looked for its achievement not to Utopia or Oceana but, once again, to a revived Elizabethan age.[9]

Such was the common denominator of positive philosophy shared by many of the back-bench members of Parliament in 1640, as it emerges, by way of protest, from their pamphlets, their diaries, their letters to their patrons, their parliamentary ejaculations both before and after that crucial date. It is astonishing how faithfully it is reflected in the letters and speeches, as afterward in the groping policy, of Oliver Cromwell. "Reformation of law and clergy," social justice for the "poor people of God" secured not by radical revolution but by patriarchal benevolence, a revival of the glories of "Queen Elizabeth of famous memory"—a protectorate over the Netherlands, a privateering war in the West Indies, and the leadership of "the Protestant interest" in Europe—all these recur in his later policy. Even the uncritical worship of Gustavus Adolphus is there. Perhaps nothing is more tragi-comic in Cromwell's romantic foreign policy than his cultivation of the robber empire in the Baltic, to which he would have sacrificed English commercial interests, and, in particular, of Queen Christina, whom he fondly courted with a pompous embassy, rich gifts, and his own portrait. For was she not both a Protestant heroine and a virgin queen—her father, the great Gustavus, and "Queen Elizabeth of famous memory" rolled into one? In fact she was not. Even as he wooed her, that flighty Nordic bluestocking was secretly being converted to popery by Jesuit missionaries, and Cromwell had to transfer his uncritical devotion to her successor.

9. Most recent writers—and not only Marxists and Fabians, for the same bias is to be found in the Roman Catholic W. Schenk's book, *The Concern for Social Justice in the Puritan Revolution* (1948)—have tended to find the evidence of such an interest in social reform only among the radical sects, who certainly made most noise about it. But I believe that just as much interest, in a more practical, less doctrinaire way, was shown by the conservative Independents. It can be discovered in their projects for law reform and Church matters, in their educational work (on which see especially W. A. L. Vincent's excellent study, *The State and School Education, 1640–1660*, 1950), in the ordinances of the Protector and Council between Dec. 1653 and Sept. 1654, and in the social policy carried out in the period of administration by major generals.

But this was in the future. In 1640 Oliver Cromwell was still, like the other country gentry who had followed their patrons to Westminster, a mere back-bencher, a lesser ally of his kinsmen the Barringtons, John Hampden, and Oliver St. John, a client of the Earl of Warwick. He never dreamed that his views would one day have more power behind them than theirs, or that the views which they all shared would be expressed otherwise than by the remonstrances of a faithful if indignant Parliament to a wayward but, they hoped (once his "evil counsellors" were removed), ultimately amenable King. None of them dreamed, in 1640, of revolution, either in Church or in State. They were neither separatists nor republicans. What they wanted was a King who, unlike Charles I, but like the Queen Elizabeth of their imagination, would work the existing institutions in the good old sense; bishops who, unlike the Laudian bishops, but like Bishop Hall or Archbishop Ussher, would supervise their flocks in the good old sense of "the sweet and noble" Anglican, Richard Hooker.[10] At first they hoped that King Charles would adjust himself, would jettison a few Stuart innovations, give a few guarantees, and become such a King of the State, such a supreme governor of the Church. It was only when King Charles had shown himself quite unadjustable that revolution, though unwanted, took place, generating its own momentum and driving basically conservative men to radical acts such as they

10. The conservatism of the opposition in secular matters is generally admitted. In Aug. 1643 Henry Marten was sent to the Tower, without a division, for expressing republican sentiments. In Church matters the "Presbyterian" clergy and the extreme sectaries naturally expressed clear anti-Anglican sentiments; but the laity (as the history of the Westminster Assembly showed) had no intention of submitting to such clerical extremists. In fact, the spiritual advisers of the Independents, William Ames, Thomas Hooker, Hugh Peter, etc., were "non-separating congregationalists," who never disowned the Anglican Church (see Perry Miller, *Orthodoxy in Massachusetts,* Cambridge, Mass., 1933, pp. 177 ff.; R. P. Stearns, *Hugh Peter,* Urbana, 1954, p. 12, etc.). It was Henry Parker, a formidable Independent thinker, whose praise of Hooker I have quoted. Parker also described Bishop Hall as "one of the greatest assertors, and in that the noblest, of episcopacy" (W. K. Jordan, *Men of Substance,* Chicago, 1942, pp. 70–71). When in power, Cromwell granted far greater liberty to Anglicans than the revengeful Anglicans of the Restoration were disposed to admit (see R. Bosher, *The Making of the Restoration Settlement,* 1951, pp. 9–14), and appointed for Archbishop Ussher a state funeral in Westminster Abbey, with an Anglican service.

would never have imagined before and would shudder to recollect afterward, and facing them with fundamental problems of which they had never previously thought. It was only by an extraordinary and quite unpredictable turn of events that one of these back-benchers, Oliver Cromwell, having ruined all existing institutions, found himself, in 1649, faced with the responsibility of achieving, or restoring, the lost balance of society. It was a formidable responsibility for one so arbitrarily brought to eminence, but Cromwell took it seriously, for he was essentially a serious and a modest man; the question was, how could it be carried out?

The radicals, of course, had their plans: they were the intellectuals, or the doctrinaires, the new men and the young men of the revolution. They intended to continue the revolution, to create new engines of force, and to impose thereby new and untried but, in their eyes, hopeful constitutions. But Cromwell was not a radical or an intellectual or a young man. He did not want to continue the revolution, which had already, in his eyes and in the eyes of his fellow gentry, got out of control. He wanted to stop it, to bring it under control, to bring "settlement" after an unfortunate but, as it had turned out, unavoidable period of "blood and confusion." Nor did he believe in new constitutions, or indeed in any constitutions at all. He did not believe, as some of his more wooden colleagues believed, in the divine right of republics any more than in the divine right of kings. Forms of government were to him "but a mortal thing," "dross and dung compared with Christ," and therefore in themselves quite indifferent. He was not, he once said, "wedded or glued to forms of government": had not the ancient Hebrews, God's own people, fared equally well, according to circumstances, under patriarchs, judges, and kings? [11] Acceptability,

11. *Clarke Papers*, I (Camden Society, 1891), 369. This indifference to forms of government, which implied a rejection of Charles I's rule without any particular constitutional alternative, was a commonplace among the Cromwellian Independents. Sir Henry Vane similarly held that "it is not so much the form of the administration as the thing administered wherein the good or evil of government doth consist" (*The People's Case Stated in the Trial of Sir Henry Vane, Kt.*, 1662, p. 106). Cf. Stephen Marshall, *A Letter to a Friend in the Country* (1643): "Among the divers kinds of lawful governments, monarchy, aristocracy and democracy, no one of them is so appointed of God as to exclude the other from being a lawful government"; and Hugh Peter, *Mr. Peter's Message with the Narration of the*

or, as he called it, "acceptance," was to him the only test of right
government. In his indignation against Charles I he might de-
nounce monarchy, but in cooler moments he would admit that a
government "with something monarchical in it" was probably the
most acceptable, and therefore the best. In his indignation against
the Earl of Manchester he might express his hope of living "to see
never a nobleman in England"; but in cooler moments he could
insist that "a nobleman, a gentleman, a yeoman" were "the ranks
and orders of men whereby England hath been known for hundreds of years," and that "nobility and gentry" must be kept up.[12]
Fundamentally, in his eyes, it was the fault of persons, not of institutions, which had been fatal to the *ancien régime:* "the King's
head was not taken off because he was King, nor the Lords laid
aside because Lords, neither was the Parliament dissolved because
they were a Parliament, but because they did not perform their
trust." [13] In politics Oliver Cromwell was not a theorist or a doctrinaire, but an opportunist.

Opportunists who do not believe in the necessity of particular
constitutions take what lies nearest to hand, and what lay nearest
to Cromwell's hand when he found himself called upon to restore
his ideal Elizabethan society was naturally the surviving debris
of the Elizabethan constitution. Parliament had been savaged—
and by none more than himself—but its rump was there; the King
had been destroyed, but he himself stood, if somewhat incongru-
ously, in his place. Naturally he saw himself as a new Queen Elizabeth—or rather, being a humble man, as a regent for a new Queen
Elizabeth; and he prepared, like her, to summon a series of defer-
ential parliaments. Surely, since he was one of them, and since they
all earnestly pursued the same honest ideal, the members would

---

taking of Dartmouth (1646), p. 2: "For it is certain that good men may
save a nation when good laws cannot"; and *A Dying Father's Legacy*
(1660), p. 110: "I nowhere minded who ruled, fewer or more, so the good
ends of government be given out . . ." Cf. the similar views of other Independents quoted in E. Ludlow, *Memoirs,* ed. C. H. Firth (1894), I, 184–85,
and T. Burton, *Parliamentary Diary* (1828), III, 260, 266.

    12. B. Whitelocke, *Memorials* (1853), III, 374; *Camden Miscellany,* VIII
(1883), 2; W. C. Abbott, *Writings and Speeches of Oliver Cromwell* (Harvard, 1937–47), III, 435, and IV, 273.

    13. MS. Tanner, III, 13, quoted in *Clarke Papers,* III (1899), p. viii, n. 1.

agree with him, just as they had agreed with "that Lady, that great Queen"? Surely he had only to address them in the Painted Chamber, to commend them in a few eloquent phrases, to leave them to their harmonious deliberations, and then, having received from them a few "good laws," to dismiss them, in due time, amid applause, complimentingly, with a "Golden Speech"?

Alas, as we know, it did not happen thus. It was not with golden speeches that Cromwell found himself dismissing his parliaments, but with appeals to heaven, torrents of abuse—and force. This was not merely because the basis of legitimacy and consent was lacking: Queen Elizabeth, like Cromwell, was disputed in her title, and Cromwell, like Queen Elizabeth, was personally indispensable even to those extremists who chafed at his conservatism. The fatal flaw was elsewhere. Under Oliver Cromwell something was missing in the mechanics of parliamentary government. It was not merely that useful drop of oil with which Queen Elizabeth had now and then so gracefully lubricated the machine. It was something far more essential. To see what that omission was, we must turn from the character to the composition and working of those uniformly unfortunate assemblies.

The methods by which Queen Elizabeth so effectively controlled her parliaments of—for the most part—unpolitical gentry are now, thanks to the great work of Sir John Neale and Professor Notestein, well known.[14] They consisted, first, in electoral and other patronage and, secondly, in certain procedural devices among which the essential were two: the presence in Parliament of a firm nucleus of experienced Privy Councillors, and royal control over the Speaker. Now these methods of control are of the greatest importance in the history of Parliament, and if we are to consider Oliver Cromwell as a parliamentarian it is necessary to consider his use both of this patronage and of these procedural devices. This, I think, has not before been attempted. My purpose in this essay is to attempt it. I believe it can be shown that it was precisely in this field that Cromwell's catastrophic failure as a parliamentarian lay.

14. Wallace Notestein, *The Winning of the Initiative by the House of Commons* (British Academy Lecture, 1924); J. E. Neale, *The Elizabethan House of Commons* (1949); *Elizabeth I and Her Parliaments* (1953).

In order to show this it will be necessary to take Cromwell's parliaments in turn and to see, in each case, how far the patronage of
the government and its supporters was used, and who formed that
essential nucleus of effective parliamentary managers, that compact "front bench" which, under the Tudors, had been occupied
by the royal Privy Council.

Of course, Cromwell did not inherit the system direct from
Queen Elizabeth. In the intervening half-century there had been
many changes—changes which had begun even before her death.
For in the last years of Elizabeth both methods of royal control had
been challenged: the Puritans had developed a formidable parliamentary "machine" independent of the Privy Council, and the Earl
of Essex had sought to use aristocratic patronage to pack the House
of Commons against the Queen's ministers. But in the event,
thanks to the parliamentary ability of the two Cecils, neither of
these challenges had been successful. It was only after the death of
the Queen, and particularly after the rejection of Robert Cecil by
James I, that the indifference of the Stuart Kings and the incom-
petence of their ministers had enabled a parliamentary opposition
to develop and to organize both patronage and procedure against
the Crown. By 1640, when the Long Parliament met, the tables
had been completely turned. In that year the opposition magnates
—the earls of Bedford, Warwick, and Pembroke—showed themselves better boroughmongers than the royal ministers, and the failure of Charles I to secure the election to Parliament, for any constituency, of his intended Speaker could be described by Clarendon
as "an untoward and indeed an unheard of accident, which brake
many of the king's measures and infinitely disordered his service
beyond a capacity of reparation." [15] Thus in 1640 both patronage

15. R. N. Kershaw, "The Elections for the Long Parliament," in *English
Historical Review*, 1923; Clarendon, *History of the Rebellion*, I, 220. The
extent to which the party of opposition in 1640 was an aristocratic party,
controlled by certain great boroughmongering lords, has, I think, been
insufficiently emphasized by historians, although Clarendon, as a contemporary, takes it for granted. Pym was a client of the Earl of Bedford
("wholly devoted to the earl of Bedford," Clarendon, *op. cit.*, I, 245);
those who afterward became Independents were largely (like the Independent preachers) clients of the Earl of Warwick, to whom Cromwell
himself remained a constant ally, even when their roles were reversed
(*ibid.*, p. 874). For the Earl of Warwick as head of a political party, see

and procedure were firmly in the hands of the opposition. But this turning of the tables did not entail any change in the system by which Parliament was operated. It merely meant that the same system which had formerly been operated by the Crown was now operated against it. John Pym, the ablest parliamentary manager since the Cecils, resumed their work. He controlled the patronage, the Speaker, and the front bench. From 1640 until 1643 Parliament, in his hands, was once again an effective and disciplined body such as it had never been since 1603.

With the death of Pym in 1643 his indisputable empire over Parliament dissolved and lesser men competed for its fragments. First St. John, then Vane among the radicals, Holles among the conservatives, emerged as party leaders; but they cannot be described as successful party leaders: the machine creaked and groaned, and it was only by disastrously calling in external force —the army—that the Independents were able, in the end, to secure their control. On the other hand, once Parliament had been purged and the King executed, a certain unity of counsel and policy returned. The Rump Parliament, which governed England from 1649 to 1653, may have been justly hated as a corrupt oligarchy, but it governed effectively, preserved the revolution, made and financed victorious war, and carried out a consistent policy of aggressive mercantile imperialism. Its rule was indeed the most systematic government of the Interregnum; and since this rule was the rule not of one known minister but of a number of overlapping assemblies operating now as Parliament, now as committees of

---

A. P. Newton, *The Colonising Activities of the Early Puritans* (New Haven, 1914), *passim*. For some of his electioneering activities, see J. H. Hexter, *The Reign of King Pym* (Cambridge, Mass., 1941), pp. 44–45. For the electioneering activities of the earls of Pembroke, see Violet A. Rowe, "The Influence of the Earls of Pembroke on Parliamentary Elections 1625-1641," in *English Historical Review*, 1935, p. 242. On the other hand, the electioneering feebleness of the government is shown by Archbishop Laud's refusal to avail himself of the borough patronage at his disposal at Reading, or, apparently, at Oxford (see Laud, *Works*, 1847-60, VI, 587; M. B. Rex, *University Representation in England, 1604-1690*, 1954, p. 145). And yet, if Laud had chosen to recommend Sir Thomas Gardiner for Reading, there would have been a sound Royalist Speaker instead of Lenthall, and the disaster so emphasized by Clarendon would never have occurred. It is difficult to overestimate the consequences which might have flowed from so slight an exertion.

Parliament, now as Council of State, while some of the administrative departments were notoriously confused and confusing, it is reasonable to ask who were the effective managers who made this complex and anonymous junta work so forcefully and so smoothly. This is a question which, in my opinion, can be answered with some confidence.

We have, unfortunately, no private diaries of the Rump Parliament which can show who managed its business or debates, but we have later diaries which show at least who claimed to have managed them; and from this and other evidence I believe we can say that, at least after 1651, the policy of the Rump was controlled by a small group of determined and single-minded men. Up to the summer of 1651 the ascendancy of these men is not so apparent, but with the policy which prevailed after that date it can, I think, be clearly seen. For in 1651, with the passing of the Navigation Act and the declaration of war against the Netherlands, the old Elizabethan ideal of a protectorate over the Netherlands was jettisoned in favor of a new and opposite policy, a policy of mercantile aggression against a neighboring Protestant power. Furthermore, this policy, we are repeatedly told, was the policy not of the whole Parliament but of "a very small number," with allies in the City of London, "some few men" acting "for their own interest," "some few persons deeply interested in the East India trade and the new Plantations." [16]

Now the identity of these few men, or at least of their parliamentary managers, can hardly be doubted, for they never tired of naming themselves. They were Sir Arthur Hesilrige and Thomas Scot. In the later parliaments of the Interregnum, whose proceedings are fortunately known to us, Hesilrige and Scot appear as an inseparable and effective parliamentary combine. Together they head the list of those republicans whom Cromwell twice excluded from his parliaments. Together they are named by Ludlow as the principal champions of sound republican doctrine. Together they appear, in the *Commons' Journals,* as tellers for strictly republican motions. Moreover, not only did they repeatedly claim for them-

16. These statements concerning the fewness of the makers of Rump policy, made by Pauluzzi the Venetian resident, Daniel O'Neil the Royalist agent, and the later Dutch ambassadors, are quoted by S. R. Gardiner, *History of the Commonwealth and Protectorate* (1894), II, 120 n.

selves all the republican virtue of the Rump Parliament in general, but, in particular, the policy for which they most extolled the Rump was always precisely that policy of mercantile aggression which had been launched in 1651 with the triumphant but, in the eyes of serious-minded Protestants, fratricidal war against the Netherlands.

For Hesilrige and Scot were not only republicans. They were also, to use a later term, "Whigs." If republics were to them the best of all forms of government, that was not merely because of classical or biblical precedents, nor because of the iniquity of particular kings: it was because republics alone, in their eyes, were the political systems capable of commercial empire. Like the later Whigs, who were also accused of a preference for "oligarchy," they found their great example in the mercantile republic of Venice. "Is there anything but a Commonwealth that flourishes?" asked Scot: "Venice against the pride of the Ottoman Empire";[17] and he never ceased to urge a reversion to the aggressive commercial policy of 1651–53. "We never bid fairer for being masters of the whole world." "We are rival for the fairest mistress in the world—Trade." "It is known abroad—the Dutch know—that a Parliament of England can fight and conquer too." "You never had such a fleet as in the Long Parliament," echoed Hesilrige; "all the powers in the world made addresses to him that sat in your chair"; "trade flourished, the City of London grew rich, we were most potent by sea that ever was known in England." When Cromwell expelled the Rump, he afterward declared, "there was not so much as the barking of a dog or any general or visible repining at it"; and his gentry supporters agreed with him: "there was neither coroner nor inquest upon it." But some squeaks there were, and it is interesting to see whence they came. At the crucial moment, when an agreed solution was almost in sight, it was Hesilrige who swept down from seventy miles away and by his presence and oratory prevented

---

17. The fashionable cult of Venice reached its height under the Commonwealth. The republicans Harrington and Neville made it their ideal; the anonymous tract *A Persuasive to a Mutual Compliance* (1652) prophesies for the Rump a future comparable with that of Venice (*Somers Tracts*, VI, 158); James Howell's laudatory *Survey of the Signorie of Venice, of her admired policy and method of government*, was published in 1651; etc., etc.

the other members from surrendering to less than force; and when they had been expelled by force, it was from the City of London that the only plea for their restoration came: a petition whose paternity is easy to recognize—for six years later it was implicitly claimed by Thomas Scot.[18]

Now it is interesting to note that this policy, the "Whig" policy of mercantile aggression which I have ascribed to Hesilrige and Scot and their allies in the City, though it was carried out by an Independent parliament carefully purged of unsympathetic elements, was flatly contradictory to the declared views and prejudices of those ordinary Independent gentry whom Cromwell represented and who, in their general attitude, foreshadowed rather the Tory squires than the mercantile Whig pressure group of the next generation.[19] Cromwell himself always favored the Elizabethan policy of an alliance with and a protectorate over the Netherlands, and it was this policy which Oliver St. John had, until 1651, pressed upon the Dutch government at the Hague. The defection of St. John in 1651 had enabled the "Whig" party to carry their war policy, but in 1653, when Cromwell had expelled the Rump, he lost no time in ending the war they had begun. Further, Cromwell and his colleagues had revolted, in part, against the centralization of trade in the City of London, which had caused the decay of local boroughs and local industry: they had no wish to fight (and pay for) mercantile wars in the interest of the City; and afterward, when they denounced the Rump, they "cast much dirt and unsavoury speech" on it as "a trading Parliament." [20] Decentraliza-

18. Abbott, *Writings and Speeches of Oliver Cromwell,* III, 453; Burton, *Parliamentary Diary,* III, 97, 111–12, etc.

19. This distinction between the "Whig" policy of the Rump and the "Tory" policy of the Cromwellian Independents is well illustrated in the person of a prominent champion of the former and enemy of the latter, Slingsby Bethel. In his pamphlet *The World's Mistake in Oliver Cromwell* (1668) he attacked Cromwell precisely because he had reversed the mercantilist policy of the Rump; in his *Interest of Princes and States* (1680) he attacks the gentry as the chief obstacle everywhere to rational mercantile policy; and in the days when Whigs and Tories existed in fact, not merely in embryo, he was Whig sheriff of London in the year of the Popish Plot.

20. Burton, *Parliamentary Diary,* I, pp. xxv, xxviii. For Independent complaints against the growth of the City of London and its monopoly of trade, see *ibid.,* I, pp. cx, 177, 343–44. For the same complaint resumed by a Tory back-bencher a generation later, see *The Memoirs of Sir John Reresby* (1875), p. 333.

tion, the provinces against the City, and the Protestant interest—
these were their political slogans, the slogans which they had ut-
tered in the 1630s and 1640s and would utter again after 1653, but
which went altogether unheeded by those Rumpers who had tem-
porarily seized control of the revolution. Finally, the Rump Parliament—and this was one of Cromwell's greatest grievances against
it—showed itself increasingly indifferent to that Protestant "concern for social justice" which loomed so large in the Independent
program. War on Protestants abroad in the interest of City merchants was accompanied at home, in those years, by a privileged
scramble for public property which seemed a mockery of Puritan
ideals. The republic of Hesilrige and Scot might call itself a "Commonwealth," but in fact, said a real republican, "it was an oligarchy, detested by all men that love a Commonwealth";[21] or, if it
were a commonwealth, it was only, according to the sour definition
of Sir Thomas More: "a certain conspiracy of rich men procuring
their own commodities under the name and title of a Commonwealth."

Thus the policy of the Rump in the years 1651–53—the years,
that is, when the army's resentment was mounting against it—
was not only the policy of a small managing group which had
obtained control of the assembly: it was also a policy essentially
opposed to the aims of those Independents who had made the
revolution. For all their insistence upon decentralization, social justice, and Protestant alliances, those Independents had proved quite
incapable of making such a policy even in their own parliament
which their own leader had purged in their interest. Unable, or
unfitted, to exercise political power, they seemed doomed to surrender it to any organized group, however small, which was capable of wielding it—even if that group used it only to pursue
policies quite different from their own. Though the "Tory" Independents had made the revolution and, through the army, held
power in the state, the "Whigs" had contrived to secure power in
Parliament. To correct this and create a government of their own,
the Independents had the choice between two policies. Either they
could preserve the republican constitution and beat the "Whigs"
at their own game—or, if that was too difficult for natural back-

21. Burton, *Parliamentary Diary*, III, 134.

benchers, they could remove their rivals by force and place over Parliament a "single person," like-minded with themselves, to summon, dismiss, and, above all, guide and regulate their assemblies. This latter course was entirely consistent with their general political philosophy; it was also the easier course; and consequently they took it. The crucial question was, did the new "single person" understand the technique of his task? He had in his hands all the power of the state; but had he in his head the necessary knowledge of parliamentary management: that is, patronage and procedure to prevent another usurpation of the vacant front benches? Would he now fill them with his Privy Councillors and thus cement, as Queen Elizabeth had done, the natural harmony between the faithful, if somewhat inarticulate, Commons and the Throne?

If this was what Cromwell hoped to do, his first opportunity after the expulsion of the Rump was perhaps his best, for the Parliament of Saints, the Barebones Parliament of 1653, was, after all, largely a nominated, not an elected, assembly. And yet, as it turned out, this experiment proved to be Cromwell's most humiliating failure. The Barebones Parliament is a classic example of an unpolitical assembly colonized from within by a well-organized minority. It was so colonized not merely because the majority of its members were unpolitical—that is true of most assemblies—but because Cromwell himself, in summoning it, was quite unaware of the real inspiration behind it, and made no attempt to convert it, by preparation or organization, into a useful or even workable assembly. As he afterward admitted, it was a tale not only of the members' weakness but of his own: "the issue was not answerable to the simplicity and honesty of the design." [22]

The evidence for this is sadly plain. For what was in the minds of Cromwell and his conservative allies when they decided, or agreed, to summon the Barebones Parliament? We look, and all we find is a well-meaning, devout, bewildered obscurity. The Independents had no political theories: believing that forms of government were indifferent, they counted simply on working with the existing institutions, and now that the existing institutions—first monarchy, then republic—had been destroyed, they were at a loss. "It was necessary to pull down this government," one of them

22. Abbott, *Writings and Speeches of Oliver Cromwell,* IV, 489.

had declared on the eve of the expulsion, "and it would be time enough then to consider what should be placed in the room of it"; and afterward it was officially stated that "until the Parliament was actually dissolved, no resolutions were taken in what model to case the government, but it was after that dissolution debated and discussed as *res integra*." [23] In other words, having expelled the Rump Parliament which had betrayed the Independent cause, the Independent officers found themselves in a quandary. They had acted, as Cromwell so often acted, not rationally nor with that machiavellian duplicity with which his victims generally credited him, but on an impulse; and when the impulsive gesture had been made and the next and more deliberate step must be taken, they were quite unprepared.

Over the unprepared the prepared always have an advantage. In this case the prepared were the new radical party which had replaced the broken Levellers: the extreme totalitarian radicals, the Anabaptists and their fighting zealots the Fifth Monarchy men. These men had already established themselves in the army through their disciplined tribunes, the chaplains; they already controlled many of the London pulpits; and for the capture of direct power they had two further assets: an organization, in the form of the Committee for the Propagation of the Gospel in Wales, which was now totally controlled by their energetic Welsh leader, Vavasour Powell, and his itinerant missionaries; and a patron at the highest level in Major General Harrison, the commissioner in charge of the Welsh Propagators and—what was now more important—the *alter ego* of the unsuspecting Cromwell. In the Rump Parliament, which after all had been the residue of a parliament of gentry, lawyers, and merchants, these radical zealots had had little influence. Indeed, they had been its most violent enemies, for the Rump, unlike Cromwell, had been well aware of their subversive activities and had for some time been preparing, in spite of constant obstruction, to discontinue the Welsh Propagators who formed their essential committee. It was largely to forestall, or avenge, so crucial a blow that Harrison had urged Cromwell to expel the Parliament.[24]

23. Ludlow, *Memoirs*, I, 351; [Anon.] *A True State of the Case of the Commonwealth* (1654), quoted by Firth in Ludlow, *op. cit.*, I, 358, n.
24. The history of the struggle over the Welsh Propagators can be followed in T. Richards, *The Puritan Movement in Wales* (1920). See also

When he had expelled it, Cromwell had played into the hands of the radicals. They had used him to destroy their enemy for them; and they now looked forward to using him still further, as a means of achieving direct political power.

As so often in the history of Oliver Cromwell, there is something at once tragic and comic in the manner of his deception by the Fifth Monarchy men. To him they were merely good religious men, and when he found that his own exalted mood of indignation against the Rump was shared by them, he followed their advice, little suspecting what deep-laid political schemes lurked behind their mystical language. "Reformation of law and clergy": was not that precisely his program? A milder, cheaper, quicker law; a decentralized, godly, Puritan clergy; were not these his ambitions? How was he to know that by the same phrase the Anabaptists meant something quite different and far more radical: wholesale changes in the law of property, abolition of tithe, the extension over England of the closely organized, indoctrinated religious tribunes who had already carried their gospel over Wales "like fire in the thatch"? Oliver Cromwell suspected no such thing. When Harrison urged him to expel the Rump as the persecutors of the "poor saints in Wales," he innocently acquiesced; and when he found that the refusal of the Rump to renew their authority had left the Welsh Propagators without a legal basis, he as innocently supplied them with a substitute, writing to them to ignore strict legality and "to go on cheerfully in the work as formerly, to promote these good things." Months afterward the greatest crime of the Rump would still seem to him to be its attempt to disband those Welsh Propagators, "the poor people of God there, who had men watching over them like so many wolves, ready to catch the lamb as soon as it was brought out into the world." [25] This romantic view of a knot of Tammany demagogues, who concealed their sharp practices behind lachrymose Celtic oratory, was soon to be sadly dispelled.

As soon as they had secured the expulsion of the Rump, the Fifth Monarchy men were ready for the next step. What they required

---

Alan Griffith, *A True and Perfect Relation of the whole Transaction concerning the Petition of the Six Counties,* etc. (1654).

25. Abbott, *Writings and Speeches of Oliver Cromwell,* III, 13, 57.

was a legislature nominated by the supposedly "independent" churches, some of which had been completely penetrated and were now safely controlled by them. Only in this way could so unrepresentative a party achieve power. Therefore when Cromwell remained poised in doubt, he soon found himself besieged by willing and unanimous advisers. "We humbly advise," the Saints of North Wales wrote to him from Denbigh (the letter was composed by the local Fifth Monarchy panjandrum Morgan Llwyd), "that forasmuch as the policy and greatness of men hath ever failed, ye would now at length, in the next election, suffer and encourage the saints of God in his spirit to recommend unto you such as God shall choose for that work." [26] Another Fifth Monarchy preacher, John Rogers, was even more precise. He urged that an interim junto of twelve, "like to Israel's twelve Judges," be first set up; that a Sanhedrin of seventy men "or else one of a county" be then nominated, in which "the righteous of the worthies of the late Parliament" might also be included; and that in all cases of doubt the General should "consult with the Saints (Deuteronomy i. 13) and send to all discerning spirited men for their proposals." [27] Through Harrison, these proposals were urged in the Council of Officers;[28] under this double pressure, direct and indirect, Cromwell easily yielded; and the Barebones Parliament, when it was summoned, was, in fact, a body constituted almost exactly as required in the Fifth Monarchy program. The twelve councillors were appointed, and the members of the new Parliament were to be elected by the local churches,[29] which the radicals had often penetrated. Some few members were to be nominated directly by the Council.

26. *Milton State Papers*, ed. J. Nickolls (1743), p. 120; cf. J. H. Davies, *Gweithiau Morgan Llwyd* (Bangor, 1899 and 1908); II, 264.

27. John Rogers, *A Few Proposals,* quoted in Edward Rogers, *Life and Opinions of a Fifth Monarchy Man* (1867), p. 50.

28. See Harrison's letters on this subject in the Jones correspondence (see below, n. 31); also Ludlow, *Memoirs,* I, 358; *Clarke Papers,* III, 4.

29. Since this essay was written, Austin Woolrych, in an interesting article on "The Calling of Barebone's Parliament," in *English Historical Review,* July 1965, has argued that whatever demands or suggestions were made, the members of that Parliament were not "elected" by the churches, but nominated by the Council of Officers, and that the various letters from the churches, proposing particular members, were not replies to requests but unsolicited proposals. Although convinced by Mr. Woolrych's argument, I have not altered my text. The effective difference is anyway slight,

Whom would the churches elect? Cromwell's own demands were moderate and sensible. He called for "known men of good repute"—that is, respectable Puritan, even if unpolitical, gentry; and such were the men he himself seems to have nominated: Lord Lisle, his own kinsmen, his own medical man Dr. Goddard, etc.[30] But the radicals had more definite, more positive, views: they were determined to send to Parliament only reliable radical party members. The chance survival of the correspondence of one of their Welsh sympathizers, Colonel John Jones of Merionethshire, clearly shows their electioneering tactics:[31] for in Wales at least there were now no "independent" churches, only Vavasour Powell's dragooned itinerant missionaries. Consequently even the formality of election was there unnecessary. "I presume," Harrison wrote to Colonel Jones, "brother Powell acquainted you our thoughts as to the persons most in them to serve on behalf the Saints of North Wales: Hugh Courtney, John Browne, Richard Price out of your parts." In other words, the three members for North Wales were simply nominated in London by Harrison and Powell and their names communicated, as a courtesy, to a prominent supporter in the district. It need hardly be added that all three were prominent Fifth Monarchy men, and all were duly "elected." No doubt the three members for South Wales—Vavasour Powell's own district —were similarly chosen. Two of them also appear to have been Fifth Monarchists.[32] Similarly in England, wherever radical preach-

since the Council naturally would be in many cases, and demonstrably was in others, guided by the local Saints. Mr. Woolrych's conclusions make the achievement of the Fifth Monarchy men in "colonizing" a purely "nominated" assembly even more remarkable.

30. Lord Lisle was evidently nominated by the Council, since he sat for Kent, but had not been nominated by the churches of Kent, whose list of nominees survives (*Milton State Papers*, p. 95).

31. Some of these letters were published in the *Transactions of the Lancashire and Cheshire Historical Society* (1861), pp. 171 ff. (The originals are now MS. 11440 in the National Library of Wales.) Colonel Jones afterward separated himself from the Fifth Monarchy men, married Cromwell's sister, and supported the Protectorate; but at this time, as his letters show, he was a complete fellow traveler with Harrison and Vavasour Powell.

32. The three members for South Wales were James Phillips, John Williams, and Bussy Mansell. According to J. H. Davies, *Gweithiau Morgan Llwyd*, II, p. lxiii, two of them were Fifth Monarchists. Louise Fargo Brown, *Baptists and Fifth Monarchy Men* (Washington, D.C., 1912), p.

ers controlled the churches, radical politicians were recommended
to the Council as members of Parliament, and Harrison, on the
Council, saw to it that they were approved.[33] So the Fifth Monarchists and their fellow travelers, a compact minority, moved *en bloc*
to Westminster. It was machine politics, and it worked like magic.
Complacently Harrison could write to a friend that "the Lord had
now at last made the General instrumental to put the power into
the hands of His people"; but that, he added, "was the Lord's
work, and no thanks to His Excellency."[34] The innocent Cromwell was still quite unaware of the revolutionary movement which
he was sponsoring.

Thus the Barebones Parliament was "elected," and when it met,
on July 4, 1653, Cromwell addressed it in his most exalted style.
Now at last, he thought, he had a parliament after his heart, a parliament of godly men, gentry of his own kind, back-benchers, not
scheming politicians—with a sprinkling, of course, of Saints. He
had a sound Speaker too, Francis Rous, a gentleman, a religious
man, and a typical Cromwellian: elderly, unpolitical, "Elizabethan," a stepbrother of Pym and a friend of Drake. Surely so pure
a body could be trusted to make good laws. Having urged them to
do so, he withdrew altogether from the scene and waited for the
good laws to emerge. He did not seek to control Parliament;
though elected to its committees, he did not sit on them; in an
honest attempt "to divest the sword of all power in the civil administration" he drew aside, as Queen Elizabeth and her Privy
Council had never done, from the business of managing Parliament,
and waited for results.

The results were as might have been expected. The Cromwellian

33, only identifies one of them, viz. John Williams, as a Baptist or Fifth
Monarchy man; but whether formally enrolled in the party or not, Bussy
Mansell certainly voted with the radicals and was one of the last-ditchers
on the radical side who were ultimately turned out by force (see his letter
in *Thurloe State Papers,* 1742, I, 637).

33. Apart from the Welsh seats, I deduce that other constituencies were
thus "colonized" from the few surviving lists sent in by the churches. Thus,
although the churches of Norfolk and Gloucester proposed miscellaneous
names, many of which were not accepted by the Council, the churches of
Suffolk and Kent proposed solid lists of radical voters (*Milton State Papers,*
pp. 92–95, 124–25).

34. S. R. Gardiner, *History of the Commonwealth,* II, 222.

back-benchers were as clumsy old bluebottles caught in the delicate web spun by nimble radical spiders. The radicals were few—there were only eighteen definitely identifiable Anabaptists or Fifth Monarchy men,[35] of whom five were from Wales; but it was enough. They made a dash for the crucial committees;[36] Harrison, unlike Cromwell, sat regularly both in the House and on its committees; and outside the clerical organizers of the party had the London pulpits tuned. The oratory of Blackfriars created for the radicals that outside pressure which in the past had enabled Pym to intimidate the Royalists and Vane to intimidate the "Presbyterians." Within six months the radicals had such control over the whole

35. Brown, *Baptists and Fifth Monarchy Men*, p. 33. It is often stated that the extremists had a "party" of about sixty (e.g., by H. A. Glass, *The Barebones Parliament*, 1899; Brown, *op. cit.*, p. 33, and *The First Earl of Shaftesbury*, New York, 1933, p. 55; Margaret James, "The Tithes Controversy in the Puritan Revolution," in *History*, 1941); but I do not think that so definite a statement can properly be made. It rests on the numbers in divisions, as recorded in the *Commons' Journals* and on two (slightly different) voting lists for the last crucial debate, one of which is quoted from Thomason E. 669 by Gardiner, *History of the Commonwealth*, III, 259 (it is also in *Thurloe State Papers*, III, 132), and the other, without reference, by Glass. But divisions were not always on a straight conservative-radical issue and it is not proper to label members permanently as "Cromwellians" or "radicals" on the basis of one imperfectly recorded division (Glass's list gives Squibb as a conservative, which is ridiculous, and the lists anyway do not distinguish, among those who did not vote on the conservative side, between radicals, abstainers, and absentees). Further, many of those who voted as radicals in 1653 afterward, when separated from the radical leaders, conscientiously served the Protectorate, having no doubt been—like Cromwell himself—innocent fellow travelers with the extremists. From a critical study of the tellers in divisions, and from other sources, it is certainly possible to identify the leaders on both sides: Sir Anthony Ashley Cooper, Sir Charles Wolseley, Sir Gilbert Pickering, Alderman Tichborne, on the conservative side; Harrison, Samuel Moyer, Arthur Squibb, Colonel Blount, John Ireton, and Thomas St. Nicholas on the radical side. No doubt there were others—like the solid bloc of Baptists and Fifth Monarchists—whose position can be as clearly defined. But it is likely that the ordinary back-benchers belonged to no "party," but voted according to the occasion, and that the success of the radicals consisted in managing floating voters as well as in having control over disciplined voters.

36. The committees most heavily colonized by the radicals were, naturally, those concerned with the essential parts of their program, viz. tithes and the law. The Committee for a New Model of the Law contained all the principal radicals, and out of its eighteen members no less than thirteen voted on the radical side in the crucial last debate.

assembly that the Cromwellian conservatives, panic-stricken at their revolutionary designs, came early and furtively to Whitehall and surrendered back to the Lord General the powers which, through lack of direction, they had proved incapable of wielding. Who were the parliamentary managers of the Barebones Parliament who thus filled the vacuum left by Cromwell's inability or refusal to form a party? Once again, I think, they can be identified. Arthur Squibb, a Fifth Monarchy man, was a London lawyer with Welsh connections,[37] and Samuel Moyer, a Baptist, was a London financier and member of the East India Company who had recently been added—no doubt by Harrison—to the Council of State. Both were sincere radicals in politics and religion, as they afterward showed in their eclipse; both had done well out of the revolution; they had worked together on important financial committees, particularly on the permanent Committee of Compounding; they are named together among the earliest public spokesmen for the Barebones Parliament;[38] and in the end, when Cromwell had discovered how he had been abused, it was Squibb and Moyer who, with Harrison and the preachers, were singled out for his revenge.[39] In the committees of the Barebones Parliament, where the radicals concentrated their strength, Samuel Moyer, their link with the Council of State, headed the list by sitting, as no other man did,

37. He had begun his career in the office of a Welsh lawyer, Sir Edward Powell, and was connected by marriage with the Welsh judge John Glyn.

38. After Cromwell's opening speech, the members adjourned till 8 A.M. next day for "a day of humiliation for a blessing upon their meeting, not any minister speaking before them (as was proposed), only themselves. Amongst the rest was Mr. Squibb and Samuel Moyer" (*Clarke Papers*, III, 9).

39. After the institution of the Protectorate, Squibb was forced to give up his offices as keeper of the prison at Sandwich and teller of the exchequer (*Cal. S.P. Dom. 1654*, pp. 116, 272). He was involved in Venner's Fifth Monarchy rising of 1656 (*Thurloe State Papers*, VI, 185). At the Restoration he and his brothers sought in vain to recover the tellership of the exchequer (*Cal. S.P. Dom. 1661–62*, p. 369; *1663–64*, pp. 121, 582; *1666–67*, pp. 182–83, 535). He was imprisoned in the Tower in connection with a Fifth Monarchy sermon in 1671 (*Cal. S.P. Dom. 1671*, p. 357). Moyer disappeared from the Council of State and all official positions at the same time. He reappeared to present the republican and Fifth Monarchy petition in Feb. 1659 (*Commons' Journals*, Feb. 9–15, 1659; Burton, *Parliamentary Diary*, III, 288) and again another petition on May 12, 1659 (*Commons' Journals*, s.d.).

on seven standing committees; and we know from Cromwell himself that Squibb's house in Fleet Street was the central office of the party, "and there were all the resolutions taken that were acted in that House day by day; and this was true *de facto*—I know it to be true." [40] Against this highly organized party machine—the Welsh electioneering machine of Vavasour Powell, the publicity-making machine of the London pulpits now controlled by the party, and the parliamentary caucus of Harrison, Squibb, and Moyer—Cromwell, for immediate purposes, had nothing: nothing, that is, except the ultimate basis of his rule—force.

It was by force, in the end, that the little group of radicals who refused to accept the suicide of the majority were expelled. While Speaker Rous, that "old bottle," as the radicals called him, who was unable to contain the new wine, went off "with his fellow old bottles to Whitehall" to surrender their authority, some thirty radical members remained in the House at Westminster. Too few to count as a quorum, they could not legally act as a parliament; but they called Samuel Moyer to the mace and began to register their protests. They were interrupted by two colonels who ordered them to leave and then, meeting with no compliance, "went out and fetched two files of musketeers and did as good as force them out; amongst whom," says a saddened Welsh radical, "I was an unworthy one." [41] "And why should they not depart," retorted a conservative pamphleteer, "when their assembly was by resignation dissolved, since they were but one degree above a conventicle, and that place, famous for the entertainment of so many venerable assemblies, was not so fit for them as Mr. Squibb's house, where most of their machinations were formed and shaped." [42]

Cromwell's reply to the collapse of the Barebones Parliament was not to devise—he never devised anything—but to accept a new constitution. Just as, after his impulsive dismissal of the Rump, he had accepted the ready-made plans of Major General Harrison and his party of Saints for a Parliament of their nominees, so now, after the sudden disintegration of that Parliament, he accepted from

40. Abbott, *Writings and Speeches of Oliver Cromwell*, IV, 489.

41. *Thurloe State Papers*, I, 637; cf. [? Samuel Highland] *An Exact Relation of the late Parliament*, 1654 (*Somers Tracts*, VI, 266–84); *Clarke Papers*, III, 9–10.

42. *Confusion Confounded, or a Firm Way of Settlement Settled* (1654).

Major General Lambert and his party of conservative senior officers the newly prefabricated constitution of the Instrument of Government. By this the new Protectorate was set up, and Cromwell, as Lord Protector, carefully limited by a council of senior officers, was required, after an interval of nine months, to summon a new parliament based on a new franchise. Since this new franchise was, basically, the realization of the plan already advanced by the conservative senior officers seven years earlier in Ireton's Heads of Proposals, it must be briefly analyzed: for if ever the Independent gentry got the kind of parliament for which they had fought, it should have been in the two parliaments of the Protectorate elected on the franchise which they had thus consistently advocated. If social composition were sufficient to secure a harmonious and working parliament, that success should now be assured.

The most obvious feature of the new franchise is that while preserving property qualifications, and thus substantially the same social level of representation, it notably altered the distribution of membership, drastically cutting down the borough representation and greatly increasing the county representation. Compared with these facts, the creation of four new boroughs or three new county seats are insignificant adjustments of detail. In fact, the new franchise, in spite of these four new boroughs, reduced the total number of parliamentary boroughs in England and Wales from 182 to 109 and the total number of borough members in Parliament from 419 to 136. At the same time the county representation was increased from 90 out of 509 seats to 264 out of 400 seats. In other words, whereas in previous parliaments borough members had occupied 83 percent and county members 17 percent of the seats, in Cromwell's parliaments borough members were now to occupy 34 percent and county members 66 percent. The county representation was thus quadrupled, the borough representation more than halved.

What is the significance of this sweeping change? The Victorian writers who saw in Cromwell an early nonconformist Liberal supposed that he had in some way "modernized" the franchise. Had he not disfranchised rotten boroughs and enfranchised new boroughs? But the overall change, the gigantic switch from borough seats to county seats, seems to me more significant than such modifications of detail. Modern Marxist historians, believing that the

Protectorate was a device of the rich, a forcing house of capitalism, suppose that the new franchise was "designed to bring the electoral system into something like correspondence with the property-distribution in the country." [43] But where was the wealth of England? Much of the new wealth was wealth from trade, concentrated—as the Independent gentry indignantly complained—more and more in the City of London. Even if we consider landed wealth only, it can hardly be argued that its distribution was better represented under the new franchise than under the old. Landed wealth was distributed among noblemen, merchants, and gentry. Cromwell's parliaments under the new franchise contained no English peers and very few merchants. [44] They were parliaments of gentry, and not necessarily of the richer gentry either. The chief difference between the new and the old members was that whereas the old had been predominantly borough gentry the new were predominantly county gentry. What does this difference between "borough gentry" and "county gentry," in fact, mean?

A glance at English parliamentary history at any time between 1559 and 1832 provides the answer. The borough gentry were client gentry; the county gentry were not—they were, or could be, independent of patronage. It was largely through the boroughs that patrons and parliamentary managers had, in the past, built up their forces in Parliament. It was through them that Essex had built up a party against Cecil and Cecil against Essex, through them that Charles I might have resisted the opposition magnates and the opposition magnates were, in fact, able to resist him. Further, at all times, it was through the boroughs that able men—lawyers, officials, scholars—got into Parliament as the clients of greater men and provided both the administration and the opposition with some of their most effective members. The "rotten" boroughs, in fact, performed two functions: first, they made Parliament less representative of the electors than it would otherwise have been; secondly, they made it less inefficient as an instrument of policy.

Now, if, as I have suggested, the Independent gentry were, in fact, the rural "back-bench" gentry, such as were afterward repre-

43. C. Hill and E. Dell, *The Good Old Cause* (1949), p. 445.
44. For merchant representation in Cromwell's parliaments, see M. P. Ashley, *Commercial and Financial Policy of the Protectorate* (1934), pp. 6–8.

sented in the Tory party of Queen Anne and the first two Georges, it is clear that they, like the later Tories, would be opposed to the borough system as being, by definition, a device of the front-bench politicians to evade the "equal representation" of "the people"—that is, of the country gentry—and to introduce "courtiers" instead of honest country gentry into Parliament. It is true, many of them had themselves been returned in this manner in 1640; but their own front-bench leaders, the "Presbyterian" magnates, had then deserted them, and by 1647 they were clamoring for decentralization in Parliament as in government, law, Church, and education. They demanded a parliament not of untrustworthy "courtiers" or experts but of sound, honest, representative men like themselves: a "more equal representative" of real Independents, uncontrolled by any professional caucus; and since, in their own language, "it was well understood that mean and decayed boroughs might be much more easily corrupted than the numerous counties and considerable cities," [45] they sought it by a reduction of "corrupt" borough seats and a multiplication of "independent" county seats.[46]

That had been in 1647, when the Independents had been in opposition. Now they were in power; but their philosophy had not changed. It was not merely that they were committed by their past: that would be too cynical an interpretation. Their philosophy was genuinely held: experience had not yet shown the inherent impossibility of a completely back-bench parliament or the inherent difficulty of decentralization by a revolutionary central government; and Cromwell no doubt supposed that honest, Independent country gentlemen, freely elected from within the Puritan fold, would naturally agree with the aims and methods of his rule. Further, from the point of view of Cromwell and his council, there were certain

45. Ludlow, *Memoirs,* II, 48. The same argument was a commonplace among the later Tories.
46. Ivan Roots, in his book *The Great Rebellion* (1966), p. 182, criticizes this part of my essay on the ground that the Instrument of Government, which changed the parliamentary franchise, was the work not of "Independent country gentry" but of "a group of officers." But this is to ignore the previous history of the reforms. The Instrument of Government merely put into effect changes which had been advocated by Independent members of Parliament, and their constituents, since 1645 (and indeed before), and which had been worked out in detail in the Rump Parliament in 1650–51. The "group of officers" realized what the "Independent country gentry" had long demanded.

compensations. If, by disfranchising the boroughs, the government had deprived itself of a system of patronage, it had equally denied that system to opponents who might, like the opponents of Charles I, be more skillful in using it. Besides, to make doubly sure, the new government prudently added to the English Parliament a new system of exclusively government patronage which had not been, and indeed could not have been, considered in 1647. The sixty new Scotch and Irish seats created by the Instrument of Government were not, of course, designed for genuine representatives of the newly conquered Scots or Irishmen: they were safe pocket boroughs for government nominees.

A parliament of congenial, unorganized, Independent country gentry, like-minded with himself, reinforced by sixty direct nominees and saved, by the franchise, from the knavish tricks of rival electioneers—surely this would give Cromwell the kind of parliament he wanted. Especially after the radical scare of 1653, on which he was now able to dwell, and which had made him appear, even to many of those "Presbyterians" who shuddered at his regicide past, a "saviour of society." Therefore, when the members had assembled in September 1654, and had listened to a sermon on the arrival of the Israelites, after their years in the Wilderness, at their Land of Rest, Cromwell felt able to apply the text to them and to congratulate them too on having at last, "after so many changings and turnings," arrived at a period of "healing and settling." Furthermore, he assured them, they were now "a *free* Parliament"; just as he had not sought to control the elections, so he would not in any way control or interfere with their deliberations. Instead, he urged them to discover among themselves "a sweet, gracious and holy understanding of one another"; and having so urged them, he once again swept off to Whitehall to await, in Olympian detachment, the results of their deliberations.

He did not have to wait long. Able men can work any system, and even under the new franchise the experienced republicans had contrived to re-enter Parliament. Once in, they moved with effortless rapidity into the vacuum created by the Protector's virtuous but misguided refusal to form a party. The speed with which they operated is astonishing: one is forced to conclude either that Hesilrige and Scot were really brilliant tacticians (a conclusion which the recorded evidence hardly warrants) or that Cromwell had no vestige of an organization to resist them. At the very beginning they nearly got their nominee—the notorious regicide John Bradshaw—in as Speaker. Having failed, they displaced the rival Speaker by the old dodge of calling for a Committee of the Whole House. At once Hesilrige and Scot were in control of the debates; the floating voters drifted helplessly into their wake; and the whole institution of the Protectorate came under heavy fire. Within a week Cromwell had repented of his words about "a free Parliament," and all the republican members, with Hesilrige, Scot, and Bradshaw at their head, had been turned out by force. Legislation was then handed back to the real back-benchers for whom the Parliament had been intended.

Ironically, the result was no better. Again and again Cromwell, by his own refusal to organize and his purges of those who organized against him, created in Parliament a vacuum of leadership; again and again this vacuum was filled. A pure parliament of back-benchers is an impossibility: someone will always come to the front; and since Cromwell never, like the Tudors, placed able ministers on the front benches, those benches were invariably occupied from behind. The first to scramble to the front were always the republicans: they were the real parliamentary tacticians of the Interregnum. But when they were removed, a second group advanced into their place. It was this second group who now, by their opposition, wrecked Cromwell's first Protectorate Parliament.

Who were they? As we look at their program, shown in their long series of successive amendments to the new constitution which had been imposed upon them, we see that, basically, it is the program of the old "country party" of 1640. The voice that emerges from those "pedantic" amendments, as Carlyle so contemptuously called them, is the voice of the original opponents of Charles I, the voice even of Cromwell himself in his days of opposition. It protests, not, of course, against the decentralization which by his ordinances he had been carrying out, which was still his policy, and of which the new franchise itself was one expression, but against the machinery of centralization whereby this policy was declared: against the new Court, the new arbitrariness, the new standing army, the new taxes of that Man of Blood, Oliver Cromwell. Cromwell was caught up in the necessities and contradictions of power and found himself faced by his own old colleagues in opposition. In his days of opposition he too, like them, had demanded a parliament of back-benchers. Now he had got it—when he was in power. By a new franchise and a new purge he had confined Parliament to the old country party just at the time when he had himself inherited the position, the difficulties, and the necessities of the old Court.

But who were the leaders who gave expression and direction to this new country party? A study of the tellers in divisions, which is almost all the evidence we possess, enables us to name the most active of them. There was John Bulkley, member for Hampshire, Sir Richard Onslow, member for Surrey, and, above all, Colonel Birch, member for Hereford; and the interesting fact about these men is that they were all old "Presbyterians"— men who had been arrested or secluded in Pride's Purge. Thus, when the republicans had been removed, it was not the Independents who had occupied the vacant front benches—that indeed would have been contrary to their nature: it was the "Presbyterians." Heirs of the original front-bench opposition of 1640, first expelled by the army, then disgusted by the act of regicide, they had now decided to stomach the usurper as the only immediate guarantee against the even greater evil of social revolution; but they were not going to accept him on his terms: they were going to fight for their own.

And did no one seek to serve the cause of Independency against these new, revived "Presbyterian" opponents? Yes, the new government had its champions, but it is interesting to note that they too were not Independents. In the Barebones Parliament it was Sir Anthony Ashley Cooper, a former Royalist, since excluded as a "Presbyterian" in Pride's Purge, who had returned to politics as a Cromwellian and had sought in vain, and without support from Cromwell, to organize parliamentary resistance against the radical extremists. He had been by far the most active parliamentarian on the "conservative" side, one of their elected representatives on the Council of State, their regular teller in controversial divisions; and when his efforts had been in vain, it was another former Royalist, Sir Charles Wolseley, who had proposed and carried out the act of resignation whereby the radicals had been cheated of their victory. Now, in the Parliament of 1654, the same two ex-Royalists emerged again as the opponents of the new "country party." Only this time their roles were reversed. Leaving Sir Charles Wolseley to inherit his position as the champion of Cromwellian government, Cooper, a far abler man, now appeared less as a protagonist than a mediator: he sought not to preserve the Protectorate in the new authoritarian form in which it stood, but to make such compromises with the opposition as would make it a tolerable form of government, a form of government such as the original Independents had always demanded. Consistent with that original program, he even sought to civilize the institution by making Cromwell king. But once again Cromwell, aloof at Whitehall, never supported this voluntary ally who now fore-shadowed the only practical solution of his problem and was after-ward to prove the most formidable parliamentary tactician of the next reign; and before the abrupt end of the session Cooper drew the consequences. Despairing of Cromwell, he crossed the floor and joined Colonel Birch in opposition. A fortnight later the Protector, now dependent entirely on the army officers, came sud-denly down to Westminster prematurely to dissolve yet another parliament. "I do not know what you have been doing," he de-clared, "I do not know whether you have been alive or dead!"— it is difficult to conceive of Queen Elizabeth or Lord Burghley making such an admission—and with the usual flood of turbid eloquence, hysterical abuse, and appeals to God, he dissolved prematurely what was to have been his ideal parliament.

For the next year Cromwell surrendered entirely to his military advisers. He still hankered after his old ideals—it is a great mis-take, I think, to suppose that he ever "betrayed" the revolution, or at least the revolution for which he had taken up the sword. But he resigned himself to the view that those ideals could best be secured by administration, not legislation. After all, "forms of government" were to him indifferent: one system was as good as another, provided it secured good results; and now it seemed to him that the ideals of the revolution—honest rule such as "suits

a Commonwealth," social justice, reform of the law, toleration—
would be better secured through the summary but patriarchal
rule of the major generals than through the legal but wayward
deliberations of even an Independent parliament. And, in fact,
the major generals did attempt such things: as Cromwell afterward admitted, even while he attacked them, "you, Major-Generals, did your parts well." [47] Unfortunately, like Archbishop
Laud before him, he was soon to discover that, in politics, good
intentions are not enough. The major generals, like the Laudian
bishops, might seek to supervise J.P.s, to reform manners, to
manage preachers, to resist enclosures; but all this was expensive,
and when the Spanish war, like Laud's Scottish war, proved a
failure, the major generals themselves begged Cromwell, for financial reasons, to do what even Laud had had to do: to face a parliament. If Cromwell, like Laud, had apprehensions, the major generals comforted him. Confident, as military men so often are, of
their own efficiency, they assured him that they, unlike the
bishops, could control the elections and secure a parliament which
would give no trouble. So, in the autumn of 1656, after the most
vigorous electioneering campaign since 1640, a parliament was
duly elected.

The result was not at all what the major generals had expected.
Ironically, one of the reasons for their failure was that very reduction of the borough seats which the Independents had themselves designed. In the interest of decentralization, Cromwell and
his friends had cut down a system of patronage which now at last
they had learned to use. In the period of direct rule by the major
generals, the government had "remodeled" the boroughs and converted them into safe supporters;[48] but alas, thanks to the new
franchise, the boroughs were now too few to stem the tide, and
from the uncontrollable county constituencies, which the new
franchise had multiplied, the critics of the government—genuine
Independent critics of a new centralization—were returned, irresistible, to Westminster. The major generals had secured their
own election, but little more: thanks to their own new franchise,

47. Burton, *Parliamentary Diary*, I, 384.
48. See B. L. K. Henderson, "The Cromwellian Charters," in *Transactions of the Royal Historical Society*, 1912, pp. 129 ff.

their heroic electioneering efforts had proved vain; and Cromwell, when he saw what they had done, did not spare them. "Impatient were you," he told them, "till a Parliament was called. I gave my vote against it; but you were confident by your own strength and interest to get men chosen to your hearts' desire. How you have failed therein, and how much the country hath been disobliged, is well known." [49] He might well rub it in, for one of the first acts of the parliament thus called was to vote out of existence the whole system of the major generals.

Thus, in spite of vigorous efforts to pack it, Cromwell's second and last Protectorate Parliament consisted largely of the same persons as its predecessor; and in many respects its history was similar. Once again the old republicans had been returned; once again, as not being "persons of known integrity, fearing God and of good conversation," they were arbitrarily removed. Once again the old back-benchers, the civilians, the new country party, filled the vacuum. But there was one very significant difference. It was a difference of leadership and policy. For this time they were not led by the old "Presbyterians." A new leadership appeared with a new policy, and the Independents now found themselves mobilized not against but for the government of Oliver Cromwell. Instead of attacking him as a "single person," they offered now to support him as king.

The *volte-face* seems complete, and naturally many were surprised by it; but, in fact, it is not altogether surprising. The new policy was simply the old policy of Sir Anthony Ashley Cooper, the policy of civilizing Cromwell's rule by reverting to known institutions and restoring, under a new dynasty, not, of course, the government of the Stuarts, but the old system from which the Stuarts had so disastrously deviated. For after all, the Independents had not originally revolted against monarchy: the "Whig" republicans, who now claimed to be the heirs of the revolution, had, in fact, been belated upstarts in its course, temporary usurpers of its aims. The genuine "Tory" Independents, who had now reasserted themselves over those usurpers, had merely wanted a less irresponsible king than Charles I. Nor had

49. Burton, *Parliamentary Diary*, I, 384.

they wanted new constitutions. They had no new doctrines: they merely wanted an old-style monarch like Queen Elizabeth. Why should they not now, after so many bungled alternatives, return to those original limited aims? Why should not Cromwell, since he already exercised monarchical power, adjust himself more completely to a monarchical position? In many ways the policy of the "Kingship party" in Parliament—however denounced by the republicans as a betrayal of the revolution which they sought to corner—was, in fact, the nearest that the Puritans ever got to realizing their original aims. Consequently it found wide support. The country party and the new court at last came together.

Who was the architect of this parliamentary coup? There can be no doubt about his identity. Once again, it was a former Royalist. Lord Broghill, a son of the 1st Earl of Cork, was an Irish magnate who had become a personal friend and supporter of Cromwell. He was now member of Parliament for County Cork, and his immediate supporters were the other members for Ireland, whom, no doubt, as Cromwell's Irish confidant, he had himself helped to nominate. There was Colonel Jephson, member for Cork City and Youghal, where Broghill's family reigned; there was Colonel Bridge, member for Sligo, Roscommon, and Leitrim; there was Sir John Reynolds, member for Tipperary and Waterford; and there was Vincent Gookin, member for Kinsale and Bandon, Surveyor-General of Ireland. In other words, Lord Broghill was a great parliamentary manager, like the earls of Warwick and Bedford in 1640. While the major generals, as officials, had organized the attenuated boroughs of England in their support, Broghill, a private landlord, wedded to an entirely different program, had organized another area of influence, in Ireland. If the "Presbyterians" had been, in some respects, a Scottish party, and the Fifth Monarchy men a Welsh party, the "Kingship-men" were, in their first appearance, an Anglo-Irish party.[50]

Once again the remarkable thing is the ease with which the new leadership secured control over Parliament. Just as the eleven "Presbyterian" leaders, whenever they were allowed to be present

50. The Irish basis of the "Kingship party" was pointed out by Firth, "Cromwell and the Crown," in *English Historical Review*, 1902, 1903.

in 1647-48, had always been able to win control of the Long Parliament from Vane and St. John; just as, after 1649, the little group of republicans dominated every parliament to which they were admitted; just as a score of radical extremists dominated the Barebones Parliament of 1653, or a handful of old "Presbyterians" the Purged Parliament of 1654, so the little group of "Kingship-men" quickly took control, against the protesting major generals, of the Parliament of 1656. Their success illustrates the complete absence of any rival organization, any organization by the government—and, incidentally, the ease with which Cromwell, if he had taken the trouble or understood the means, could have controlled such docile parliaments.

For there can be no doubt that Cromwell himself, though he stood ultimately to gain by it, was at first completely surprised by Broghill's movement. As he afterward said, he "had never been at any cabal about the same."[51] Indeed, when Broghill's party first made itself felt in Parliament, it was positively opposed to the declared policy of the Protector; for Cromwell was still committed to the system of government by major generals, and his faithful shadow, Secretary Thurloe, had already drafted a speech urging the continuation of that system—a speech which the sudden, belated conversion of his master and himself to the "Kingship party" left undelivered in his files.[52] Furthermore, the previous advocate of kingship, Sir Anthony Ashley Cooper, had been firmly excluded from the present parliament by order of Cromwell himself. We are obliged to conclude that Cromwell at first genuinely intended to support the major generals, and that, in jettisoning them, he did not follow any deliberate course. He simply wearied of them, as he had wearied in turn of the King, of the "Presbyterians," of the Levellers, of the Rump, of the Saints; and having wearied, he surrendered once again to a new party, just as, in the past, he had surrendered in turn to Vane, to Ireton, to

51. Burton, *Parliamentary Diary*, I, 382.
52. The draft is in *Thurloe State Papers*, V, 786-88, where it is described as "minute of a speech in Parliament by Secretary Thurloe"; but, in fact, I can find no evidence that it was ever delivered, and I presume that it is a draft. In any case, delivered or undelivered, it shows that Thurloe, and therefore Cromwell, had intended to continue the major-general system, which, in fact, they jettisoned.

Harrison, to Lambert—successive mentors who had successively promised to lead him at last out of the "blood and confusion" caused by their predecessors to that still elusive elixir, "settlement."

Having captured a majority in Parliament, the "Kingship party" set methodically to work. The government of the major generals was abolished; the kingship, and the whole political apparatus which went with it—House of Lords, Privy Council, State Church, and old parliamentary franchise—was proposed. Except for the army leaders, whom such a policy would have civilized out of existence, and the obstinate, doctrinaire republicans, all political groups were mobilized. The officials, the lawyers, the Protectoral family and clients, the government financiers—all who had an interest in the stability of government—were in favor. At last, it seemed, Cromwell had an organized party in Parliament. He had not made it: it had made itself and presented itself to him ready-made. It asked only to be used. What use did Cromwell make of it?

The answer is clear. He ruined it. Unable to win over the army leaders, he wrestled with them, rated them, blustered at them. "It was time," he protested, "to come to a settlement and leave aside these arbitrary measures so unacceptable to the nation." [53] And then, when he found them inexorable, he surrendered to them and afterward justified his surrender in Parliament by describing not the interested opposition of serried brass hats but the alleged honest scruples of religious Nonconformist sergeants. Of course, he may have been right to yield. Perhaps he judged the balance of power correctly. Perhaps he could not have maintained his new monarchy without army support. There was here a real dilemma. And yet the army could certainly have been "remodeled"—purged of its politicians and yet kept strong enough to defend the new dynasty. As Monck afterward wrote, and by his own actions proved, "there is not an officer in the Army, upon any discontent, that has interest enough to draw two men after him, if he be out of place." [54] Cromwell's own personal ascendancy over the army, apart from a few politically ambitious generals,

53. Burton, *Parliamentary Diary*, I, 382.
54. *Thurloe State Papers*, VII, 387.

was undisputed. Instead of pleading defensively with the "Army Grandees" as an organized party, he could have cashiered a few of them silently, as examples to the rest, and all opposition to kingship would probably have evaporated; for it was nourished by his indecision. The total eclipse first of Harrison, then of Lambert, once they had been dismissed—though each in turn had been second man in the army and the state—sufficiently shows the truth of Monck's judgment.

Be that as it may, Cromwell never, in fact, tried to solve the problem of army opposition. After infinite delays and a series of long speeches, each obscurer than the last, he finally surrendered to it and accepted the new constitution only in a hopelessly truncated form: without kingship, without Lords, without effective Privy Council. Even so, in the view of Lord Broghill and his party, it might have been made to work. But again, Cromwell would not face the facts. Neither in his new Upper House nor in his new Council would he give the "Kingship men" the possibility of making a party. Spasmodic, erratic gestures now raised, now dashed their hopes, and led ultimately nowhere; the leaders of the party wrung their hands in despair at the perpetual indecision, the self-contradictory gestures of their intended king; and in the end, in January 1658, when the Parliament reassembled for its second session, the old republicans, readmitted under the new constitution, and compacted by their long exile, found the "Kingship men" a divided, helpless, dispirited group, utterly at their mercy.

At once they seized their opportunity. The lead was given by their old leader, Sir Arthur Hesilrige. Why, he asked, had the preacher, in his opening address, said nothing in praise of "that victorious Parliament," the Rump? "I cannot sit still and hear such a question moved and bide any debate." Whereupon that other oracle of the republicans, Thomas Scot, "said he could not sit still but second such a notion, to hear one speak so like an Englishman to call it a victorious Parliament." From that moment the incorrigible combine was at work again, each seconding the other, filibustering unchecked with long, irrelevant speeches on the horrors of the *ancien régime,* boastful personal reminiscences, the divine right of parliaments, the virtue of regicide, the glories of the Rump. Hesilrige, who once spoke for three hours on past history, beginning with the Heptarchy, prophesied a two months' debate and "hoped no man should be debarred of speaking his mind freely, and as often as he pleased." As for himself, "I could speak till four o'clock." Within ten days all constructive business had become impossible: the Parliament, the French ambassador reported to his government, *"était devenu le parlement de Hesilrige,"* and as such Cromwell angrily dissolved it, "and God judge between you and me."[55] Before he could summon another, he was dead.[56]

If Oliver Cromwell's parliaments were thus consistently hamstrung through lack of direction, the one parliament of his son Richard was, if anything, more chaotic—and that in spite of immense efforts to prepare it. For weeks before it met, Secretary Thurloe and the Council, on their own admission, did "little but prepare for the next Parliament."[57] The old franchise, and with it the old opportunities of borough patronage, was restored. The council, as Ludlow sourly remarks, "used their utmost endeavours to procure such men to be chosen as were their creatures and had their dependencies on them."[58] But the result was as unsatis-

55. Burton, *Parliamentary Diary,* III, 874, 117, 141, and II, 437 (and cf. III, 140); Bordeaux to Mazarin, Feb. 18, 1658, cited in F. Guizot, *Histoire de la république d'Angleterre* (Paris, 1864), II, 629.

56. For the failure of the "Kingship party" in Cromwell's last year see the analysis of their tactics in R. C. H. Catterall, "The Failure of the Humble Petition and Advice," in *American Historical Review,* Oct. 1903 (IX, 36–65). Catterall concludes that Cromwell was wiser than the "Kingship men" and was working, more slowly, more prudently, and more patiently than they, to the same result: "Time was the essential requisite. . . . Time, however, was not granted." What one thinks of Cromwell's plans and prospects of success must depend on one's estimate of his character as revealed by his previous career, and here I must dissent from Catterall. I cannot agree that patience was "a quality always at Oliver's disposal and always exercised by him," nor find, in his career, evidence of a slow and prudent progress toward a clearly envisaged political aim. Rather he seems to me to have successively borrowed and then impatiently discarded a series of inconsistent secondhand political systems; and I see no reason to suppose that he was any nearer to a final "settlement" at the time of his death than at any previous time in his history of political failure.

57. *Thurloe State Papers,* VII, 562.

58. Ludlow, *Memoirs,* II, 49, and references there cited, cf. *Calendar of State Papers (Venetian),* XXXI, 276–77, 282, 284, 285.

factory as ever. The "Kingship party" was now dead: they would have fought to make Oliver king, but who would fight to put the crown on Richard's head rather than on that of Charles II? Lord Broghill did not even sit in the new parliament. On the other hand, the republicans were full of confidence. The demoralization of the Cromwellians gave them hope; in organization they were supreme; and when the Parliament met it was soon clear that Hesilrige and Scot were once again its masters.

Masters for what? Certainly not to lead it to constructive legislation. Republicanism in England, except in their fossilized minds, was dead: perhaps it had never been alive outside that limited terrain. Certainly it had not inspired the beginning of the rebellion, and certainly it was extinct at the end of it. From 1653 onward, when the "Whig" policy which they had grafted onto the revolution had been repudiated, Hesilrige and Scot and their friends were simply obstructionists. They had a doctrine and a parliamentary organization. Thanks to that doctrine, and that organization, and the absence of any rival organization, they had achieved power for a time; but when their policy had been rejected, and they proved incapable of modifying it or making it acceptable, they could never recover power and they could use their clear, hard, narrow doctrine and their unrivaled parliamentary organization solely to destroy every rival party in Parliament, until the enemy they hated most of all, the monarchy of the Stuarts, returned to crush them and their rivals alike. From 1653 onward the republicans were simply the saboteurs of every parliament to which they could gain admittance. The weakness of the executive was their opportunity: an opportunity not to advance a cause, but simply to destroy their own rivals; and in no parliament was that weakness so tempting to them, or that destruction so easy, as in the parliament of Richard Cromwell, who was too feeble to adopt his father's methods and expel them.

Consequently the record of Richard's parliament makes pitiful reading—even more pitiful than that of Oliver's parliaments, which at least is enriched by the serious purpose and volcanic personality of the Protector. In vain Richard's Speaker, regularly rebuked for his inability to control the debate, protested at the irrelevancy of members: "we are in a wood, a wilderness, a labyrinth. Some affirmative, some negative, which I cannot draw into one question. . . . The sun does not stand still, but I think you do not go forward." Even a new and more forceful Speaker, who himself pitched into the debate, answering everyone and laying about him "like a Busby among so many school boys," proved hardly more effective.[59] Most pitiful of all was the fate of Mr. Secretary Thurloe, the chief representative of the Protector in his parliament, the man who was accused of having packed Parliament with at least eighty of his nominees. If only he had done so, as it was his duty to have done, the government might have fared better.[60] In fact, attempting to defend the indefensible, romantic, irrational foreign policy of the government, Thurloe found himself hopelessly left behind as one speaker after another carried the debate off into irrelevant byways. Before long, Thurloe, instead of defending his foreign policy, was defending himself against a charge of having sold English subjects into slavery in the West Indies; and in a debate on the constitution he even found himself in a minority of one.[61]

The Secretary of State in a minority of one! The mere thought of such a possibility would have made Mr. Secretary Cecil or Mr. Secretary Walsingham—if they could even have conceived such a thought—turn in their graves. And yet this is the man whom historians have supposed—merely on account of the number of letters which he either wrote or received or steamed open—to be the genius of Cromwellian government! [62] When such a thing could happen it was clear that the old Elizabethan system of which the Cromwellians had dreamed, and indeed any parliamentary system, had indeed broken down.

59. Burton, *Parliamentary Diary*, III, 192, 269–70, 281, 333, and IV, 205, 213, 234, 243.

60. In fact, Thurloe protested, "I know not of three members thus chosen into the House." Burton, *Parliamentary Diary*, IV, 301.

61. Burton, *Parliamentary Diary*, III, 399, 287; and cf. [Slingsby Bethel] "A True and Impartial Narrative . . . ," in *Somers Tracts*, VI, 481.

62. The political ability of Thurloe seems to me to have been greatly overrated by historians. His skill in counter-espionage is attested by his own state papers, and it excited such admiration at the time that it afterward became legendary; but otherwise he seems to have been merely an industrious secretary who echoed his master's sentiments (and errors) with pathetic unoriginality. A good secretary is not necessarily a good Secretary of State.

Thus Oliver Cromwell's successive efforts to govern with and through Parliament failed, and failed abjectly. They failed through lack of that parliamentary management by the executive which, in the correct dosage, is the essential nourishment of any sound parliamentary life. As always with Cromwell, there is an element of tragic irony in his failure: his very virtues caused him to blunder into courses from which he could escape only by the most unvirtuous, inconsistent, and indefensible expedients. And the ultimate reason of this tragic, ironical failure lies, I think, in the very character of Cromwell and of the Independency which he so perfectly represented. Cromwell himself, like his followers, was a natural back-bencher. He never understood the subtleties of politics, never rose above the simple political prejudices of those other backwoods squires whom he had joined in their blind revolt against the Stuart Court. His first speech in Parliament had been the protest of a provincial squire against popish antics in his own parish church; and at the end, as ruler of three kingdoms, he still compared himself only to a bewildered parish constable seeking laboriously and earnestly to keep the peace in a somewhat disorderly and incomprehensible parish. His conception of government was the rough justice of a benevolent, serious-minded, rural magistrate: well intentioned, unsophisticated, summary, patriarchal, conservative. Such was also the political philosophy of many other English squires who, in the seventeenth century, turned up in Parliament and, sitting patiently on the back benches, either never understood or, at most, deeply suspected the secret mechanism whereby the back benches were controlled from the front. In ordinary times the natural fate of such men was to stay at the back, and to make a virtue of their "honesty," their "independency," their kinship rather with the good people who had elected them than with the sharp politicians and courtiers among whom they found themselves. But the 1640s and 1650s were not ordinary times. Then a revolutionary situation thrust these men forward, and in their indignation they hacked down, from behind, the sharp politicians and courtiers, the Royalists and "Presbyterians," who had first mobilized them. Having no clear political ideas, they did not—except in the brief period when they surrendered to the republican usurpers—destroy institutions, but only persons.

They destroyed parliamentarians and the King, but not Parliament or the Throne. These institutions, in their fury, they simply cleaned out and left momentarily vacant. But before long the vacancy was refilled. By careful tests and a new franchise, Parliament was reopened—to Independents (that is, back-benchers) only; under careful reservations and a new title, the Throne was reoccupied—by an Independent (that is, a back-bench) ruler. At last, it seemed, Crown and Commons were in natural harmony.

Alas, in political matters natural harmony is not enough. To complete the system, and to make it work, something else was necessary too: an Independent political caucus that would constitute an Independent front bench as a bridge between Crown and Parliament, like those Tudor Privy Councillors who gave consistency and direction to the parliaments of Henry VIII and Elizabeth. Unfortunately this was the one thing which Cromwell always refused to provide. To good Independents any political caucus was suspect: it smacked of sharp politicians and the Court. An Independent front bench was a contradiction in terms. Even those who, in turn, and without his support, sought to create such a front bench for him—Sir Anthony Ashley Cooper, Sir Charles Wolseley, Lord Broghill—were not real Independents, but, all of them, ex-Royalists. Like his fellow squires (and like those liberal historians who virtuously blame the Tudors for "packing" their parliaments), Cromwell tended to regard all parliamentary management as a "cabal," a wicked interference with the freedom of Parliament. Therefore he supplied none, and when other more politically minded men sought to fill the void, he intervened to crush such indecent organization. In this way he thought he was securing "free parliaments"—free, that is, from caucus control. Having thus secured a "free parliament," he expected it automatically, as a result merely of good advice, good intentions, and goodwill, to produce "good laws," as in the reign of his heroine Queen Elizabeth. He did not realize that Queen Elizabeth's parliaments owed their effectiveness not to such "freedom," nor to the personal worthiness of the parties, nor to the natural harmony between them, but to that ceaseless vigilance, intervention, and management by the Privy Council which worthy Puritan back-benchers regarded as a monstrous limitation of their freedom. No wonder Cromwell's parliaments were uniformly barren. His ideal was an Elizabethan Parliament, but his methods were such as would lead to a Polish Diet. Consequently, each of his parliaments, deprived of leadership from him, fell in turn under other leadership and were then treated by him in a manner which made them feel far from free. Only in Cromwell's last year did a Cromwellian party manager, without encouragement from him, emerge in the House of Commons and seek to save the real aims of the revolution; but even he, having been tardily accepted, was ultimately betrayed by his inconstant master. In that betrayal Cromwell lost what proved to be his last chance of achieving the "settlement" which he so long and so faithfully but so unskillfully pursued.

Thus it is really misleading to speak of "Cromwell and his parliaments" as we speak of "Queen Elizabeth and her parliaments," for in that possessive sense Cromwell—to his misfortune—had no parliaments: he only faced, in a helpless, bewildered manner, a succession of parliaments which he failed either to pack, to control, or to understand. There was the Parliament of Hesilrige and Scot, the Parliament of Squibb and Moyer, the Parliament of Birch, the Parliament of Broghill, and the Parliament of Hesilrige once again; but there was never a Parliament of Oliver Cromwell. Ironically, the one English sovereign who had actually been a member of Parliament proved himself, as a parliamentarian, the most incompetent of them all. He did so because he had not studied the necessary rules of the game. Hoping to imitate Queen Elizabeth, who, by understanding those rules, had been able to play upon "her faithful Commons" as upon a well-tuned instrument, he failed even more dismally than the Stuarts. The tragedy is that, whereas they did not believe in the system, he did.

G. D. RAMSAY

Industrial Laisser-Faire and the Policy of Cromwell

AT THE CLOSE of the Middle Ages there was never a hint
that the political sovereign was not entitled to regulate the
economic life of his principality, and it is nowadays a commonplace among economic historians that industry in England was in
fact regulated with varying thoroughness by the government in
the century or so preceding the outbreak of civil war in the 1640s.
It is also agreed that long before the end of the eighteenth century
the triumph of *laisser-faire* was assured and indeed that this was
one of the main factors in precipitating the ultimate heightening
of manufacturing speed and skill that passes under the name of
"the industrial revolution." As to when and how the change in
governmental policy was effected there is at present less certainty.
It is the purpose of this essay to suggest further clues to the solu-

From *The Economic History Review*, Vol. XVI, No. 1, August 1946, by
permission of the author and the Economic History Society.

tion of the problem and, in particular, by examining the effectiveness of industrial regulation during the Protectorate of Oliver Cromwell to determine the attitude of Puritan government in its heyday toward industry and incidentally thereby to help toward elucidating the significance—or insignificance—of the Civil Wars and the subsequent religious changes in English economic history.

The regulation of industry in Tudor England by external authority was spurred by motives various and intertwined. It might be, as to a large extent in the case of the Statute of Artificers, the care of the government for the preservation of the manpower and of the social tranquillity of the kingdom. Or it might be a grant of monopoly designed to raise money for a hard-pressed Crown. On the other hand, the series of acts by which the textile industry was bound in the sixteenth century was instigated, it can hardly be doubted, by the merchant adventurers, a powerful and well-organized body of wealthy Londoners. Sometimes an ancient guild organization, such as the Company of Hostmen of Newcastle-on-Tyne, was wrested by a rising local capitalist clique to its own special ends,[1] though commonly the bodies of medieval provenance were the bulwark of the smaller men. But whatever the class interest in which the restrictive forms might be used, the idea of regulation itself was not questioned.

State interference with industry may be considered to have been at its most intense during the final decades of the sixteenth century, when the government was in the hands of an abler set of persons than was to be the case for some time to come. The machinery then employed for the regulation of industry was largely of medieval origin, though it was undergoing considerable refurbishing. Broadly speaking, it falls into three component pieces. There was, firstly, Parliament, a cumbrous and intermittent organ of government no doubt, but essential if any new departures in policy or amendments to existing industrial rules were to be assured

1. J. U. Nef, *The Rise of the British Coal Industry*, II (1932), 119–33. The complexity of industrial associations is set out in G. Unwin, *Industrial Organization in the Sixteenth and Seventeenth Centuries* (1904), pp. 103–47; cf. also F. J. Fisher, "Some Experiments in Company Organization in the Early Seventeenth Century," *Economic History Review*, IV (1932–34), 177–94.

of the backing of the common-law courts and the publicity which the passage of a bill through the House of Commons would lend. Secondly, there was the King's Council, armed with both administrative and judicial powers. And lastly, there was the whole congeries of local administrative agencies of varying authority: the justices in the counties, the corporations and guilds in the boroughs, and a series of *ad hoc* companies springing into existence here and there for the control of specific industries, sometimes as a simple matter of fiscal convenience. Yet even at the time of greatest governmental activity many sectors of industrial life were left largely untouched save by the most general statutory regulations.

To begin with, the most weighty organ of government virtually ceased to function after the change of dynasty. Throughout the later sixteenth century—an epoch of rapid economic development but hardly more so than the succeeding period—successive parliaments were busy in passing supplementary statutes to keep the industrial code up to date. For the much-regulated textile industry alone, for instance, there were passed before the death of Elizabeth no less than eleven acts in amplification or amendment of the fundamental statute of 1552.[2] But, by contrast, in the only slightly shorter period between the accession of James I and the outbreak of civil war only two clothing acts were passed, the first of which reached the statute book as early as 1607; the other was a short confirmatory measure of transient validity, enacted in 1624.[3] Thenceforth, no more statutes were passed to prevent the industrial code from becoming obsolete in its special application to individual branches of the textile industry. The explanation of this neglect lies not, of course, in any deliberate policy of withdrawal on the part of the government, but in the reluctance of the Crown to summon Parliament and in the absorption of the latter, when summoned, in political and constitutional controversy to the exclusion of other business.

Yet even before Parliament had sunk into temporary ineffective-

2. 5 & 6 Ed. VI, c. 6. The eleven acts were: 7 Ed. VI, c. 9; 8 Mar. I, c. 6; 4 & 5 P. & M., c. 5; 1 Eliz., c. 14; 8 Eliz., c. 12; 14 Eliz., c. 10; 27 Eliz., c. 17 and 18; 35 Eliz., c. 9 and 10; 43 Eliz., c. 10.
3. 4 Jac. I, c. 2 and 21 Jac. I, c. 18.

ness as a legislative body there were notable fields of industrial activity which had either escaped specific regulation or were dropping out of it. In the middle of the sixteenth century the remolding of industry associated with the vastly accelerated substitution of coal for wood and other fuels, that was felt in activities from the making of salt to the manufacture of munitions, had begun with little or no interference from the central authority.[4] It was also during the reign of Elizabeth that the "new draperies," introduced by religious refugees from France and the Low Countries, which transformed the textile industry in East Anglia and powerfully affected it elsewhere, took root outside the ambit of specific governmental control.[5] A further stimulus to industrial change was delivered in the next century by the drastic curtailment, owing to the outbreak of the Thirty Years' War, of the Continental market, which for so long had been the mainstay of the staple export industries of the kingdom. It gave producers a pressing incentive to experiment with new methods and materials in the hope of finding substitute markets; thus it was that in the West Country a new range of textile products was developed in the reign of Charles I without reference to statutory materials or sizes.[6] Meanwhile, too, in Lancashire the cotton industry was taking root in almost complete freedom.[7] Indeed, in the guilds generally before 1640, it has been pointed out that the efforts to enforce qualitative standards were coming to an end, save in the textile crafts.[8]

In sum, despite the will of the Stuart government to supervise the industrial activity of the kingdom, its efforts were bounded by

4. J. U. Nef, *The Rise of the British Coal Industry,* I, 165–89, and II, 201–315, and "The Progress of Technology and the Growth of Large-scale Industry in Great Britain, 1540–1640," *Economic History Review,* V (1934), 3–24.

5. G. Unwin, *Studies in Economic History* (1927), pp. 292–93, and J. E. Pilgrim, "The Cloth Industry in Essex and Suffolk, 1558–1640," thesis summary in *Bulletin of the Institute of Historical Research,* XVII (1939–40), 144.

6. G. D. Ramsay, *The Wiltshire Woollen Industry in the Sixteenth and Seventeenth Centuries* (1943), pp. 85–100.

7. A. P. Wadsworth and J. L. Mann, *The Cotton Trade and Industrial Lancashire, 1600–1780* (1931), pp. 54–70.

8. F. J. Fisher, "The Influence and Development of the Industrial Gilds in the Larger Provincial Towns under James I and Charles I," thesis summary in *Bull. Inst. Hist. Res.,* X (1932), 47.

the paralysis of the lawmaking body to such limited fields as lay within administrative or fiscal reach and could be covered by the authority of the King's Council alone—for instance, by the publication of proclamations, the issue of charters or patents of privilege, or the manipulation of local bodies by the use of the prerogative courts. It is difficult to exaggerate the importance of the clogging of the legislative machine during the first half of the seventeenth century in hastening the emancipation of a rapidly developing industry from governmental control, though it may admittedly be doubted whether, even if the apparatus of government had been functioning freely, it would have been able to conjure up the administrative ways and means requisite for the regulation of an industrial society in such rapid flux, particularly in view of the failure of the government of Elizabeth to cover all the ground. But the point to observe is that long before the outbreak of civil war increasing sections of the national economy—and generally the least stagnant and therefore the most vital ones—were slipping outside the terms of statutory reference, so that the country as a whole was coming to be covered by little beyond general enactments concerning wages, prices, and conditions of labor.

The disastrous impact of the Civil War upon the administrative framework of industrial regulation was assuredly considerable, though it may be assumed that the weight of the blow varied from county to county.[9] Following the Civil Wars came some years of weak and unsettled government, but with the seizure of power by Oliver Cromwell, strong in the support of an invincible army, toward the end of 1653 the country once more enjoyed a firm rule that was to last until the death of the Protector in September 1658. This resolute Puritan government could dispose of the administrative organization evolved during centuries of monarchy, and had every opportunity of putting its industrial policy into practice. As to its activity there is no doubt. Warrants bearing the signature

9. The disturbance caused by the Civil Wars to the industrial life of the country was not without limits. For instance, the Company of Cutlers of Hallamshire, though it operated over a large and disturbed area, was hardly affected by the strife in Yorkshire. R. E. Leader, *History of the Company of Cutlers in Hallamshire,* I (1905), p. 41.

of the Protector, letters from the president of the Council, missives signed by the secretary Thurloe, these were sent all over the countryside with a thousand varying instructions. Local officials were appointed and removed at will, care was taken that justices of the peace should execute their office, instructions and advice were dispatched to borough functionaries—or even given by word of mouth, as when the authorities of London and Westminster attended upon the Council of State and "several matters were propounded to them in relation to the good government of the cities." [10] Municipal problems of all sorts were scrutinized and resolved by it; indeed, the steadily growing interest on the part of the central government during the later sixteenth and early seventeenth centuries in the affairs of the borough has been said to have reached its climax during the years of the Protectorate.[11] And, to compensate for the loss of the prerogative courts, in the last resort the government held at its disposal for the enforcement of its orders and the coercion of the refractory—were they Bristol apprentices or Derbyshire miners— the powerful weapon, unknown to its predecessors, of a standing army.[12]

There is little in the extant letters and speeches of Oliver Cromwell to suggest that he was tempted to the pursuit of any distinct policy in the field of industrial regulation by forces other than the fundamental opportunism of a conservative mind. Nor is it easy to discern any positive outlook among his councillors of state. Indeed, the only individual who could be said to belong to the ruling oligarchy and whose views on the economic structure of the Commonwealth are available for posterity was William Sheppard, a country lawyer of Gloucestershire origin who had early been summoned to London by the Protector to advise him in legal affairs and was granted a clerkship in the Court of Upper Bench; later, he attained the office of sergeant-at-law. On one occasion he drew up, by order of the Council, a scheme of law reform which was duly propounded before that body, to the consternation of lawyers

10. *C.S.P.D., 1654*, p. 1.

11. *C.S.P.D., 1654–58, passim;* S. and B. Webb, *English Local Government,* I (1906), 305–06.

12. J. Latimer, *Annals of Bristol in the Seventeenth Century* (Bristol, 1900), p. 32; *C.S.P.D., 1653–54*, p. 222.

and the City. He later published his proposals in a small volume entitled *England's Balme*, preceded by an epistle dedicatory to His Highness and Council.[13]

In this he offered a wide survey of existing legal institutions and their bearing upon the life of the country. He professed himself open to argument on the question of a compulsory seven years' apprenticeship, the restriction of aliens, or indeed in any case where the law appeared to bear harshly upon the subject, but his specific proposals were confined to other matters. In general he advocated the more severe enforcement of existing laws and their particular reinforcement so as to prevent deceitful trading and the use of false weights and measures. He favored a stricter assessment of wages and its corollary, the more stringent enforcement of the assize of bread and ale. His attitude toward the whole problem of poverty and unemployment was Elizabethan; an elaboration of existing poor-law machinery and the transportation of incorrigible vagrants was all that he could suggest. As a general preventive against social derangement he urged, with his eye on the Continent, the establishment of new industries and the compulsory cultivation of flax and the encouragement of spinning by countryfolk. This led him to his most remarkable proposal—a reduction of the privileges of the corporate towns. Their jurisdiction was to be confined to freemen and, to stem the tide of corruption, county magistrates were to exercise an appellate jurisdiction within the boroughs; this, however, was suggested not as a step toward local freedom but in order to establish local enforcement of the law more surely.[14]

Although Sheppard's proposals were never put into practice, they serve to indicate the drift of opinion in the immediate entourage of the Protector concerning the regulation of industry. They are also of significance owing to the part played by Sheppard in the widespread remodeling of borough charters during the Protectorate.

13. There is an article on Sheppard in the *D.N.B.* See also *C.S.P.D.*, *1655-56*, pp. 169, 189, 340-41, 370; *1656-57*, pp. 121, 149, 161, 181, 191; *1657-58*, p. 178; C. H. Firth (ed.), *Clarke Papers*, III (1899), 61, 64; Wm. Sheppard, *England's Balme* (1657), preface.

14. Wm. Sheppard, *England's Balme* (1657), pp. 25 *et seq.*, 135, 164-65, 167-71, 175-76, 184, 185, 188-91, 203-04.

The government was driven to interfere with the chartered cities and towns to ensure both that local government lay in the hands of politically reliable men and also that supporters of the regime should be returned to Parliament by the boroughs. A Committee for Charters including Sheppard and three other legal advisers was set up by the Council of State for the inspection and replacement of instruments of incorporation; the manner in which business was referred to "Mr. Sheppard and the rest of the Committee" affords some ground for supposing that he was the most prominent member thereof. By force or fraud many towns were induced to surrender their charters and received in return new documents of incorporation confiding power to the loyal clique.[15] While the significance of this revolution in local government was primarily political, its economic interest should not be missed. The boroughs were not only electoral districts and agents of local government: they were the economic pivots of the Commonwealth. On the activity of their rulers depended the regulation of urban industries. If any desire to dilute such control had actuated the government, it must assuredly have found expression in the new articles of incorporation with which so many towns were now endowed. The great majority of such borough charters has unfortunately long since perished; three at least have, however, survived and the contents of a few others may be gleaned from incidental references.

In general, democratic government was discouraged; the new borough councils were co-optative rather than elective. For political reasons this was inevitable, and no economic implication need be read into the change. Although in the Chipping Wycombe instrument the law officers of the Protectorate secured the omission of provisos of doubtful legality concerning the enforcement of a seven

15. The widespread nature of the inquisition into borough charters under the Protectorate and the importance of the part played by Sheppard is brought out by B. L. K. Henderson, "The Commonwealth Charters," in *Transactions of the Royal Historical Society*, 3rd ser., VI (1912). In addition to those incorporations noted by Mr. Henderson, there are traces of attention being directed to charters at Chippenham and Stratford-on-Avon. F. H. Goldney (ed.), *Records of Chippenham* (1889), p. 222, and J. O. Halliwell, *Council Book of Stratford-on-Avon* (1863), p. 420. Cf. also *C.S.P.D., 1653-54,* p. 344; *1655-56,* pp. 121-22, 364, 370; *1656-57,* p. 224.

years' apprenticeship[16] and the control of non-freemen by the mayor, it is evident that the Cromwellian charters were no less kindly than their predecessors; the grants everywhere proved the conservatism of the government. The charter issued to Newport, Isle of Wight, was a mere exemplification of that which had been bestowed by Edward VI. The privileges to be enjoyed by Abergavenny were substantially those which Charles I had authorized. For Salisbury the old rights were maintained—including the restraints upon non-freemen—with the addition of jurisdiction over the cathedral precincts. Indeed, the town politicians sought fresh privileges; so it was at Reading and at Uxbridge, and it was hardly in the interest of the Protector to offend his partisans.[17] The charter granted to Swansea is of particular interest, for Swansea was a fresh incorporation and greater scope was thus afforded to its framers for the exposition of their policy. The new borough, however, was governed on familiar lines. A monopolistic guild merchant was established, whose composition was controlled by the mayor and common council. The latter were empowered to issue by-laws for the regulation of trade and to enforce these by the customary fines. The usual fairs and markets were granted. It is clear that the government of the Protectorate fully supported the privileged and authoritative status of the chartered boroughs in the national economy.[18]

The erection of restrictive corporations in the traditional style was by no means confined to the framework of municipal government. A corporation for the weavers of Norfolk had already been set up at their desire in 1650 and the act of incorporation was renewed in 1653. On further petition the Protectorate Parliament permanently established this corporation in 1656. It was given power over all worsted manufacturers in the county except makers of

---

16. For most trades this was normally enforceable under the terms of the Statute of Artificers.

17. *C.S.P.D., 1655–56*, pp. 253, 371; *1656–57*, pp. 233–34, 267; B. L. K. Henderson, "The Commonwealth Charters," *Trans. Roy. Hist. Soc.* 3rd ser., VI (1912), 135–39, 153, 161; *H.M.C. Reading*, p. 192; H. Hall (ed.), "The Commonwealth Charter of the City of Salisbury," *Camden Miscellany*, XI (1907), 187–88 *et passim*.

18. C. G. Francis (ed.), *Charters Granted to Swansea* (1867), pp. 25–27, 33–35, 39, 45, 249 *et passim*.

satins and fustians, and saving the privileges of the weavers of Great Yarmouth and King's Lynn. We learn that before the final confirmation the system of regulation had been imperiled by the frivolous suits of certain clothiers who were alleged to hanker after "their former deceits," and that the Council of State in answer to the petition of the "honest" weavers ordered the local major general to consult with the justices of assize at their next circuit for the maintenance of "lawful" supervision. The terms of incorporation granted wide powers of search, inspection, and regulation to the officials of the corporation, who were entitled if necessary to call upon the county and borough authorities in their endeavors to bring defaulters to justice.[19] The success of the Norfolk manufacturers may have stimulated the makers of perpetuanas and serges in Exeter and Devon to present their petition for incorporation to the Commons in December 1656. It was, however, an unpropitious moment for the airing of industrial projects; a bill was duly introduced upon the report of the Committee for Trade, but the House became more and more engrossed with the burning question of Cromwell's kingship, and its consideration was again and again postponed. It passed the first reading and then gradually disappeared from the agenda. Had the Taunton cloth manufacturers not likewise presented their petition at an unseasonable time, two other clothing corporations might have been established on the Norfolk model.[20]

A fourth incorporation project came to naught because of opposition from local interests. The clothiers of Leeds in 1654 attempted to make use of the member for their newly enfranchised borough to secure the incorporation of all practicing their trade in the West Riding, "that Soe many officers may be Chosen by the holle Num-

19. C. H. Firth and R. S. Rait (eds.), *Acts and Ordinances of the Interregnum,* 1642–60, II (1911), 775 and 1137; *C.S.P.D., 1655–56,* p. 201; B. L. K. Henderson, "The Commonwealth Charters," *Trans. Roy. Hist. Soc.* 3rd ser., VI (1912), 159, 161.

20. *Commons' Journals,* 1653–59, pp. 349–50, 452, 459, 475, 480, 492, 494, 495, 515, 521, 524, 527, 540; J. James, *History of the Worsted Manufacture in England* (1857), p. 153. The contents of the Somerset petition are not known; they may have concerned the excise, but probably were a request for incorporation (*C.S.P.D., 1655–56,* pp. 260–61).

ber of Clothyers as may be thought Requisit" for regulating the
industry. This was alleged to be desirable because the lax supervision of the rural clothiers by the Riding justices had lowered the
standard of Yorkshire cloth and injured the trade of the town
manufacturers.[21] When nothing came of this, the Leeds authorities
petitioned the Riding quarter sessions "that every Clothyer may be
strictly enjoyned to set his scale of lead to the fore end of his Cloth
thereby declareing the just length and waight." The Riding justices refused to permit joint searching, but promised to control
tentering more effectually. In turn, the country clothiers petitioned
the Council of State, while Captain Baines, M.P. for Leeds, prepared bills for the desired incorporation in the two sessions of the
Parliament of 1656. In both they survived the first reading, but
were faced by a powerful opposition. The city of York disliked
the whole project and one of the county members spoke strongly
against it. The House finally rejected the bill in January 1657, but
ordered the Committee for Trade to inquire into the clothing
industry and suggest suitable methods for regulating it.[22] It is
difficult to determine the interests at work in terms of trade and
class, but it is at least clear that the Leeds project was not shipwrecked upon any opposition to regulation itself as such.[23]

A final example to indicate the survival under the Protectorate
of the royal practice of regulating industry by means of corporate
monopolistic associations of producers is furnished by the case of
the framework knitters. Their art had been invented too late to

21. British Museum, *Additional Manuscripts*, 21,417, Baines Correspondence, f. 210.
22. Baines Correspondence, f. 224; H. Heaton, *The Yorkshire Woollen
and Worsted Industries* (1920), pp. 230 *et seq.; C.S.P.D., 1655-56*, p. 187;
B. L. K. Henderson, "The Commonwealth Charters," *Trans. Roy. Hist. Soc.*
3rd ser., VI (1912), 161; *Commons' Journals*, 1653-59, pp. 467, 475, 478, and
588; Thomas Burton, *Diary*, ed. J. T. Rutt, I (1828), 126-27, quot. M. James,
Social Problems and Policy during the Puritan Revolution (1930), pp.
163-64.
23. Baines, even if supported financially by the wealthier clothiers—and
the payment of M.P.s would naturally come from their better-off constituents
—was also the nominee of their poorer colleagues and had indeed been
elected despite the opposition of the oligarchic corporation of Leeds, as represented by the returning alderman (Baines Correspondence, ff. 199 and
203). See also H. Heaton, *The Yorkshire Woollen and Worsted Industries*
(1920), pp. 232 *et seq.*

come within the purview of the Elizabethan code, and the interests of the framework knitters had been flouted by ambitious or greedy individuals; it was alleged that through the multiplication of apprentices and the spread of faulty manufacture the whole industry would be lost to the Commonwealth, to the ruin of its more honest—or conservative—indigenous practicers. The latter were emboldened by the example of the needlemakers to present in 1655 a petition for incorporation to the Protector. It was referred to the lord mayor and aldermen of London, to the attorney-general, and at length to the Committee for Trade, and finally in 1657 the required charter was prepared and issued.[24] The corporate regulation of the framework-knitting industry endured until the early eighteenth century.[25]

Scattered throughout the length and breadth of the Commonwealth were the multitudinous local authorities upon whom devolved the responsibility for the enforcement of industrial regulation. As to the large segments of economic activity which were slipping beyond their competence something has already been said, but there is considerable evidence to suggest their activity in enforcing fixed wages, prices, and terms of apprenticeship during the years of the Protectorate. Most of the signs of this vigilance are in the forms of indictments and presentments in local courts for alleged

24. Anon., *To the Lord Protector. The Humble Representation of the Promoters and Inventers of the Art of Frameworke-Knitting, that they may be incorporated by Charter under the Great Seale of England* (1656), pp. 1–2, 12–13 *et passim;* W. Felkin, *History of the Machine-Wrought Hosiery and Lace Manufactures* (1867), pp. 61–67; F. A. Inderwick, *The Interregnum, 1648–60* (1891), p. 90; *C.S.P.D., 1655–56*, p. 336; *1656–57*, pp. 64–65, 268; J. D. Chambers, "The Worshipful Company of Framework Knitters (1657–1779)," *Economica*, no. 27 (1929), pp. 296–329; B. L. K. Henderson, "The Commonwealth Charters," *Trans. Roy. Hist. Soc.* 3rd ser., VI (1912), 159; M. James, *Social Problems and Policy during the Puritan Revolution* (1930), p. 172; E. Lipson, *Economic History of England,* II (1931), 105.

25. J. D. Chambers, *Nottinghamshire in the Eighteenth Century* (1932), pp. 111–16. It may be added here that the Bench during the Protectorate does not appear to have been unfriendly to grants of monopoly; Hale in pronouncing favorable judgment upon the Soapmakers' Company patent of 1637 was at pains to point out in 1656 that—with familiar qualifications—patents for the well regulating and ordering of trades were perfectly legal. T. Hardres, *Reports of Cases Adjudged in the Court of Exchequer in the Years 1655, 1656, 1657, 1658, 1659 and 1660* (1693), pp. 53–55.

breaches of law and custom, so that at first sight this evidence might seem to indicate the decay of regulation. But a trickle of charges and convictions reveals rather the frailty of human nature and the will of the authorities to maintain the law; any collapse of the system of industrial regulation would generally be attested more by silence in the records than by minutes of legal proceedings.[26]

Of all the varied tasks imposed by law and custom upon local authorities none possessed a greater significance than the duty of enforcing specified wage rates. These rates were essentially maxima, and any combination to extort higher wages was a misdemeanor.[27] The latter was always a possibility, since the labor problem in seventeenth-century England was caused by the scarcity rather than the abundance of hands; the evasion of service by young unattached folk who preferred to remain at home or eke out their living by crude subsistence farming was condemned by the Wiltshire justices in 1655 and no doubt met with scant favor elsewhere.[28] Wage assessment engaged the attention of the Commons in October 1656, when they appointed a committee "to consider of the Statutes and Laws touching the Wages of Artificers, Labourers, and Servants, and to present a Bill . . . for the more effectual putting the same in Execution." This committee was requested further "to take into Consideration the Habits and Fashions of Servants and Labourers; and to prepare a Bill for the remedying of Abuses therein."[29] No doubt sumptuary legislation would have eased a general reduction of wages; but the activities of this committee—despite a distinguished membership—left no mark on the course of events.

During the years of the Protectorate there is definite evidence that new wage assessments were drawn up by the justices in nine

26. On the interpretation of the records, cf. S. Kramer, *The English Craft Gilds* (1927), pp. 186–90, and R. K. Kelsall, *Wage Regulation under the Statute of Artificers* (1938), pp. 15–28, 53–66.

27. The question of wage assessments is treated by R. H. Tawney, "The Assessment of Wages by the Justices of the Peace," *Vierteljahrschrift für Sozial und Wirtschaftsgeschichte,* XI (1913), and the most recent evidence is summarized by R. K. Kelsall, *Wage Regulation under the Statute of Artificers* (1938), to both of which this and the following paragraph are indebted.

28. *H.M.C. Wilts,* pp. 132 *et seq.*

29. *Commons' Journals,* 1653–59, p. 435.

counties;[30] in many districts the existing rates were simply maintained, as in Shropshire, Nottinghamshire, and Hertfordshire.[31] In Cheshire and the North Riding of Yorkshire the justices were reminded of their duties in enforcing wage assessments by the grand jury.[32] In the boroughs, the rating of wages was founded upon medieval custom and far antedated the Statute of Artificers. The city of Chester in December 1653 secured a reduction in the wages of workmen in the building trades, as did the court of aldermen of the city of London rather more than a year later.[33] The mayor and burgesses of Pontefract in 1654 similarly fixed the remuneration of tailors' journeymen and apprentices.[34] Possibly a more typical example is furnished by the cordwainers of Oxford, who in December 1653 in the course of a general reconstruction of guild rules settled the wages to be paid by masters to journeymen;[35] it may be believed that in most boroughs the guilds unobtrusively went their way while the municipal council watched from the background.

Complementary to the regulation of wages was the control of prices. There was a deliberate effort on the part of the government

30. A list of these assessments will be found in R. K. Kelsall, *Wage Regulation under the Statute of Artificers* (1938), p. 115.

31. O. Wakeman, *Shropshire Quarter Sessions Records* (1905), pp. 5, 14, 26, 56; H. H. Copnall, *Nottinghamshire County Records* (Nottingham, 1915), p. 113; W. Le Hardy, *Calendar to the Sessions Books and Sessions Minute Books and Other Sessions Records of the County of Hertford,* V (Hertford, 1928), 112, 116.

32. Chester Castle, Cheshire Quarter Sessions Minute Book of Presentments and Indictments, 1654–62; J. C. Atkinson, *North Riding Quarter Sessions Records,* V (1886), 178.

33. Chester Town Hall, Order Book of the Chester Corporation, 1624–84; E. B. Jupp and W. W. Pocock, *An Historical Account of the Worshipful Company of Carpenters of the City of London* (1887), p. 316; B. L. Hutchins, "The Regulation of Wages by Gilds and Town Authorities," *Economic Journal,* X (1900), 408; M. James, *Social Problems and Policy during the Puritan Revolution* (1930), pp. 178–79. It should be remembered, however, that there was constant friction in the sixteenth and seventeenth centuries between the boroughs and the various building trades: G. Unwin, *Industrial Organization in the Sixteenth and Seventeenth Centuries* (1904), pp. 64–67.

34. R. Holmes (ed.), *Booke of Entries of the Pontefract Corporation* (Pontefract, 1887), p. 406.

35. Bodleian, MS. Morrell 14, Company of Cordwainers, Oxford, minutes of meetings, 1614–1711.

to lower the price of sea coal in London.[36] Wine prices in June
1657 were fixed by statute,[37] and in January 1655 the rates at which
the three qualities of beer were to be sold were proclaimed. To this
topic the inquiries of the Commons were directed in September
1656, although in the preceding months Whalley and the other
major generals had been required to diminish the "imoderate gayne"
of innholders.[38] Local authorities throughout the Commonwealth
were actively concerned with the enforcement of the assize of bread
and ale and its ancillary regulations; among the towns as to which
positive evidence is available may be instanced Bristol, Clitheroe,
Dorchester, Ipswich, Manchester, Newport (Isle of Wight), Northampton, Preston, Reading, Shrewsbury, and York,[39] while the
counties include Cheshire, Derby, Hertford, Nottingham, Somerset,
Surrey, Wiltshire, and Worcester.[40] Sometimes drastic expedients
were necessary to control the price of bread; the authorities of
London and Nottingham traded in grain, the former regularly,

36. J. U. Nef, *The Rise of the British Coal Industry*, II (1932), 130; F. W.
Dendy (ed.), *Extracts from the Records of the Company of Hostmen of
Newcastle-on-Tyne* (Durham, 1901), pp. xxiv, 109, 114.

37. C. H. Firth and R. S. Rait (eds.), *Acts and Ordinances of the Interregnum*, II (1911), 1057.

38. C. H. Firth (ed.), *Clarke Papers*, III, 75; T. Birch (ed.), *A Collection
of the State Papers of John Thurloe*, IV (1742), 686 et passim; F. A. Inderwick, *The Interregnum, 1648–60* (1891), pp. 63, 65.

39. J. Latimer, *Annals of Bristol in the Seventeenth Century* (Bristol,
1900), pp. 32–33, 38; W. S. Weeks, *Clitheroe in the Seventeenth Century*
(Clitheroe, 1927), p. 47; C. H. Mayo, *The Municipal Records of Dorchester*
(Exeter, 1908), p. 649; W. E. Layton, "Notices from the Great Court and
Assembly Books of the Borough of Ipswich," *The East Anglian*, new ser., II
(1887–88), 157, 173, 196; J. P. Earwaker (ed.), *The Court Leet Records of
Manchester*, IV (Manchester, 1887), 100–03 et passim; Newport, Isle of
Wight, offices of the Town Clerk, Newport Lawday Book, April 1654 and
Court Book of the Piepowder Court, passim; J. C. Cox (ed.), *Northampton
Borough Records*, II (Northampton, 1898), 79; Hewitson, *Preston Court
Leet Records* (1905), pp. 2, 29, 37, 45, 59, 81; J. M. Guilding (ed.), *Reading
Records*, IV (1892–96), 497, 540; H. W. Adnitt, "The Orders of the Cor-
poration of Shrewsbury, 1511–1735," *Trans. Shropshire Archaeol. Nat. Hist.
Soc.*, XI (1888), 185; B.M. Add. MS. 34,604, Accompt Book of the Bakers'
Company of York, 1584–1835, ff. 169–81. I am indebted to L. P. Addison for
examining the Newport documents on my behalf.

40. Chester Castle, Minute Books of Indictments and Presentments at
Cheshire Quarter Sessions 1640–54 and 1654–62, Easter and Midsummer Ses-
sions 1654, and Midsummer Sessions 1655; J. C. Cox, *Three Centuries of
Derbyshire Annals*, II (1890), 255; W. Le Hardy, *Calendar to the Sessions*

the latter when the occasion warranted it. From this it was but a step to the free distribution of loaves, as was done at Leicester in June 1656. The regulation of prices merged insensibly into the provision of poor relief.[41]

It should be recalled too that the control of prices was also largely dependent upon the due punishment of all who infringed the contemporary commercial code. Over all the Commonwealth it was insisted that buying and selling should take place in shop or market place; convictions of forestallers, regrators, and engrossers were everywhere recorded. Sometimes individuals were charged with the more heinous offense of extortion. The conviction of a Hertfordshire currier for buying parcels of leather and selling them again without altering "the forme or property thereof" illustrates the prevalence of medieval economic conceptions.[42] This, however, is not the place for an examination of commercial ethics in theory or practice during the Protectorate; it is sufficient to observe that the control of prices, at least so far as the necessities of life were concerned, was no less effective than the statutory regulation of wages.

The evidence with regard to the maintenance of the apprenticeship laws is no less strong. Various examples of town guilds endeavoring under the Protectorate to ensure that their new members should have completed the customary period of apprenticeship might be quoted—such were the drapers of Bristol, the mercers of Durham, the drapers, tailors, mercers, hardwaremen, coopers,

---

Books of the County of Hertford, V (Hertford, 1928), 121; H. H. Copnall, *Nottinghamshire County Records* (Nottingham, 1915), pp. 49, 52; E. H. Bates (ed.) (Harbin), *Quarter Sessions Records for the County of Somerset,* III (1912), 250; *V.C.H. Surrey,* IV, 434; W. W. Ravenhill, "Some Western Circuit Assize Records of the Seventeenth Century," *Wiltshire Archaeol. Nat. Hist. Soc. Mag.,* LXXIII (1890), 74; *H.M.C. Wilts,* p. 132; County Hall, Worcester, Quarter Sessions Rolls of Indictments and Recognisances for Worcestershire, 1653–56, *passim;* G. Unwin, *Industrial Organization in the Sixteenth and Seventeenth Centuries* (1904), pp. 67–69.

41. H. Stocks (ed.), *Records of Leicester,* IV (Cambridge, 1923), 433, 439, 442–43; M. James, *Social Problems and Policy during the Puritan Revolution* (1930), p. 269; T. Bailey, *Annals of Nottinghamshire,* III (Nottingham, 1853), 856.

42. W. Le Hardy, *Calendar to the Sessions Books and Sessions Minute Books and Other Sessions Records of the County of Hertford,* VI (Hertford, 1928), 11. See also, for example, J. C. Atkinson, *North Riding Quarter Sessions,* V, 159, 168, and VI, 7.

and chandlers of Gateshead, the cordwainers of Leicester, the colliers, paviors, and carriagemen of Newcastle-on-Tyne, the tailors of Oxford, the mercers of Sandwich, and in the city of London the drapers', goldsmiths', and weavers' companies.[43] It was, however, with the municipal councils that the effective sanction rested, and there are widespread indications of the interested conservatism of the boroughs, alike in preventing unapprenticed strangers from settling within their precincts to ply a trade and in expelling those whose titles in this matter were defective; active measures to these ends are known to have been taken, for instance, at Bedford, Carlisle, Chester, Clitheroe, Hull, Ipswich, Leicester, Maidstone, Newport (Isle of Wight), Nottingham, Preston, Reading, Rye, and Salisbury.[44] In the counties the justices enforced the statutory ap-

43. S. Kramer, *The English Craft Gilds* (1927), pp. 24–26, 31, 42; A. Hamilton Thompson, "On a Minute-Book and Papers Formerly Belonging to the Mercers' Company of the City of Durham," *Archaeologia Aeliana*, 3rd ser., XIX (1922), 228–29; C. Walford, *Gilds, Their Origin, Constitution, Objects and Later History* (1888), p. 202; H. Stocks (ed.), *Records of Leicester*, IV (Cambridge, 1923), 416; M. H. Dodds, *Extracts from the Municipal Accounts of Newcastle-on-Tyne* (Newcastle-upon-Tyne, 1920), pp. 11, 104–05; Bodleian, MS. Morrell 6, Election and Order Book of the Company of Tailors, Oxford, f. 157; B.M., Add. MS. 24,462, Gildbook of the Company of Mercers, Linen Drapers, Woollen Drapers and Merchant Taylors of Sandwich, Co. Kent, 1655–1772, ff. 3–7; A. H. Johnson, *History of the Worshipful Company of Drapers of London*, III (Oxford, 1922), 233; W. S. Prideaux, *Memorials of the Goldsmiths' Company of London*, II (1897), 35, 56, 68; E. B. Jupp and W. W. Pocock, *An Historical Account of the Worshipful Company of Carpenters of the City of London* (1887), p. 635.

44. J. Brown, *Life of John Bunyan* (1885), p. 98; R. S. Ferguson and W. Nanson, *Some Municipal Records of the City of Carlisle* (Carlisle, 1887), pp. 97 *et seq.;* Chester Town Hall, Chester Corporation Order Book and Chester City Assembly Book, entries for September 1657; W. S. Weeks, *Clitheroe in the Seventeenth Century* (Clitheroe, 1928), pp. 39, 41; J. M. Lambert, *Two Thousand Years of Gild Life, with a Full Account of the Gilds and Trading Companies of Kingston-upon-Hull* (Hull, 1891), p. 175; W. E. Layton, *Notices from the Great Court and Assembly Books of the Borough of Ipswich*, III, 177; H. Stocks (ed.), *Records of Leicester*, IV (Cambridge, 1923), 443; W. S. Martin, *Records of Maidstone* (1926), p. 135; Newport Sessions Book, August 17, 1654 and Lawday Book, October 1656; W. T. Baker, *Records of the Borough of Nottingham*, V (Nottingham, 1900), 291; Hewitson, *Preston Court Leet Records*, pp. 31–32, 52; J. M. Guilding (ed.), *Reading Records,* IV (1892–96), 488, 510, 513, 517, 522, 527, 535; *H.M.C. Rye*, p. 230; F. A. Inderwick, "Rye under the Commonwealth," *Sussex Archaeol. Coll.*, XXXIX (1894), p. 10; R. Benson and H. Hatcher, *History of Salisbury* (1843), p. 441.

prenticeships in Devonshire, Hertfordshire, Northants, Worcester-shire, and doubtless elsewhere.[45]

The interest of the municipalities in the enforcement of the apprenticeship laws was heightened by the fact that "servitude of apprenticeship" to a freeman was a normal way of acquiring the freedom of any town. This often gave valuable rights to the possessor and hence in some boroughs the freemen, unwilling to share their privileges but recognizing the needs of the inhabitants, were prepared to allow the admission of strangers who might practice their trades on payment of fines whose tariff varied according to the usefulness of the newcomer. Occasionally, if there were a lack in any particular trade—whether a plumber or a carpenter at Chester, for instance, or an up-to-date chimneysweep at Exeter[46]—the corporation would try to entice an immigrant upon terms. Sometimes both guild and borough were ready to admit a newcomer, particularly if he could claim kinship with a freeman, for a gift of plate or money. During 1655 the tailors of Oxford received into their guild three individuals who had not served apprenticeship, on payment of sums ranging from £2. 10s. to £12, and in 1657 a fourth was admitted for £16.[47] The freedom of Worcester was very occasionally sold to strangers for sums ranging from £8 to £10 and upon one occasion was bestowed upon an individual who promised to give the city "a silver sword to be borne before the mayor." [48] But such saleable privilege was within the reach only of those who were in some measure well-to-do and in special circumstances. Nor was the phenomenon of freedom by purchase known only after the Great Rebellion; it was practiced in the first half of

45. A. H. A. Hamilton, *Quarter Sessions from Queen Elizabeth to Anne* (1878), p. 164; W. Le Hardy, *Calendar to the Sessions Books of the County of Hertford* (Hertford, 1928), *passim;* J. Wake (ed.), *Quarter Sessions Records of the County of Northampton* (1924), p. 132; Worcester, County Hall, Quarter Sessions Rolls of Indictments and Recognisances, *passim.*

46. Chester Town Hall, Chester Corporation Order Book, entries for March 1657 and March 1658; *H.M.C. Exeter,* p. 328.

47. Bodleian, MS. Morrell 6, Election and Order Book of the Company of Tailors, Oxford, ff. 160–61.

48. Worcester Guildhall, Chamber Order Book, no. 3, 1650–78, ff. 14, 19, 21—as to the sword, an entry in a different hand indignantly records that "it apeared to be a very inconsiderable sword."

the century,[49] no doubt as widely. It represented, indeed, the homage of the industrial administrative system to the persistent current of change, and as long as it remained exceptional it witnessed as much to the vitality as to the decay of the former.

Indeed, silent evasion and neglect were the real foes of industrial regulation in the seventeenth century and were later to compass its downfall. But now the moneyed interloper was anxious to come to terms. He paid for the privilege of entering the charmed circle of guild and borough, and thenceforth he had strong reason to be an ardent defender of the vested rights of his own company. Meanwhile, the economic *cursus honorum* lay smooth for the native; it is worthy of notice that in March 1654 the Bristol common council announced that any freeman who might "desire to be admitted into the Company of the Trade to which he have served as an apprentice upon a reasonable fine" might appeal to the municipal authorities to fix the latter for him if the company proved greedy. The indications are that deviations from custom met with scant favor; for instance, the Leicester town council in February 1656 ordained that no non-resident freeman might have power to bind apprentices to succeed to the freedom of the borough. And the Chester company of blacksmiths, plumbers, pewterers, and girdlers saw fit to inflict the severe penalty of disfranchisement upon one of their number "for making his prentice free of City when he served him but 5 years."[50]

The evidence is thus that under the Protectorate the enforcement of the apprenticeship laws and customs continued as usual. It is not without interest to observe that several of the indentures of the company of carpenters in the city of London were for eight and a few for nine years' service. In Newport, Isle of Wight, periods ranging from eight to fifteen years were common, nor was an eight

49. Cf. F. J. Fisher, "The Influence and Development of the Industrial Gilds in the Larger Provincial Towns under James I and Charles I," thesis summary in *Bull. Inst. Hist. Res.*, X (1932), *passim*.

50. H. Stocks (ed.), *Records of Leicester*, IV (Cambridge, 1923), 430; Simpson, "The City Gilds of Chester: The Smiths', Cutlers' and Plumbers' Company," *Journ. Chester and North Wales Archaeol. and Hist. Soc.* new ser., XX (1914), 44; B.M., Egerton MS. 2,044, Register of Ordinances of the Bristol Corporation, 1551–1656, ff. 66–67.

years' apprenticeship unknown in York and Ipswich.[51] The imposition of terms in excess of the statutory seven years well illustrates the deeply rooted strength of medieval and local tradition and helps to explain how the efforts of the government to dispense with the condition of apprenticeship in the settlement of former Parliamentary soldiers met with little response.

An ordinance to enable Parliamentary veterans to set up shop where they chose was issued in September 1654 and Cromwell followed it up by summoning the lord mayor and aldermen of London and obtaining from them "a promise of compliance and obedience," which suggests that he felt doubts as to the effectiveness of the edict by itself.[52] Such uncertainty would not have been without justification. The Sandwich company of mercers was indeed defied by an ex-soldier, and two or three settled down in Bristol;[53] but these are the sole available examples of entirely and immediately successful exploitation of the privileges granted by the ordinance. There was, despite the promise of lord mayor and aldermen, trouble in London, where the goldsmiths, for instance, showed little forwardness over the case of an ex-soldier.[54] Another veteran who sought to establish himself in Leicester did not dare to do so without first petitioning the corporation, which yielded permission only upon payment of £5.[55] In general, however, the striking rarity of entry into trade or industry by ex-soldiers—while records of

---

51. E. B. Jupp and W. W. Pocock, *An Historical Account of the Worshipful Company of Carpenters of the City of London* (1887), p. 277; Newport, Isle of Wight, Office of the Town Clerk, Newport Convocation Book, *passim;* M. Sellers, *The York Mercers and Merchant Adventurers, 1356–1917* (Durham, 1918), p. 284; B.M., Add. MS. 10,407, Account-book of the Company of Silk Weavers of York, ff. 145–49; W. E. Layton, "Notices from the Great Court and Assembly Books of the Borough of Ipswich," *The East Anglian,* IV, 220.

52. C. H. Firth and R. S. Rait (eds.), *Acts and Ordinances of the Interregnum,* II (1911), 1132; *C.S.P. Ven., 1653–54,* pp. 264–65; *C.S.P.D., 1654,* pp. 343, 346.

53. B.M., Add. MS. 24,462, Gild-book of the Company of Mercers, Sandwich, f. 6; J. Latimer, *Annals of Bristol in the Seventeenth Century* (Bristol, 1900), p. 32.

54. W. S. Prideaux, *Memorials of the Goldsmiths' Company,* II (1897), 74–75.

55. H. Stocks (ed.), *Records of Leicester,* IV (Cambridge, 1923), 425.

"freedom by servitude of apprenticeship" are plentiful and of "freedom by composition" by no means unknown—would seem to testify that but few veterans were in a position during the years of the Protectorate to avail themselves of their nominal privilege to set up shop wherever they wished.

The facts set forth in the preceding pages are in a broad sense capable of the most diverse interpretation. Here they illustrate the efforts of small craftsmen to use their corporate privileges to defy an ambitious capitalist master, there they show how medieval forms could be appropriated to shield a clique of wealthy entrepreneurs, elsewhere they reflect the rivalry of town and country or borough and borough, while in a fourth instance they are perhaps explicable only in terms of hidden personal relationships. But to attempt any elucidation of the complex fabric of English society in the seventeenth century is not the purpose of this essay. If the arguments propounded above are well founded, then it must be accepted that under the Protectorate the administrative structure of industrial regulation inherited from medieval times and reinforced by the Statute of Artificers and other parliamentary enactments was still a vital ingredient in the economy of the country and that the government of Cromwell had no wish that it should be otherwise. Or, to put it in another way, that Cromwell in what in the twentieth century would be called his industrial policy was as much a conservative as he was, for instance, in his conduct of foreign affairs. In respect of the former he was, if this be so, the heir of Burleigh and even of Charles I, despite the change of religion.

This is not to deny what has already been pointed out—that for lack of an adaptable and all-embracing industrial code whole sections of English industry, notably textiles, were slipping more and more beyond all save the most general statutory control; this, however, was a process whose origins can be traced back to the reign of Elizabeth and which was forwarded mainly by the disuse of Parliament as a legislative body under the first Stuart kings and the consequent failure of the regulative laws to keep pace with the march of production.[56] As a result of the progress of technical

56. *Supra.*

change, it is doubtless true that English industry, willy-nilly, was freer in 1655 than it was in 1635, just as in 1635 it was freer than it had been in 1615. But the essential point is that as far as the evidence of the actual working of the machinery of industrial regulation is concerned the latter in its diminishing sphere was still an effective limb of authority under the Protectorate. Here and there individuals were seeking to evade the law for their own profit, as their forefathers had done, but the idea of regulation and restriction was in itself not rejected. It had not yet occurred to the employing classes that they would fare best if industrial law and custom were as far as possible put on one side.

We are therefore left with the conclusion that under the rule of Cromwell the administrative network of industrial regulation functioned much as it had done during the Eleven Years' Tyranny and that the dislocation caused by the Civil Wars was for the most part local and momentary.[57] Even in the textile industries, which had undoubtedly continued in the 1640s to move toward industrial freedom—since with their steady technical development the statutory qualitative standards were growing more and more obsolete —there was during the Protectorate a not wholly unsuccessful movement to put the clock back; it failed to achieve its full aim mainly because the legislature, as under the monarchy, was too deeply embroiled in political disputes to attend to economic affairs. It is thus evident that the final permeation of English economy by *laisser-faire* must be dated to some period after 1660.

With the return of Charles II, however, the central government lost most of its effective control over local authorities—a fact which in itself was of enormous long-term effect; it is difficult to generalize about the organization of English industry from the reign of Elizabeth onward, but it becomes next to impossible after the Restoration, when industrial organization, development, and regulation came to vary from shire to shire and borough to borough. All that can here be done is to point briefly to a few straws in the economic wind which may help in assessing the checkered and gradual nature of the final victory of *laisser-faire*. The creation of regulative associations of producers continued in the eighteenth century

57. *Supra.*

despite the decay of many trading companies in the later seventeenth century; the blanket makers of Witney, for instance, were incorporated in 1711[58] and the Spitalfields silk weavers received special legislative protection as late as 1773.[59] Wage assessments continued to be made in some counties long after the great dispute over the Gloucester rating in 1756, though the general effectiveness of wage regulation may have diminished from the last quarter of the seventeenth century onward.[60] The custom of apprenticeship is not completely dead even in the twentieth century and it retained its normal vitality up to the end of the seventeenth century.[61] The triumph of individualism in the Yorkshire textile industries has been placed in the early eighteenth century,[62] a period in which the London city companies also ceased to perform their regulative functions.[63] Throughout the country as a whole it would seem that effective power had passed from the guild organizations by the middle of the eighteenth century, though in some cases fifty years earlier.[64] Yet it was not until 1776 that the copestone was laid to two centuries of economic evolution with the publication of *The Wealth of Nations,* which adorned a largely unwanted and unconscious social process with academic justification.

It is possibly unwise to put forward any date as marking the crucial period in the advent of industrial *laisser-faire* in England, but in view of these scattered indications it might very tentatively be suggested that it was mainly in the years on either side of 1700 that the final emergence of a free industrial economy may be discerned. There is a good *prima facie* case for believing that the great expansion of production which accompanied the tapping of a

58. A. Plummer (ed.), *The Witney Blanket Industry* (1934), pp. 114–21.
59. 13 Geo. III, c. 68; cf. E. Lipson, *Economic History of England,* III (1931), 270.
60. R. K. Kelsall, *Wage Regulation under the Statute of Artificers* (1938), p. 27, urges that "the case for a divergence between assessed and economic rates before, say, the sixteen-eighties is still not proven."
61. T. K. Derry, "The Enforcement of a Seven Years' Apprenticeship under the Statute of Artificers," in *Abstracts of Dissertations for the Degree of Doctor of Philosophy in the University of Oxford,* IV (1931), 13–14.
62. H. Heaton, *The Yorkshire Woollen and Worsted Industries* (1920), pp. 241–42.
63. G. Unwin, *The Gilds and Companies of London* (1908), pp. 345–46.
64. S. Kramer, *The English Craft Gilds* (1927), p. 176.

newly opened world market in the generation after the Restoration did much to strain and snap the ancient bonds of restriction and regulation. In this period the general temper of the times became less friendly to restraints on trade and Chief Justice Holt was the most famous member of the Bench to forward the progress toward a *laisser-faire* economy.[65] It was in these years too that the energy and character of Dissenters, who were denied entry to political and professional careers by the Anglican monopoly, bore fruit in industrial and commercial life and that an economic individualism perhaps developed in concert with Puritan ethics.[66] The present writer has not found any satisfactory evidence of the working of "economic Puritanism" during the Interregnum, which was for the national economy a period of some disorder followed, as argued above, by a conservative reconstruction under Cromwell.

65. W. S. Holdsworth, *A History of English Law*, VI (1924), 333-49, 516-23. Holt is noticed in the *D.N.B.*

66. It has been pointed out by R. H. Tawney, *Religion and the Rise of Capitalism* (1926), p. 236, that "a systematic and theoretical individualism did not develop" until after the Restoration. Much further study of local industries is required before the period of the advent of *laisser-faire* can be satisfactorily determined.

ROGER CRABTREE

The Idea of a Protestant Foreign Policy

IN ENGLISH HISTORIOGRAPHY "the idea of a Protestant foreign policy" may be referred to the concept of Oliver Cromwell's diplomacy as being inspired more by religious than by commercial or geopolitical considerations. As such it implies condemnation. With the eccentric exception of Carlyle, historians writing since the middle part of the nineteenth century have called Cromwell's foreign policy Protestant principally as an aid to pointing out, and explaining, its deficiencies. This interpretation has had for its theme that Cromwell's view of the European situation was anachronistically orientated toward that of Elizabeth's day, or at least of the Thirty Years' War, when religious antipathies were

Reprinted from *The Cromwell Association Handbook 1968–69* with the kind permission of J. Roger Crabtree and The Cromwell Association, Mr. Maurice Ashley, President.

more relevant to national interests. In consequence the words "Elizabethan" and "anachronistic" have been used here as virtual synonyms for "Protestant." Gardiner made the identification explicitly: "His mind still worked on the lines of the Elizabethan period, when the championship of Protestantism was imposed on Englishmen by interest as well as by duty."[1] The idea is that Cromwell, pursuing this "chimera,"[2] was led to neglect real problems, such as the trade rivalry of the Dutch and the danger of French domination of the Continent, for involvement in a Spanish war destructive of English commerce, and an alliance with France detrimental to the balance of power. Protagonists of this view have also been able to apply it to Cromwell's attitude to Baltic affairs: his insistence that the main trouble there was caused by imperial ambitions, as part of a Catholic conspiracy to extirpate Protestantism, impelling him to attempt to form a Protestant league against the Habsburgs analogous to those of the sixteenth and early seventeenth centuries; so, again, his apparent inability to distinguish Charles X of Sweden from Gustavus Adolphus blinded him to the position as it really was, Sweden not Austria being now the main threat to stability in the area. Several assumptions are implicit in the theory—that Cromwell's Protestantism was of an order that permitted him to subordinate his country's interests to some otherworldly end; or, alternatively, that he mistakenly thought the two could still be reconciled, that while he could effect a reasonable conjunction or compromise between spiritual zeal and worldly wisdom at home, a similar resolution escaped him abroad; and, finally, that he *did* commit errors of judgment in foreign affairs of a kind which require some such explanation. It is the intention in this essay to question the validity, in its own terms, of the whole argument and propose instead that the idea of a Protestant foreign policy may best be understood to have been conceived, and to some extent practiced, exactly as its chief exponent claimed all his public actions were:

1. S. R. Gardiner, *History of the Commonwealth and Protectorate* (1903), II, 188.
2. The appellation is from M. Prestwich, "Diplomacy and Trade in the Protectorate," *Journal of Modern History*, XXII. Other exponents include C. V. Wedgwood and J. Buchan in their biographies of Cromwell.

if any whosoever think the interest of Christians and the interest
of the nation inconsistent, I wish my soul may never enter into
their secrets . . . And upon these two interests, if God shall
account me worthy, I shall live and die. And I must say, if I
were to give an account before a greater tribunal than any earthly
one, and if I were asked why I have engaged all along in the late
war, I could give no answer but it would be a wicked one, if it
did not comprehend these two ends.[3]

. . . "if it did not comprehend these two ends . . ."—how
could Cromwell think that his war with Spain was justifiable in
this way? Here is the major difficulty in reconciling these words
with his actions. Allow, as most of his modern critics do, that he
envisaged the expedition to Hispaniola as conveniently agreeable
to the requirements of profit and piety and patriotism, the interesting question arises why, when the project met with disaster, he
persisted in a war which most historians have thought to be ill-
advised.[4] To say that he was "on this point a belated Elizabethan"[5]
is not an answer; at best it pushes the problem back a stage.
Instead part of the solution may be found in reconsidering what
was involved in the conflict. The beginning of the commission
of General Venables presents the official English view:

> Whereas we are resolved through the blessing of God, to send an
> army into America, for securing and increasing the interest of this
> commonwealth in those parts, and for opposing, weakening, and
> destroying that of the Spaniards, who under a pretence of the pope's
> donation claims all that part of the world, as belonging unto him,
> and thereupon hath not only exercised inhuman cruelties upon the
> natives, and prohibited all other nations to have any trade, com-
> merce, or correspondence with those parts; but hath, contrary to
> the laws of all nations, by force of arms, expelled the people of
> these islands from several places in America, whereof they were
> the rightful possessors, destroying and murdering many of their
> men, and leading others into captivity; and doth still continue all
> manner of acts of hostility upon us, and the people aforesaid in

3. T. Carlyle, *Letters and Speeches of Oliver Cromwell* (1888 ed.), Speech
VIII, April 1657.
4. An odd exception is F. Harrison, *Oliver Cromwell* (1899), who regarded it as a justified attempt to secure the "free commerce of the ocean."
5. J. Buchan, *Oliver Cromwell* (1934), p. 413.

those parts, as against open and professed enemies; thereby threatening the ruin and destruction of the English plantations in those parts, when he shall have opportunity for the same.[6]

It was not all just verbiage—even the seemingly empty phrase ". . . resolved through the blessing of God" was possibly significant in the context of the breakdown of negotiations: was Cromwell thinking England had again been meddling "with an accursed thing"? Whether so or not, he had proposed on this, as on that previous occasion, quite reasonable terms for an accommodation, reasonableness obscured by the Spanish ambassador's famous complaint that his master's two eyes were being asked for.[7] Trade to the Spanish Indies was not really in question: what was demanded was freedom of access to English settlements in the West Indies[8]—and the refusal of this is the major grievance referred to in Venables' commission. As for the question of religious toleration for English merchants residing in Spain, there was nothing revolutionary in the proposal: the nineteenth article of the Anglo-Spanish treaty of 1630 had made provision for the discreet exercise of Protestant worship; the problem was what constituted discretion and who was to determine whether its bounds had been exceeded. Cromwell's request for the omission of the words *"modo ne dent scandalum"* from the concessionary clause was only an attempt at regularizing a situation productive of difficulties and misunderstandings. In implicitly suggesting that the English should be arbiters in their own cause, he was after all being no more obdurate than the Spanish were in insisting on the Inquisition retaining the function: the English merchants had no financial interest in being scandalous; arguably the Inquisition had in judging them to be such. If this was a narrowly Protestant policy, it was not in any case peculiar to Cromwell: the pro-Spanish Merchant Adventurers made complete freedom of worship a condition of their residence in Bruges in September 1649,[9] the Council of State—not then dominated by Cromwell's party—complained in

6. *Thurloe State Papers* (1742) (hereafter *TSP*), III, 16. Dated August 18, 1654.
7. *Ibid.*, I, 759–63. Thurloe's account of Spain and France.
8. *Ibid.*
9. *Ibid.*, I, 129.

March 1651 of the Inquisition's molesting English merchants at Malaga,[10] and, in November 1652, the Rump had included an article extending the existing toleration in the draft of a commercial treaty offered to Cardenas.[11] There seems little reason, therefore, to suppose Cromwell insatiable or extraordinary in his requirements of Spain; the freedoms sought were moderate, limited, and quite consistent with God's and England's interests, as even the opponents of the Spanish war saw them to be. Their *immoderate* rejection might have been enough to precipitate an adventure like the West Indies expedition even if an agreement with the Spanish was ultimately being sought—there is a possible analogy here with the gunboat diplomacy which reduced Portugal to terms.

This last, however, would presuppose that war in Europe was not apprehended as a likely consequence, which is at variance with the extravagant expressions in Venables' orders, Blake's instructions vis-à-vis Portugal being tied more closely to the issue of the negotiations then in progress with that country. Gardiner, and many historians have followed him, assumed Cromwell to have been captivated by the idea of a separate war in the Indies, something he found quite inexplicable, except on the assumption of "his admiration for Elizabethan methods which led him to suppose that the existing Spanish Government would be as ready as that of Philip II to put up with a system which kept peace in Europe whilst war was being waged in America." [12] This exegesis requires some modification. In the first place there was more room for doubt about the outcome than hindsight allows for. There was a precedent—more recent than Elizabeth's activities —for assuming aggressive action would not necessarily entail formal war: the English conquest of parts of French America and Blake's attack on the French fleet sent to succor Dunkirk in 1652. True, there was then a naval war and a trade embargo, but perhaps Spain was too preoccupied to resent an injury in this way? Sir Benjamin Wright, writing to Thurloe from Madrid in April 1655, thought an attack *on Hispaniola* would lead to war, though

10. *Ibid.*, I, 175.
11. Gardiner, *op. cit.*, II, 184.
12. S. R. Gardiner, *Oliver Cromwell* (1962 ed.), p. 168.

not one south of the Equator, unless "they find themselves here so weak, and so environed with enemies on all sides, that they must pass by and put up any thing that you will do against them." [13] Nor was it a desperate hope: Spain was very much in this position, as witness Philip IV's humiliating necessity to keep on good terms with the Dutch.[14] James Wilson from Cadiz about the same time told Cromwell that an attempt on the West Indies would not be provocative "so far as may be judged by the disposition of these people," if Cuba and the "galleons" were left alone.[15] Probably the general view was that war was likely, but not inevitable, and that it was the scale and objectives of the attack which made it so, rather than its official character. Since the whole operation was meant to rely heavily upon the surprise factor, the government could scarcely canvass this sort of opinion when it was relevant: it is significant only as showing that a separate war policy, if mistaken, was not ludicrously inapposite. Indeed, long after real war began Lord Jermyn imagined that Cromwell and Spain were in treaty, which "gives some apprehension of an agreement between them, that may import, that the war beyond the line should induce no consequence of a breach on this side," and involve instead an alliance in Europe against France and the Stuarts.[16]

More important than this question—which is basically not susceptible of resolution—is how far the likelihood of war with Spain was taken into consideration when the West Indies expedition was decided upon. There is no real evidence that Cromwell was unduly surprised by the Spanish reaction. Thurloe merely states that "O. himself was for a war with Spain, at least in the West Indies, if satisfaction was not given for the past damages, and things well settled for the future," and again, "so it was resolved . . . to send a fleet and land forces into the West Indies, where it was taken for granted the peace was already broken by the Spaniard contrary to the former treaties; and not to meddle with anything in Europe, until the Spaniard should begin, unless

13. *TSP,* III, 366.
14. *Correspondance de la Cour d'Espagne sur les Affaires des Pays-Bas au XVIIe Siècle,* ed. H. Lonchay (Brussels 1933), IV, *passim.*
15. *TSP,* III, 389–90.
16. *Ibid.,* I, 692–93. To Charles II, Paris, February 4, 1656.

the American fleet should be met with, which was looked upon as a lawful prize."[17] If this last phrase is a true rendering of the grounds of the decision, a naval war in Europe was thought possible, and the possibility deliberately accepted, even welcomed. At least the chances of a trade embargo were realistically assessed: English merchants were warned not to venture capital too deeply in Spain some six months before the breach occurred.[18] It is true that the argument that Spain's "necessity of our trade" would require peace was used in debate in the Council,[19] but other reasons were urged why the war could not be destructive if it broke out. On this basis, then, it would seem that Cromwell, while not definitely resolved on war, was not ignorant of or averse to the possibility—it may be that he was simply allowing events to guide him and that Thurloe's "at least in the West Indies" is a reference to irresolution rather than to crude Elizabethanism. This would be consistent with his behavior on other occasions: his first attempting to come to terms with Charles I, with the Presbyterians, the Levellers, the Rump, then, in each case when he saw divine providence at work in their obstinacy, switching over to the offensive. At home, however, his ability not to know where he was going produced in the end something like a stable government, and a settlement roughly consistent with the interests of the country as a whole. By whatever kind of coincidence, or tortuous self-deception, even—for it is unwise to reject any possibility on *a priori* grounds—of heavenly guidance, waiting on events seemed to work. Sagredo, an extraordinary ambassador from Venice, attributed this success in part to "Fortune," explaining: "I call the effect of Fortune that opportunity which came as it were toward him, to make the path to greatness easy for him."[20] However stupid the Spanish war has appeared to those who came after him, Cromwell himself lost no faith in his "dispensations." How then could he think that his policy was in England's interests?

17. *Ibid.,* I, 759–63. Thurloe's account of Spain and France.
18. C. H. Firth (ed.), *Clarke Papers* (1899), III, 52. Army newsletter, September 1655. Bordeaux to Mazarin, April 8 and 29, 1655, quoted in Gardiner, *op. cit.,* III, 390. Other references to warnings include *TSP,* III, 637, IV, 21, 47, and *Correspondance de la Cour d'Espagne,* IV, 497.
19. *Clarke Papers,* III, 205–06.
20. E. Momigliano, *Cromwell,* pp. 309–10.

One objection is easily disposed of: the contention of Slingsby Bethel that Cromwell made an "unjust war with Spain and an impolitic league with France, bringing the first thereby under, and making the latter too great for Christendom; and by that means broke the balance betwixt the two crowns of Spain and France, which his predecessors, the long-parliament, had always wisely preserved"[21]—an accusation echoed by Ludlow in his memoirs in remarkably similar language: "This confederacy was dearly purchased on our part; for by it the balance of the two crowns of Spain and France was destroyed, and a foundation laid for the future greatness of the French, to the unspeakable prejudice of all Europe in general, and of this nation in particular, whose interest it had been to that time accounted to maintain that equality as near as might be."[22] (Incidentally, neither takes account of Cromwell's scoffing reminder, "I could instance how it was said, 'We will have a war in the Indies, though we fight them not at home,'"[23] which throws an interesting sidelight on "Elizabethan" attitudes.) It proved a popular criticism echoed throughout the eighteenth century—particularly trenchantly by Bolingbroke[24] and the authors of the Old Parliamentary History[25]—and survived into the present.[26] The objection is not so much that Mazarin's France was not Louis XIV's (though it is interesting historiographically to see how popular the idea was when France represented a threat to England and how it gradually went out of fashion when that threat receded)—the anachronism is a deeper one. In Cromwell's day it was generally regarded as an act of folly to ally with a weak state against a strong one, if it could be avoided. Not everyone thought like this of course. Sir Benjamin Rudyerd, in a speech apprehensive of growing French power, argued in 1641 that "our aptitude is rather to balance, which being rightly used may make the King that great arbiter of all

21. *Harleian Miscellany* (1810 ed.), VII, 349.
22. C. H. Firth (ed.), *Ludlow Memoirs* (1894), II, 2–3.
23. Carlyle, *op. cit.,* Speech V, September 1656.
24. Bolingbroke, *Letters on the Study and Use of History* (1752), I, 258–59.
25. *Old Parliamentary History* (1751–62), XX, 473.
26. D. A. Bigby, *Anglo-French Relations 1641–1649* (1933), p. 31.

the affairs of Christendom, by withholding or opposing . . ."[27] but this was an exceptional and to some extent an archaic view. There was a strong feeling that switching sides was unwise; Ormonde thought that it devalued the credit of the defaulting party[28] and Clarendon refers to "the old mistaken and unhappy maxim that the Crown of England could balance the differences which fell out between the princes of Europe by its inclining to either party," as having "made the ministers of that State too negligent in cultivating the affections of their neighbours by any real obligations . . ."[29] The accent was on what one could get from one's ally in the way of military[30] and financial[31] support, even of territory,[32] rather than on diminishing the strength of an enemy. For this purpose powerful friends were sought, the arguably reasonable implication being that it was safer to make sure of being on the winning side, thus neutralizing any possible threat thence. De la Court made the point negatively in 1622 when he said that, because it was not in France's interest to make war on the United Provinces, the Dutch had no need of a French alliance, that because Spain was weak a Spanish alliance was superfluous too, and that "we are to take care that we do not suffer ourselves for fear of a war with *England,* to be inveigled into an alliance jointly to carry on an offensive war against any nation . . ."[33] Parenthetically this idea is helpful in putting the Anglo-Dutch negotiations of 1653 and 1654 into perspective—the English propositions of a close union and alliance being a natural demand for a stronger power to make of a weaker. As respects the Anglo-

27. *Ibid.*
28. *Nicholas Papers* (1920), IV, 8–9. May 1657.
29. Clarendon, *History of the Rebellion and Civil Wars in England* (1958 ed.), IX, s. 170.
30. *Vide* Whitlocke's "Relation of the Swedish Embassy to the House," *Old Parliamentary History,* XX, 341: "They [the Swedes] have store of men, arms and shipping, to join with us upon any occasion, and whereby both you and they may be strengthened against your enemies, and be more considerable throughout the world."
31. Cromwell's negotiations with Spain and France bear this out.
32. E.g., Cromwell's asking Spain for a Flanders port and the question of Swedish Bremen being pledged to England.
33. *The True Interest and Political Maxims of the Republic of Holland* (London, 1746 ed.), pp. 232, 235, 242–43.

French alliance, on the other hand, Thurloe adduces in its favor France's ability to harm England both in the Mediterranean and with regard to Charles II.[34] On the French side Bordeaux concurred; he found it astonishing that Cromwell should hesitate to close: "I can hardly believe," he wrote in June 1655, "that the lord protector doth know himself so ill, that the power of the king, and the weakness of Spain, can cause him to hope any advantage from a war with the one, and from a strict league with the other . . ."[35] Even the great shibboleth of English foreign policy, the Baltic "balance," was not a sophisticated attempt to keep Danish and Swedish power equal. Divided control of the Sound was an *ad hoc* solution: the usual feeling seems to have been that the one essential was the preserving of free access to the Baltic and that this was the best way of doing it—analogous rather to arguments against monopolies than to Slingsby Bethel's fear of Sweden and France dividing "the western empire betwixt them."[36] In Cromwell's fear of a Dutch-Danish-Polish-Austrian combination overwhelming Sweden, in his opponents' complementary worry about the growing commercial power of that country, there was only the faintest prevision of the later theory. Surely, if it had been otherwise, those who spoke against the Spanish war in Richard's Parliament would have made something of the danger of French aggrandizement?

Instead they concentrated on the commercial disadvantages of the war. Here the question to be considered is whether there was any justification for incurring whatever losses took place, or whether, on this count, Cromwell must be charged with fanaticism in continuing to fight. In doing this some provisional estimate of the damage must be arrived at. Apart from the financial cost which must be treated in conjunction with the advisability of the war as a whole, criticisms come under two heads: the destruction of English shipping and the disruption of the two-way trade with Old Spain. Estimates of the number of ships lost vary between

34. *Somers Tracts* (1809–15 ed.), VI, 329. Concerning the Foreign Affairs in the Protector's Time.

35. *TSP*, III, 468. Gardiner points out that Venables' commission was dated the same day (August 18, 1654) that the news of the French relief of Arras reached England.

36. *Harleian Miscellany*, VII, 350.

about 1,200 and something over 2,000.[37] None of them comes from
a source friendly to Cromwell's government and all may be suspected on that ground alone. Richard Baker was concerned with
making a case against the release of a captured pirate when he
spoke in 1657 of a loss of 1,800 ships. Bampfield in Richard's
Parliament made the number 1,500 only (February 1659). Next
month Hesilrige, arguing the same point, revised the figure to
"at least" 1,200. Obviously there was no very reliable source of
information behind all this. Three other guesses may be dis-
counted: Barwick wrote to Hyde a few days after Hesilrige's
speech and that was probably his source for the same figure;
Slingsby Bethel in 1668 referred his estimate specifically to that
of Bampfield; and the anonymous author of a pamphlet entitled
Awake O England, or the People's Invitation to King Charles
(1660) need not be taken very seriously (over 2,000 was his
figure). More confidence may be placed in Garroway's contention
in the Cavalier Parliament, "We lost sixteen hundred ships in
the last *Spanish* war, great and small," for it contains its own
corrective—but he too was arguing a case. Interestingly the numbers suggested roughly balance the number of prizes taken in
the Dutch war—a fortunate, and perhaps genuine, coincidence for
those who condemned both war with Spain and the peace with
the Dutch. However, after making allowances for these doubts,
the losses were still heavy, there being numerous references to
ships sunk or captured in the letters of Thurloe's informants and
others. In fact, this may have been one reason why the war was
persisted in. Most of the damage was done by privateers from the
Spanish Netherlands and by ships holding Charles II's commission. Baker thought the latter alone chiefly to blame, "the subjects
of this commonwealth, who have gone to the enemy, taken up
commissions, and assisted them like parricides . . ." The perma-

37. *Calendar of State Papers, Domestic, Commonwealth, and Protectorate
Series* (hereafter *CSPD*), XI, 245, Petition of Richard Baker 1657 (?)—1,800.
Burton's Diary (1828), III, 402, Bampfield; February 1659—1,500. *Ibid.*, IV,
364, Hesilrige; April 1659—at least 1,200. *TSP*, VII, 662, Barwick to Hyde;
April 1659—over 1,200. *Harleian Miscellany*, VII, 103, Royalist; 1660—over
2,000. *Ibid.*, VII, 229, Royalist; 1661—1,200. *Ibid.*, VII, 353, Slingsby Bethel;
1668—1,500. Anchitel Gray, *Debates of the House of Commons* (1769), II,
213, Garroway; 1673—1,600.

nent elimination of this threat was a legitimate war aim—naval war with France or Spain the only way to bring these Royalists to battle. War with Spain had the additional advantages of offering the chance to gain control of the privateering bases in Flanders. Dunkirk in particular was long a thorn in England's side: Sir John Suckling, writing to the Commons of Charles I's third Parliament,[38] spoke of the merchants "daily damnified by the spoil of Dunkirkers" in the war then in progress. Between 1655 and 1660 complaints of ships lost and navigation threatened nearly always refer to the activities of Dunkirkers and Ostenders.[39] In 1698 the loss of Dunkirk was described by a critic of Ludlow's Memoirs as "too sadly lamented in these last wars with France." [40] Later during the War of the Spanish Succession over 900 ships were seized by Dunkirk privateers, more than the number taken by those of Brest and Calais, the great French base, put together.[41] In this context it is not surprising that Cromwell was praised, even by some of his opponents, for acquiring the town. Modern prejudice against the holding of fortified outposts in foreign countries has obscured the genuine advantages. What objection can be urged after all? It was true enough that the English could not hold territory in Flanders indefinitely without the assistance of the United Provinces or France or Spain in a war with any other of those powers: but it is difficult to imagine such a conflict. The place was envisaged not as a bastion against, but as a gateway into, Europe, a base for operations in support of an ally, and as such the military problems entailed in holding it were commensurate with those of a bridgehead, not a fortress. Even from the point of view of the "balance of power," an English presence there was a better guarantee for the Dutch than a French, or a Spanish one soon to be replaced by the French. Thurloe, who is really the only authority on Cromwell's motives in this, says that a footing on the Continent, by way of Dunkirk, Ostend, and Nieuport, was aimed at for a variety of reasons: to secure Eng-

38. *Somers Tracts,* IV, 113.
39. *Vide TSP, CSPD, passim.*
40. *Somers Tracts,* VI, 442.
41. J. S. Bromley, "The French Privateering War," in *Historical Essays presented to David Ogg* (1963), p. 214.

land against invasion by Charles II, to restrain the French from
making a separate peace with Spain, to make France vulnerable
to England in the event of its contracting alliances of a prejudicial
nature, to encourage Flemish and French Protestants, to make it
easy to interfere in the Protestant interest, to be a "bridle on the
Dutch"—there being English harbors on both sides of the Channel
—and finally, "It seemed of great importance to have this interest
in Flanders, in point of safety to our own trade, which was at all
times disturbed, and greatly prejudiced by the Dunkirkers and
Ostenders, in whose hands soever they were." [42] That Cromwell
recognized the peculiar strategic significance of the Flanders seaboard is shown by his asking a Flemish port as a condition of
alliance with Spain and refusing to consider an alternative in
French territory.[43] Given the assumption that the West Indies
expedition was envisaged as possibly provoking war, the whole
policy makes sense—success in the Indies would lead to peace;
failing that, a useful objective could be pursued in a European
war against Spain waged in concert with the French. Short-
term shipping losses were irrelevant if one of the chief potential
dangers to commerce were removed.

The loss of the rich trade with Spain was another matter. Contemporaries were agreed that this would be a disaster. Bullion
came from Spain, the fine Spanish wool necessary now that English wool had become coarser—an indirect result of the enclosures
—cochineal and indigo used as dyes, wines, fruits, olive oil, silk,
tobacco, iron. In return there was the best market for English fish
and the new draperies, this last of increasing importance with the
decline of cloth exports to northwestern Europe, and a significant
vent for hats, glass, and earthenware. Commerce with the Spanish
Netherlands was also important. One branch which was particularly vulnerable was the importation of Bruges thread into
England, where it was made into lace and sent back again. Furthermore, Spain was in a good position to interfere with England's

42. *Somers Tracts,* VI, 331. Concerning the Foreign Affairs in the Protector's Time.
43. *TSP,* I, 705. A Paper in the Handwriting of Thurloe—a draft of the
first part of Thurloe's Account of Spain and France—but this statement is
not repeated there.

trade in the Mediterranean. But, as the government believed, it could not afford a complete cessation. Thurloe's answer to Scott and Bampfield and Lloyd's complaints on this score was the bland assertion that "You export as much commodity, and import as much from Spain, as ever you did." [44] Five months before this, in September 1658, Bordeaux wrote from England to Mazarin that "the war has not been hitherto so burdensome to England as not to yield as great advantages by continuing it as by coming to an accommodation; for it is proved by the registers of the Custom-house that the exports and imports of merchandise have been as great since the rupture as they were before the war began." [45] A pamphlet published in 1661[46] appealed to the customs figures to prove the reverse, but the writer was neither so well informed as Thurloe, nor so unprejudiced as Bordeaux.[47]

Wars in the period were not incompatible with trading relations and official bans could be circumvented. The Dutch had successfully evaded an embargo on the carrying of Portuguese and French goods to Spain.[48] Whatever the Spanish king might say, his subjects considered their own profit first—as late as March 1658, Antwerp was still refusing to prohibit English goods.[49] A letter of intelligence written in November 1655 put the case succinctly: "The king of Spain has made a prohibition to bring any English merchandize in his estates although he can hardly be without." [50] Some of the methods which suggested themselves whereby his deficiencies could be supplied involved sending ships with Dutch papers,[51] under a Tuscan flag of convenience,[52] and suspending the Act of Navigation as it applied to fish exports.[53]

---

44. *Burton's Diary*, III, 487.
45. F. Guizot, *History of Richard Cromwell* (London, 1856 ed.), I, 234–35.
46. *Harleian Miscellany*, VII, 229.
47. M. Ashley, *Financial and Commercial Policy under the Cromwellian Protectorate* (1962 ed.), 143–44, argues for Bordeaux's objectivity on this point.
48. *TSP*, II, 74. Letter of intelligence from the Hague, February 1654.
49. *Ibid.*, VII, 15.
50. *Ibid.*, IV, 110.
51. *Correspondance de la Cour d'Espagne*, IV, 579, September 1657.
52. *TSP*, VI, 607. Longland, November 1657.
53. *CSPD*, XI, 7, June 1657. *Burton's Diary*, I, 296, January 1657.

The ruses seem to have worked fairly well, or could even have been dispensed with. Morrell wrote to Thurloe from Paris on April 22, 1656, to say that he had had an audience with Lestrade, Mazarin's favorite, and that the latter "grew inquisitive, whether Spain and we were enemies. I replied yes. Said he, have your merchants trade there? Yes we have. I find they fear our closing with Spain yet." [54] Morrell had no objection to alarming the French, and the progress of the embargo was irregular and dilatory: it was only two days earlier that the placards banning English goods had been published at Cadiz. Yet it is interesting as bearing out the calculation that war need not automatically prevent commerce. In November of the next year Longland reported from Leghorn that many English ships were still trading with Spain.[55] Any shrinkage of the Spanish market could also have been compensated for, in part at least, by an increase in the profit of cloth exports to Portugal and the Mediterranean—made possible by the favorable terms of the 1654 Anglo-Portuguese treaty and by the removal of the threat of French privateers. The first alternative was mentioned explicitly, the second implicitly, when the Hispaniola project was being debated: "it is said that a full trade with Portugal (which we can have as we will) will be near as good as the other." [56] This sounds odd, but the discrepancy in population between Portugal and Spain in the seventeenth century was much less than it is now. Market requirements for cloth were almost identical. Major General Haynes in June 1656, hearing that "the peace with the crown of Portugal is over," hoped that it would prove "welcome news to our clothing towns now their trade with Spain is shut up." [57] The last presumption was legitimate early in the war when ways of circumventing the embargo cannot have been fully put into operation. Two other points are worth making: Ultimately good trading relations with the Portuguese were inconsistent with friendship with Spain,[58] and

54. *TSP,* IV, 693.
55. *Vide* n. 52 above.
56. *TSP,* III, 206.
57. *TSP,* V, 165. Quoted by Christopher Hill, *The Century of Revolution* (1961), p. 158.
58. *Vide* V. H. Shillington and A. B. Wallis Chapman, *The Commercial Relations of England and Portugal,* pp. 207–08, for Spanish intolerance of

the balance of trade with Portugal was, or soon became, more favorable than that with Spain—though this was due to the comparative paucity of the import trade.[59] On the other hand, imports were much less affected by the breach. There is no question but that wines and fruits continued to be brought to England from Spain—their prices were discussed in Parliament in October and November 1656,[60] duties on Spanish products (wine and tobacco) in January 1657,[61] an act regulating wine prices was passed in June 1657,[62] and in April 1659[63] there was a vote to ban all Spanish goods.

Their importation was unlikely to have been by way of English or Spanish shipping so much as by the Dutch, in contravention of the Act of Navigation. The export of merino wool from Biscay was already almost a Dutch monopoly[64]—probably one way or another they were now bringing it to England. Samuel Lamb, arguing for a bank in January 1659, mentions with disapproval "the practice suspected to be now used, to employ Dutch shipping as much as ever to bring home Spanish goods, by colourably making bills of sale of them in trust to the freighters, to secure them against the act for increase of navigation." [65] A surprising variety of people[66] attributed "the decay of trade" to the Dutch rather

---

trade with her "rebels" in 1694. An undated paper (c. 1645) entitled *Brief Considerations concerning the Trade that may be expected hereafter between England and Portugal,* State Papers Foreign, IV, f. 68, refers to the other side of the coin—Portuguese interruption of Anglo-Spanish trade.

59. Shillington, *op. cit.,* pp. 206–07, for merchants' assertion under Charles II that Portuguese trade was more valuable. B.M. Add. MS. 36,785, *London Exports and Imports,* gives a figure for the value of imports from Portugal less than a third that for Spain (1662–63). By 1668–69 the ratio given is less than a sixth. J. O. McLachlan, *Trade and Peace with Old Spain* (1940), quotes Godolphin as saying in 1712 that the Portuguese trade "brought to England in times of war double the wealth of the trade of Spain in time of peace."

60. *Burton's Diary,* I, clxxxvi–vii.

61. *Ibid.,* I, 325.

62. *CSPD,* XI, 7.

63. *Nicholas Papers,* IV, 84.

64. Four-fifths of the quantity exported: *TSP,* I, 200, c. July 1651.

65. *Somers Tracts,* VI, 446.

66. Thurloe among them, perhaps not surprisingly. *Burton's Diary,* III, 487, February 1659. Earlier the same day Serjeant Maynard contributed to the debate his opinion that "it is rather a Dutch war, under the Spaniard's name." *Ibid.,* p. 461.

than to the Spanish war as such. Fears were expressed that besides expanding their carrying trade they would usurp the market for English-style cloth in Spain—a possibility which to some extent carried its own remedy with it: if the Dutch could imitate English cloth so successfully, it was going to be difficult to enforce a discriminatory embargo against the genuine article. For many Spanish exports, besides wool, alternative sources existed: olive oil could come from Portugal, France, and Leghorn,[67] silk from the United Provinces, the Levant, or directly from the East, wines from France and Portugal, iron from Sweden, raisins from the Levant, tobacco from English colonies in the West Indies— something the government wished to encourage. Dyes were more of a problem—indigo was another colonial product, but cochineal, a brilliant red pigment made from the crushed bodies of South American beetles, was irreplaceable. However, even had the cloth industry been completely deprived of the dye,[68] the result was unlikely to have been catastrophic; the sophisticated color range of the new draperies included crimson, but also black, "sad grey," "stone grey," "liver," "mussel," "beaver," "partridge grey," azure, pink, peach, gold and silver.[69] All this is not to suggest that the war did not produce any dislocation of trade or cause hardship to some (it would certainly have added to insurance rates and freight charges, for instance), only that its effects have been exaggerated, perhaps grossly.

How can this exaggeration be accounted for? Modern critics may have been over-influenced by their reading of a "separate war" policy, and by the complaints of contemporaries. Many at the time were prejudiced by their political opinions, but genuine anxiety understandably existed. Bordeaux, though he thought the losses were bearable, makes it clear that the merchants bitterly

67. McLachlan, *op. cit.,* p. 9. Portugal and Leghorn were suggested by a pamphleteer, "the Sussex Farmer," during the war of Jenkin's Ear. *Vide* Add. MS. 36,785 for this and other alternatives.

68. Cochineal was shipped from the Canaries—*vide* Add. MS. 32,093 f. 367, an undated remonstrance of merchants trading to the Canaries about the iniquities of the Spanish governor. Wines and fruit were coming in from the same source during the war. In Cromwell's as in Elizabeth's war at least one cargo of the dye was captured.

69. The list is from B. E. Supple, *Commercial Crisis and Change in England 1600–1642* (1959).

opposed the war.[70] Paradoxically, his unconcern about the contradiction renders an explanation of it unnecessary to the present argument, though one may be ventured. Certain interests, who were vocal and influential, were disproportionately affected. Those involved in formulating the Navigation Act—which *may* include the Eastland and Levant Companies—and the anti-Dutch lobby —which included almost everyone except Cromwell and some of his "courtiers"—could not have approved the modifications of the policy which the war made necessary. The Spanish merchants themselves were an interesting case: trade to Spain was "open," but obviously it was now, in a sense, more open. Men who had ventured capital too deeply to pull out quickly were badly hit by the confiscation of their goods; their only hope of redress lay in peace. Since these would be the bigger merchants, they were peculiarly liable to resent the irregular way in which trade was being carried on—sometimes in foreign bottoms, probably often by adventurous interlopers seizing their opportunity. Many people, Royalists, republicans, protagonists of the Navigation Act, important merchants, had the same interest in promoting a campaign to heighten apprehension as much as possible. The formidable shipping losses helped them: when examined, most of the contemporary laments about the ruin of clothiers seem to have had these as their basis. Bampfield, sitting for Exeter (an important center for the production of cloth for Spain and Portugal) in Richard's Parliament said "the consequences of that war have been the decay of our trade in *all* parts . . ."[71] (my italics)— words susceptible of interpretation as referring to privateers rather than to the embargo, as most of these complaints were. A Royalist put it explicitly: "The trade of the West of England is almost ruined since the war with Spain, most of their vessels being taken and carried to St. Sebastians by Spanish frigates which wait daily about Land's End"[72]—*not*, as has been assumed, by the closure of the Spanish market to them, or the cessation of the supply of Spanish wool, for which there is little evidence. And if this was where the war was felt most grievously, Cromwell's policy is

70. Guizot, *op. cit.*, pp. 234–35 *et al.*
71. *Burton's Diary*, III, 402.
72. *CSPD*, XI, Mompesson to Nicholas, January 1658.

comprehensible: Dunkirk and Ostend once conquered would prevent much of this sort of thing in the future—albeit no provision could be made for St. Sebastians. Right or wrong, the calculation was made on *secular* grounds.

Against this background of sizable but supportable losses directly related to a specific war aim, must be seen the reasoning behind Cromwell's persistence in the war. One positive gain, which historians have often been content to gloss over, was the preservation of an independent Portugal [73]—a positive boon for England as it was a country easily bullied into making substantial concessions, a negative one as its survival was a better guarantee against Dutch expansion in America than Spain proved during the "captivity." The picture is one of long-term gains set against immediate disadvantages—not the least of which was the crushing financial burden that the war brought with it. Cromwell may have made mistakes—his contention[74] that the war in the West Indies would pay for itself is an obvious idiocy; that much of the "Elizabethan" theory may be retained—but the *whole* policy was answerable to the conditions of the period. However, this interpretation is incomplete without an understanding of how it can be related to what is known of Cromwell's personality. The most important source for Cromwell's thinking on the Spanish war is the report, in the handwriting of Edward Montagu, of the debate which took place in the council in July 1654.[75] One passage may be quoted:

> We consider this attempt, because we think God has not brought us thither where we are but to consider the work that we may do in the world as well as at home, and to stay from attempting until you have superfluity is to put it off for ever, our expenses being such as will in probability never admit that. Now Providence seemed to lead us hither, having 160 ships swimming: most of Europe our enemies except Holland, and that would be well considered also: we think our best consideration had to keep up

73. *Vide TSP,* VII, 516. Instructions to Downing c. November 1658. Also Bischoffshausen, *Die Politik des Oliver Cromwell* (Innsbruck, 1899), 198, for mention in one of the drafts Thurloe made for Clarendon at the Restoration (B.M. Stowe MS. 185, ff. 187–200).

74. *Clarke Papers,* III, 208.

75. *Ibid.,* p. 207.

this reputation and improve it to some good, and not lay up by the walls. Thence we came to consider the two great crowns, and the particular arguments weighed, we found our opportunity point this way.

The consideration of the two great crowns, the weighing of the particular arguments, these problems had been discussed earlier;[76] again the starting point was what to do with the fleet released from the Dutch war. This was a difficulty in its own right—its maintenance was necessary for national security; Parliament would be reluctant to vote money for it except for some tangible purpose. Maintaining a diminished number of ships was not an answer: men of war and merchantmen no longer had easily interchangeable roles, and, once laid up, the usual fate of seventeenth-century ships was to lie rotting (and their crews would go to add to the groundswell of discontent at home). But "Providence" is the clue to Cromwell's attitude in this as in all things. Oliver's dispensations had led him to believe that the Stuarts by a special dialectic both were and ought to be on the losing side, and he carried this idea over into his foreign policy. No one has described his fighting the Stuarts as an Elizabethan or anachronistically Protestant policy—yet his diplomacy abroad, as well as at home, can be referred to this end.

The first reason for a peace with France (and by contextual implication for a war with Spain) given in that earlier council meeting was "The hindering of a peace between the two crowns," feared by the Protectorate, greatly hoped for by Charles II as an aid to his restoration. Thurloe at the accomplished Restoration confirms this as the order of priority; numbering the grounds of the alliances of the time he begins: "I. To deprive his majesty of foreign assistance in his restitution: hence it was that the alliance with France was preferred to that of Spain . . ."[77] In fact, the only people in a position to restore Charles II were the French and the Dutch. When Oliver came into the Protectorate, reports were coming home[78] that the Orange party, the pro-Royalist, pro-French party in the United Provinces, was gaining ground as a

76. *Ibid.,* pp. 203–06.
77. *Somers Tracts,* VI, *op. cit.,* 329.
78. *TSP,* I, *passim.*

result of the war with England. France had apparently welcomed Charles and his court. Only Spain, weak and useless as an ally, was positively estranged from the Stuarts, had been the first power to recognize the Commonwealth, was now the first to recognize the new government. England was "deeply engaged in a war with the Portuguese . . . And not only this, but we had a war with Holland . . . At the same time also we were in a war with France." [79]

The whole thing must have seemed wrong. For a moment the Stuarts seemed likely to regain abroad the credit they had lost at home, in spite of all God's witnesses against them. Yet to disrupt this pattern forcibly would have been untypical. Every major decision Cromwell had made to this point in his career he could represent as having been forced upon him, as being entailed in the natural procession of events. He believed in acting in accordance with that procession, that close study of it would reveal the trend of God's will, that the consummation of that will was inevitable, but that one had the freedom to move with it or against it. Though there were inconsistencies in his position as it can be gleaned from his letters and speeches, it was analogous to that of a man swimming in a river: the river would reach the sea, whatever he did—this was the factor of historical determinism in his approach—the man would be carried to the sea or drowned, whatever he did, the current was so strong—that was the concept of personal predestination, but he had freedom to point himself up river or down, freedom to will but not freedom to act to save himself—the force of the current was infinite, the strength of the man finite. Thus, when drowning stands for damnation and the sea for heaven, the doctrine of predestination and the feeling of personal moral responsibility were uneasily reconciled. [80] Confronted

79. Carlyle, *op. cit.*, Speech II—to the first Protectoral Parliament.

80. It would be impracticable to give even a representative selection of references for Cromwell's religious views as he expressed them. For outward dispensations see Carlyle, *op. cit.*, Letters LXVII, LXX, LXXIII, LXXXV, CXLVIII, etc.; W. C. Abbott, *The Writings and Speeches of Oliver Cromwell* (1937), I, 719, II, 82, etc. For fatalism especially frequent references. Freedom of will is implicit in Cromwell's appeals to the Dutch and Scots to repent seeing God's hand against them, and elsewhere. I have attempted to synthesize these elements, believing that Cromwell was a deeply *introverted*

by a current which apparently changed direction and stopped trying to drown the Stuarts en route, Cromwell could only wait and
try to discern what must be its mainstream and what were deceptive eddies. What signs were there that God was working to
deprive the Stuarts of useful allies abroad? How could he associate
himself and his country with this inevitable process? The Dutch
were applying for peace. The prospect of a French-Orangist alliance to restore Charles II—likely enough to Cromwell—and to
Thurloe (who, for all his sagacity, was at the mercy of his informants in the last analysis) receded. It had been the Rump's
war. That institution had miraculously brought its own destruction to pass. *He,* Cromwell, had not dissolved it; it had *made*
him do so by breaking faith in repudiating the promise not to
vote its perpetuation. Apart from Cromwell's kindly feelings
toward another Protestant republic—he distrusted that sort of
subjective reaction—here was an objective indication that something was wrong with the Dutch war. But he proceeded cau-
tiously. No armistice was granted. Only when good conditions
were obtained and the Orange party, godless by virtue of their
association with the Stuarts, were excluded from holding office in
Holland, was peace renewed. Commercial matters were not neg-
lected—this was the second part of the doctrine of dispensations—
swimming against the current was arduous, swimming with it was
easier, an inevitability rather than a reward, material benefits seen
as a probable indication of righteousness.[81]

Now the next step was to fight France or Spain. This is not
apparent to our generation, but it made sense in Cromwell's
peculiar terms and hence, indirectly, in ours. The dispensations
suggested another war—the persecution of Huguenots in France
(so the government was told) and in Savoy, Spain's maltreatment
of English merchants and colonists, the "160 ships swimming,"
the necessity of preventing a Stuart restoration. As yet the choice

---

man (as his scanty medical history suggests) and must himself have tried
to reconcile these different aspects of his belief.

81. The idea was commonly perverted into one of killing two birds with
one stone. Examples in M. James, *Social Problems and Policy during the
Puritan Revolution* (1930), pp. 22–23. Thomas Gage on the *English-Ameri-
can* (v. him also in *TSP,* III, 59) was a particularly cynical exponent.

of whom to fight was not obvious. So Oliver waited again, pursued parallel negotiations with each of the crowns, considered the relative profit of a war with either. The signs pointed to a Spanish war—as we have seen in the way negotiations with Spain broke down. But this was not enough. The crucial test was whether such a war was likely to involve material blessing for England. In many ways it was decided that it would. Above all politically, and providentially, it would be a good thing if the Stuarts looked for help from Spain rather than from France. In the Council debate recorded by Montagu in April 1654, a French alliance was regarded as "discountenance to our rebels in Scotland and fugitives." Thurloe[82] enumerates the disadvantages of unfriendly relations with France in this respect: that crown had close ties of blood and marriage with the Stuarts, they had Protestant subjects to employ on Charles II's behalf (this was not a completely fanciful notion: Lord Jermyn was pursuing the possibility in 1652.[83] Admittedly he was being fairly fanciful in his own right), and their friendship with the Scots was dangerous (again there had been signs toward the end of the Civil War of French diplomacy operating in this direction). On the other hand, he says, "It was foreseen that the excluding the king out of France would cast him upon Spain, which some thought a difficulty, but the protector an advantage. 1. Because his being in the hands of the Spaniards would make his return more difficult, the religion and interests of that crown being hated generally, both by the English and Scots, and affected only by the Irish. 2. And in case the Spaniard by the help of the Irish, had by a war attempted the restitution of the king; it was conceived to be the likeliest means of uniting the several divided interests of the kingdom together in that quarrel." Another reason given for welcoming the move was that while the Spaniard had "no interest here but the papist; the presbyterian party, whom O. was desirous enough to engage in his affairs" had "ever shewed the greatest aversion to the Spaniard."[84] So the resolution mirrored that effected at home: the Irish Catholics, the Levellers, and the republicans were heavily sup-

82. *Somers Tracts*, VI, *op. cit.*, pp. 329–30.
83. Clarendon, *op. cit.*, XIII, ss. 131–32.
84. *TSP*, I, 759–63, *op. cit.*

pressed there, the Scots and the English Presbyterians were to be accommodated if possible. Out of the possible menace of a grand alliance of Orangists, their Brandenburger and Danish relations, the Scots, the French, the Presbyterians, Charles has been removed and left to make what headway he can with unsympathetic Spaniards and republicans! Soon enough in the eyes of the government this alternative pattern was seen to be forming: "The Spaniard, cavalier, papists and levellers, are all come into a confederacy . . . The commonwealths men look also for a sudden turn, and hope they shall play next." [85] Now, said Cromwell of Spain, "that is the party that brings all your enemies before you: It doth: for so it is now, that Spain hath espoused that interest which you have all along hitherto been conflicting with—Charles Stuart's interest. And I say, it doth not detract at all from your course, nor from your ability to make defence of it, that God by His providence hath so disposed that the King of Spain should espouse that person." [86] In the rest of his discourse he associated the opponents of the war with Charles' party: and according to Ludlow[87] he specifically accused him and his followers of "clandestine correspondances" with the Spanish. But these combinations were less to be feared than the other—it was the "presbyterian" party which restored the Stuarts in the final analysis. The parties ranged against the Protectorate were at present an unnatural grouping— if it was providence, it was also sound politics. As for the modern notion that Cromwell would have been better off not having a war at all, it is by no means certain that any firm and lasting agreement could have been made with France respecting the Stuarts *and* the trade rivalry between the countries, without England fighting Spain. This contingency was in large part implicit in the negotiations. The point where the policy is most difficult to justify on material grounds is at its inception. Here it is important to insist that a European war was envisaged from the beginning —that is the decision to be assessed—and in the absence of further evidence relating to his motivation at the time, it is legitimate to guess that Cromwell was leaving the decision to fate, that he

85. *Ibid.*, V, 45. Thurloe to Henry Cromwell, May 1656.
86. Carlyle, *op. cit.*, Speech V, to the Second Protectoral Parliament.
87. *Ludlow Memoirs*, II, 11–12, 1656.

wanted a real war with Spain and that he convinced himself it might not follow the West Indies expedition in order that he could accept it as another dispensation when it did. Perhaps this is unfair: there was a faint chance of it not occurring. But however unsatisfactory this way of reaching a decision (or rather of executing it) may seem, it must not be allowed to obscure the genuine advantages of the war. These may now be collected: (1) France was committed to hindering a Stuart invasion; (2) the Stuarts were placed in an untenable position; (3) Portugal was secured; (4) the elimination of the privateering threat from Flanders was worked for, and partly achieved; (5) French cooperation in the Mediterranean was secured; (6) a basis for English expansion in the West Indies was established; (7) Dunkirk's acquisition became an insurance policy against a separate peace by France, against a future Dutch war, against any untoward happenings in the Spanish Netherlands, where England had vital strategic interests. On the other side, losses were not so great as is often assumed. Above all, a profitable peace might have been made had Cromwell lived longer.[88] In this rough way the dialectic was working again—war was suggested by signs; once entered into, it was found to be, if not so advantageous as predicted, at least not hurtful enough *on balance* for Cromwell to think God was witnessing against it. This was his idea of a Protestant foreign policy, not crudely fanatical, not oblivious of political and economic considerations, but in fact dependent on these for its spiritual force.

The same process is evident in other aspects of his diplomacy. Blake's aggressive trip round the Mediterranean neatly fulfilled the "interest of Christians and the interest of the nation." And the dual requirement was also met by the peace which was made with the United Provinces, although it has been heavily criticized: "The negotiations that ended in the peace of 1654 illustrate to what lengths Cromwell would go in his neglect of English economic interests for the sake of the Protestant chimera" writes one

88. Thurloe argues that only internal divisions prevented the government doing this after his death; *TSP*, I, 759–63, *op. cit.* Ludlow quotes Vane to the same effect; *Memoirs*, II, 170.

modern historian,[89] condemning his advocacy of a union between the countries and quoting Slingsby Bethel[90] with approval on "suddenly making a peace with Holland without those advantages for trade, as they who beat them, did intend to have had." The same writer continues to complain, among other matters, that Cromwell did not support those English merchants who wanted direct trade with Antwerp without paying dues to the Dutch at the mouth of the Scheldt. The argument will not bear much examination: Slingsby Bethel and his colleagues condemned Cromwell for not pushing the union plan as a *sine qua non*—dropping it showed a commendable grasp of realities. Two main points were conceded to England: there was to be no trading with each other's enemies and the supremacy of the English flag was acknowledged—thus prejudicing the disputed Dutch right to fish in "English" seas. That some of the limited gains in the treaty were not secured and many issues left debatable was unavoidable. Any further requirements—free trade up the Scheldt was a preposterous demand as striking at the root of Amsterdam's prosperity—would either not have been observed, if granted, or, refused, have prevented the conclusion of the peace.[91] English naval stocks were in no shape for this eventuality. Here especially Cromwell's Protestant policy displays more attention to common sense than the secular criticisms of his opponents. The Puritan Protestant league to include the United Provinces, Denmark, Sweden, France, and various German princes was an ideal: we need not censure Cromwell's dreams except so far as they impinged on his actions. In practice he took realities both as a test and as a guide.

Nowhere is this seen more clearly than in his Baltic policy. If we take his public utterances as our standard, we are compelled to conclude he was fighting the Thirty Years' War all over again: "Look how the House of Austria on both sides of Christendom,

89. Prestwich, *op. cit.*
90. *Ibid.*
91. *Calendar of State Papers Venetian, 1653–54,* p. 237—Pauluzzi, the Venetian ambassador, thought war might result from insistence on this point.

are armed and prepared to destroy the whole Protestant interest
. . . Who is there that holdeth up his head to oppose this danger?
A poor Prince—indeed poor; but a man in his person as gallant,
and truly I may say as good, as any these last ages have brought
forth; a man that has adventured his all against the Popish interest
in Poland . . ." [92] This ability to see a Habsburg round every
corner, Cromwell's undoubted affection for Charles X of Sweden,
the "poor Prince," are misleading. It is essential to distinguish between his predilections and his conception of his duty; knowing
he could be led astray by enthusiasms, he disciplined them by
reference to hard facts—the whole process being comprisable
within his religious outlook. In consequence, his Baltic policy can
be explained without relating it to religious principle at all—
though this was precisely why it was a Protestant policy in Cromwell's own terms. He was not inveigled into an alliance with
Sweden. Initially[93] he was prepared for an *ad hoc* understanding
against the Dutch and Danes to open the Baltic to English shipping. When the reason for this departed with the cessation of hos-
tilities with the Dutch, his aim was to reconcile Sweden and
Denmark and prevent either being in a strong enough position to
close the Sound. Meadowes' mediating embassy to Denmark in
September 1657 was the result. As he himself puts it, his role
in the treaty of Roskilde, concluded in spring of the following
year, was hardly pro-Swedish: "The English mediator had two
parts to act in this scene; one was to moderate the demands as
far as he could in favour of the sufferer, without disobliging the
Swede by a too notorious partiality" [94]—the other was to watch
that nothing was concluded against English interests. When it
was moved that the whole kingdom of Norway be united with
Sweden, he comments: "This entrenched upon England as giving
the Swede the sole and entire possession of the chief materials, as
masts, deal, pitch, tar, copper, iron, etc. needful for . . . the equi-
page of our ships, too great a treasure to be entrusted in one hand.

92. Carlyle, *op. cit.,* Speech XVII.
93. *Vide* his instructions to Whitlocke, *Journal of the Swedish Embassy*
(1772), pp. 13–15, 33, 95.
94. P. Meadowes, *A Narrative of the Principal Actions Occurring in the
Wars betwixt Sweden and Denmark* (1677).

The mediator in avoidance of this was the first who insinuated the proposal of rendering Scania and Bleking to the Swedes . . . safe for England, because by this means the Swede is become master of one bank of the Sound as the Dane is of the other." [95] The "temporary success of the peace of Roskilde" [96] endured, at least in its main territorial clauses, for the next three hundred years and is still with us. Meadowes wrote truer than he knew when he said that, apart from some small adjustments, "the Roskilde treaty is renewed and reconfirmed, and remains to this day the standard and measure betwixt these two Northern crowns." Meadowes' version is borne out by other references to Cromwell's attitude. [97] The alternative criticism—of failing to act in concert with the Swedes against Dutch trade in the area—has been dealt with in an article by Michael Roberts[98]: there he argues that England dare not risk war with the Dutch (owing to the depletion of naval stores) and that in any case it was questionable whether such an agreement could have been effected at all. But the Swedish-Danish struggle was only one facet of the imbroglio. There was the Swedish-Polish war to be considered as well. In the context of Swedish belligerence, the idea of directing the Swedish armies southward was quite sensible. Cromwell was certainly prepared to ally himself with the Swedes against Austria, though one may wonder how significant he intended England's contribution to be. The drawback to this might appear to be that a Swedish conquest of Poland and monopoly of the southern Baltic seaboard was dangerous for the Eastland Company—but these campaigned for a *more* vigorous policy in support of the Swedes.[99] In the long run there was no chance of Sweden raising tolls exorbitantly: England was an important customer for Danzig, whoever possessed the place. Besides, Sweden may have been expansionist in

95. *Ibid.,* pp. 58–60.
96. Prestwich, *op. cit.*
97. *Vide* Van Dorp to De Witt, November 1657, quoted in M. Roberts, "Cromwell and the Baltic," *English Historical Review,* LXXVI. Thurloe confirms it; *Somers Tracts,* VI, 323.
98. Roberts, *op. cit.*
99. *CSPD,* III, 273–74, July 1650, 1651; 392, September 1651; *TSP,* V, 88, June 1656, for complaints of Polish and Danzig exactions. For the Eastland Company's policy, see R. W. K. Hinton, *The Eastland Trade and the Common Weal in the Seventeenth Century* (1959), pp. 126–28.

its motions, but it was fundamentally weak and overextended; if
we allow that everything of which he disapproved was Habsburg
and papist to Cromwell (though if the presence of an Imperial
army in Jutland was an anachronism, no one seems to have informed Vienna of the fact), then forget it, and look at the actual
situation, it will be seen that the combination of Danes, Dutch,
Brandenburgers, and Poles would ultimately have overwhelmed
the Swedes. It does not matter much whether they were Habsburg puppets—they were not—the net effect would be the same.
Meadowes explained the sending of an English fleet in the spring
of 1659—a course Cromwell was considering when he died—in
these terms: "it was not with any intention as some vainly suggested to assist Sweden in the conquest of Denmark; that had
been impolitic and irrational, for 'tis evident the conservation of
Denmark is the common interest as well of England as of Holland, neither was there at that time the least fear or danger of
any such supposed conquest. The elector had an army in Jutland
of near thirty thousand men, Brandenburgers, Poles and Austrians,
and could have had as many more if either the country could
have supported their numbers, or the service required them." He
contends that, properly united, their forces "had been sufficient
not only to have beat the Swede out of the Danish isles and
dominions, but out of Sweden itself . . . England though sorry
for this second rupture with Denmark, thought it not their interest
to see Sweden overset and sinking under the mighty weight of so
powerful a confederacy." [100]

Here as elsewhere it is possible to find reasons, sometimes ex-
cuses, for Cromwell's policy. The exercise is not a work of
supererogation, because it is impossible to understand a policy by
condemning it—no course of action ever impressed itself upon
a man's mind as being desirable on account of the objections
which could be raised against it. For Cromwell the idea of a
Protestant foreign policy was simply the consummation of God's
will, and as a part of this, the benefiting a nation devoted to that
will. He might believe he knew what was to be done—but he was
suspicious of himself and little tied to preconceptions, "Eliza-

100. Meadowes, *op. cit.,* pp. 111–14.

bethan" or otherwise. It is possible to see his foreign policy as perhaps he saw it himself—looking for a sign as to which way to move but testing that sign strictly in accordance with profane principles. In this context a distinction between spirituality and materialism represents a false dichotomy. Of course there are *a priori* reasons for suspecting the application of the principle: could God's and England's interests really always be identical? The end of this essay is only to suggest that in his diplomacy in the Baltic, in the Dutch treaty, in the Spanish war and the French alliance, Cromwell's motives were neither anachronistic nor fanatical. The success of his policies is another question: I have merely proposed ways in which he can be justified in secular terms, as an aid to understanding his Protestantism.

CHRISTOPHER HILL

Providence and
Oliver Cromwell

I am one of those whose heart God hath drawn out to wait
for some extraordinary dispensations, according to those
promises that he hath held forth of things to be accomplished
in the later time, and I cannot but think that God is beginning of them.

CROMWELL, at Putney, November 1, 1647

An higher force him pushed
Still from behind, and it before him rushed.

MARVELL, *The First Anniversary of the
Government under O.C.*

The reference to Providence was with Cromwell an infallible
indication of a political change of front.

S. R. GARDINER, *The Great Civil War* (1894), IV, 288

From *God's Englishman,* by Christopher Hill. Copyright © 1970 by
Christopher Hill. Reprinted by permission of the publisher, The Dial Press.

"This doctrine of predestination is the root of puritanism, and puritanism is the root of all rebellions and disobedient untractableness in Parliament, etc., and of all schism and sauciness in the country, nay in the church itself; making many thousands of our people, and too great a part of the gentlemen of the land, very Leightons in their hearts,"—which Leighton had published not long before a most pestilential seditious book against the bishops, . . . in which he excited the people to strike the bishops under the fifth rib, reviling the Queen by the name of a daughter of Heth.

> MATTHEW BROOKS, Master of Trinity College, Cambridge, to Archbishop Abbott, December 12, 1630, quoted by P. Heylyn, *Historical and Miscellaneous Tracts* (1681), p. 539

PREDESTINATION is at the heart of Protestantism. Luther saw that it was the only guarantee of the Covenant. "For if you doubt, or disdain to know that God foreknows and wills all things, not contingently but necessarily and immutably, how can you believe confidently, trust to and depend upon his promises?" Without predestination, "Christian faith is utterly destroyed, and the promises of God and the whole Gospel entirely fall to the ground: for the greatest and only consolation of Christians in their adversities is the knowing that God lies not, but does all things immutably, and that his will cannot be resisted, changed or hindered." [1] *Ein' feste Burg ist unser Gott.* Luther declared that he would not have wanted free will, even if it could have been granted to him: only God can make salvation *certain,* for some if not for all.[2] Indeed the whole point for Luther lies in the *uniqueness* of the elect. Once touched with divine grace they are differentiated from the mass of humanity: their consciousness of salvation will make them work consciously to glorify God. The psychological effects of this *conscious* segregation of a group from the mass is enormous.

Calvin went a step further and boldly proclaimed that God was useless to humanity unless he had knowable purposes which we can trust and with which we can cooperate. "What avails it, in short, to know a God with whom we have nothing to do? . . .

1. Luther, *The Bondage of the Will,* trans. H. Cole (1823), pp. 31–32.
2. *Ibid.,* pp. 369–70.

How can the idea of God enter your mind without instantly giving rise to the thought that since you are his workmanship, you are bound, by the very law of creation, to submit to his authority?" [3] "Ignorance of Providence is the greatest of all miseries, and the knowledge of it the highest happiness." [4] Faith gives us "sure certainty and complete security of mind," of a sort that is self-evident to those who possess it and inexplicable to those who do not.[5]

Men have often commented on the apparent paradox of a predestinarian theological system producing in its adherents an emphasis on effort, on moral energy. One explanation that has been offered is that, for the Calvinist, faith revealed itself in works, and that therefore the only way in which an individual could be assured of his own salvation was by scrutinizing his behavior carefully night and day to see whether he did in fact bring forth works worthy of salvation. It is by means of works performed through grace, in Calvin's view, that the elect "make their calling sure, and, like trees, are judged by their fruits. . . . We dream not of a faith which is devoid of good works, nor of a justification which can exist without them." [6] This attitude is expressed by Sir Simonds D'Ewes. After listing sixty-four signs or marks from several graces which gave him assurance to a better life, he added: "I found much comfort and reposedness of spirit from them; being more careful than ever before to walk warily, to avoid sin and lead a godly life." This fact convinced him that papists and Anabaptists were utterly mistaken in arguing that assurance of salvation brings forth presumption and a careless and wicked life. On the contrary, "when a lively faith and a godly life are joined together, and are the groundwork of the signs and marks of a blessed assurance, here the very fear of losing that assurance, which is but conditional, will be a means rather to increase grace and virtue than to diminish it." [7] "Nothing is more industrious than saving faith," as Thomas Taylor put it.[8]

3. J. Calvin, *The Institutes of the Christian Religion,* trans. H. Beveridge (1949), I, 41; cf. p. 47.
4. *Ibid.,* I, 134.
5. *Ibid.,* II, 70, 157.
6. *Ibid.,* II, 97–98.
7. Sir S. D'Ewes, *Autobiography and Correspondence,* ed. J. O. Halliwell (1845), I, 369.
8. T. Taylor, *Works* (1653), pp. 178–79.

But I am not entirely convinced that this is the sole explanation. It is highly sophisticated. Most of the evidence for it among the preachers comes from the later seventeenth century, when for other reasons works were being emphasized once more. I believe that the resolution of the paradox is psychologically simpler, if philosophically more complex. Salvation, consciousness of election, consisted of the turning of the heart toward God. A man knew that he was saved because he felt, at some stage of his life, an inner satisfaction, a glow, which told him that he was in direct communion with God. Cromwell was said to have died happy when assured that grace once known could never be lost: for once he had been in a state of grace. We are not dealing here with the mystical ecstasy of a recluse; we are dealing rather with the conscience of the average gentleman, merchant, or artisan. What gave him consciousness of election was not the painful scrutiny of his works, for the preachers never tired of telling him that none could keep the commandments, that "we cannot cooperate with any grace of God" unless there is "a special spirit infused." [9] It was the sense of elation and power that justified him and his worldly activities, that gave him self-confidence in a world of economic uncertainty and political hostility. The elect were those who thought they were elect, because they had an inner faith which made them feel free, whatever their external difficulties. This sense of liberation they could recognize in one another. It was natural that they should want freedom to gather in churches with others of God's people.

Philosophically the argument is circular. But Calvinism did not exist primarily as a philosophical system.[10] It gave courage and confidence to a group of those who believed themselves to be God's elect. It justified them, in this world and the next. Professor Haller seems to me to have expressed this better than anyone else when he writes that the Puritan preachers were "dealing with the psychological problems of a dissatisfied minority"; their object was "to inject moral purpose into men who felt lost in moral confusion." "Men," he adds, "who have assurance that they are to inherit

---

9. D. Rogers, *A Practicall Catechisme* (3rd ed., 1640), p. 253.
10. For Calvin's attempts at reconciliation, see especially *Institutes,* I, 187, 202–05, 229, 241, 254, 264; cf. Bunyan, *Works,* I, 299, II, 123, 312.

heaven, have a way of presently taking possession of the earth." [11]
This courage and confidence enabled them to fight, with economic,
political, or military weapons, to create a new world worthy of
the God who had so signally blessed them: a world remolded in
their image, and therefore in his. As the *Homily on the Salvation
of all Mankind* put it: "These great and merciful benefits of God,
if they be well considered, do neither minister unto us occasion to
be idle, and to live without doing any good works . . . but con-
trariwise, if we be not desperate persons, and our hearts harder
than stones, they move us to render ourselves unto God wholly,
with all our will, hearts, might and power to serve him in all
good deeds, obeying his commandments during our lives, to seek
in all things his glory."

Those who most eagerly accepted Calvinism were men whose
mode of life was active. The philosophical reconciliation of God's
eternal decrees and their own inner impulse to labor for the glory
of God was not a subject which occupied them overmuch. They
were wise in this, for even the judicious Hooker virtually gave up
the attempt at reconciliation of God's foreknowledge and man's
free will, after noting that Augustine himself had changed his
mind on the subject. In trying to analyze the Puritan attitude,
therefore, we must not press them too hard for a philosophical
consistency which they, in common with other theologians, lacked.
We must consider rather how their theology helped them to live
in and change the world as they found it.

Our period is one in which the literate public became increasingly conscious of scarcity.[12] Famine and starvation were as old as
human history. But in the sixteenth and seventeenth centuries a
growing proportion of the working population, town dwellers
and rural industrial workers, was dependent on others for its food;
and an increasing proportion was literate and vocal. The traditional
ruling class had no need to bother about scarcity: whoever else
starved, it always had enough. The poorest peasantry and wage

11. W. Haller, *The Rise of Puritanism* (Columbia University Press,
1938), pp. 141, 162.
12. Cf. C. B. MacPherson, "The Maximization of Democracy," in *Philosophy, Politics and Society,* 3rd Series (ed. P. Laslett and W. G. Runciman),
pp. 97–100.

laborers had no other perspective than intermittent starvation: the Land of Cockayne and even the very material advantages of heaven in *Pilgrim's Progress* testify to this. The Digger Gerrard Winstanley was less concerned with *individual* scarcity than in sharing what little there was and in increasing it for and by the community. It was the yeomanry and artisanate who stood at the margin, who could lift themselves into relative abundance by a combination of hard work and good fortune. Some may even have conceived of the possibility of total escape for society from the curse of scarcity, from the burden which had rested on humanity's back since the beginning of history. Protestantism emphasized the duty of working hard on behalf of the community, the common-wealth. But even individual escape involved tremendous effort and concentration. It might also involve breaches with what was cus-tomarily regarded as correct behavior. It was important that men who had to follow new courses should have an inner certainty and confidence. Theories of predestination suggest the colossal power of the blind forces from which individuals were feeling the first beginnings of liberation. In folk tales men hope to overcome or outwit destiny by magic: but the prophecies on which they rely invariably turn out to be fallacious; as in *Macbeth,* destiny won by cheating.[13] But *the* book of prophecy was the Bible, and it would not deceive. If by intensive study men could master its prophecies, they would understand destiny and so become free. This was not the view only of simple-minded Bibliolaters or Fifth Monarchists; intellectuals as diverse as Joseph Mede and John Milton, John Napier and Sir Isaac Newton passionately held it: so did John Bunyan.

The "common man's logic" of the Huguenot Peter Ramus, which so many Puritans adopted, may have helped the more philosophically minded to feel that they had produced a system of thought,[14] or they may, with Bacon, simply have excluded the sphere of faith from rational criticism. The great scientific and political advances in our period, to which religious thought con-tributed so much, extended human control over the environment,

13. *Moby Dick* is a relatively late example.
14. See my *Intellectual Origins of the English Revolution,* pp. 291–93, and references there cited.

and man's control over the social and political institutions under which he lived. The triumphs of Puritan thought, in the last analysis, were this-worldly. Faith was something given: if there seemed to be contradictions, that was because of the fallibility of human reason. "Down reason then, at least vain reasonings down." So Milton concluded, the man who of all those normally regarded as Puritans had perhaps the greatest confidence in the human intellect. There was a contradiction, but it could not be resolved within the framework of theology. We should marvel at the way in which a Bacon, a Milton, a Winstanley, tortured their Procrustean framework, rather than at their failure to break it up and start anew.

For Calvin, works are not a means whereby a man can persuade himself he is saved when he doubts it, but are the necessary and actual fruits of the faith of an honest man engaged about a worldly job. (The fact that it is necessary to explain this is evidence of the extent to which faith, in the Calvinist sense, has ceased to be regarded as a source of inner psychological strength, at least by the historians who write about it.) Must not the elect, Calvin asked, "conceive a greater horror of sin than if it were said to be wiped off by a sprinkling of good works?"[15] A man who really believed that God had included him among the handful who were saved from eternal damnation rather naturally felt under an obligation to make some voluntary return for this voluntary grace. The price of goodness, Calvin thought, is eternal vigilance. God can preserve truth, he told Cranmer: "Nevertheless, He would by no means have those persons inactive whom He Himself has placed on the watch."[16] "God crowns none but well-tried wrestlers."[17] The Puritan Thomas Taylor neatly summed up the distinction between justification by faith and justification by works in a passage which illuminates the social context of the two doctrines: "We teach that only Doers shall be saved, and by their doing though not for their doing. . . . Though then we cannot do so much as to *merit* heaven, yet we must by grace do so much

15. Calvin, *Institutes,* II, 102.
16. Ed. H. Robinson, *Original Letters relative to the English Reformation* (Parker Soc.), II (1847), 712. Cf. Calvin, *Institutes,* II, 5.
17. Calvin, *Commentary on Genesis,* trans. J. King (1965), I, 171.

as *keep* the way. . . . The profession of religion is no such gentle-manlike life or trade, whose rents come in by their stewards, whether they sleep or wake, work or play." [18]

That was the distinction that mattered. Catholicism was a rentier religion. Provided the landlord performed the appropriate cere-monies on the appropriate occasions, the priestly steward brought in the rents for him to spend. But Protestantism was for doers only; for those who, as Taylor goes on to explain, often look into their debt books and cast up their reckonings; "but a bankrupt has no heart to this business." [19] This hostility to the mere rentier lies very deep in Puritan theology, and is the basis of the "bour-geois" doctrine of the calling. For William Perkins, "such as live *in no calling,* but spend their time in eating, drinking, sleeping and sporting, because they have . . . lands left by their parents," are guilty of rebellion and disobedience against God.[20] Popery, Richard Sibbes thought, was "set up by the wit of man to man-tain stately idleness." [21] There is no admission by purchase to the corporation of the godly, added John Cotton: all who hope for grace must serve an apprenticeship.[22]

Doers were saved by their doing, but not for it. The elect were active and courageous by definition, not in order to become elect. "The thing which we mistake is the want of victory," wrote Sam-uel Rutherford. "We hold that to be the mark of one that hath no grace. Nay, say I, the want of *fighting* were a mark of no grace; but I shall not say the want of *victory* is such a mark." "With-out running, fighting, sweating, wrestling, heaven is not taken." [23] Francis Bacon transferred this spirit—the spirit of Milton's *Areo-pagitica*—to science when he said: "Not to try is a greater risk than to fail." [24] This attitude gave the believer freedom from fear of hell or furies, courage to fight alone if need be. Samuel Butler wrote

18. T. Taylor, *Works,* pp. 166–67.
19. *Ibid.,* p. 172.
20. W. Perkins, *A Cloud of Faithfull Witnesses,* pp. 63–64, in *Works* (1616–18), III.
21. R. Sibbes, *Works* (Edinburgh, 1862–64), I, 91; cf. p. 88.
22. J. Cotton, *The Covenant of Gods Free Grace* (1645), pp. 19–20.
23. Ed. A. A. Bonar, *Letters of Samuel Rutherford* (1894), p. 399.
24. F. Bacon, *Works,* ed. J. Spedding, R. L. Ellis, and D. D. Heath (1862–74), III, 617.

from the enemy point of view, and after the event, but he too was saying that Puritanism gives revolutionary élan, that its effects are internal and psychological. "Ordinary wicked persons, that have any impression of human nature left, never commit any great crime without some aversion and dislike, although it be not strong enough to prevail against the present motives of utility or interest, and commonly live and die penitent for it. But the modern Saint that believes himself privileged and above nature engages himself in the most horrid of all wickednesses with so great an alacrity and assurance, and is so far from repentance, that he puts them upon the account of pious duties and good works." [25]

The importance of being a doer is neatly brought out in one of Cromwell's letters, written to the Speaker after the fall of Bristol in September 1645. As it was brought up to him for signature, it spoke of "the people of God with you and all England over, who have waited on God for a blessing." As Cromwell read it through, the words did not seem to convey exactly what he wanted to say. We do not know whether his secretary had taken the letter down incorrectly, or whether the more fitting phrase came into Cromwell's mind as he read it through. He took up his pen, crossed out the words "waited on" and altered the phrase to read "who have *wrestled with* God for a blessing." Passivity was intolerable even when face to face with God himself. God would allow the world to be changed only by those who helped themselves. "Our rest we expect elsewhere," Cromwell assured St. John three years later. Nor were these principles peculiar to Oliver: in 1641 Hanserd Knollys wrote in *A Glimpse of Sions Glory*: "It is the work of the day to give God no rest till he sets up Jerusalem as the praise of the whole world." [26] Here, as in Cromwell's letter, God is regarded almost as an impersonal force; it is like the desire of Zhelyabov, the nineteenth-century Russian conspirator, "to give

---

25. S. Butler, *Characters and Passages from Notebooks* (Cambridge University Press, 1908), p. 307. Butler was referring primarily no doubt to the more radical sectaries. But he would have said (and I agree) that their actions were justified by principles put forward earlier by more conservative Puritans.

26. H. Knollys, *A Glimpse of Sions Glory* (1641), in Woodhouse, *Puritanism and Liberty*, p. 233.

history a push." [27] "We cannot wait for favors from Nature," said the Soviet scientist Michurin; "our task is to wrest them from her." [28]

The Puritan integration of freedom and necessity is also an integration of the individual in the historical process. It comes at the point at which a man says: "Trust in God and keep your powder dry." God works through human agents. The active cooperation of the elect expedites the accomplishment of his purposes. Sloth and dishonoring God by refusing to cooperate in this way, Calvin tells us, are the greatest evils.[29] "The work of God will go on," Hugh Peter said in December 1648; but "I am not in the mind we should put our hands in our pockets and wait what will come." [30] By so cooperating we "make our destiny our choice," as Andrew Marvell and the Matchless Orinda put it.[31]

Such an attitude demands very careful consideration of time and place, accurate assessment of each political situation. "God permitteth not his people to fight when it seemeth good to them," said the Geneva Bible's marginal note to Deuteronomy XX.1.[32] "We must not put all carelessly upon a providence," Richard Sibbes warned, "but first consider what is our part; and, so far as God prevents [i.e., goes before] us with light, and affords us help and means, we must not be failing in our duty. We should neither outrun nor be wanting to providence. . . . When things are clear, and God's will is manifest, further deliberation is dangerous, and for the most part argues a false heart." [33] It might be Lenin discussing on which precise day in October the Russian Revolution should take place. "That which . . . goes nearest to my heart,"

27. D. Footman, *Red Prelude* (1944), title page.
28. *Soviet News,* June 8, 1951.
29. Calvin, *Institutes,* I, 192, 223–25, 231; cf. pp. 212–13.
30. *Clarke Papers,* II, 90.
31. A. Marvell, *Upon Appleton House*; K. Philips, *L'Accord du Bien,* in *Minor Poets of the Caroline Period* (ed. G. Saintsbury, Oxford, 1905), I, 564; cf. p. 599.
32. "When thou goest out to battle against thine enemies, and seest horses, and chariots, and a people more than thou, be not afraid of them: for the Lord thy God is with thee, which brought thee up out of the land of Egypt."
33. Sibbes, *Works,* I, 209; cf. p. 211.

cried Sir Henry Vane in the Commons in 1641, "is the check which
we seem to give to divine providence if we do not at this time
pull down this [ecclesiastical] government. For hath not this
Parliament been called, continued, preserved and secured by the
immediate finger of God, as it were for this work?" [34] The political implications of cooperating with destiny are clear. Hooker
shrewdly pointed out that "when the minds of men are once er-
roneously persuaded that it is the will of God to have those things
done which they fancy, their opinions are as thorns in their sides,
never suffering them to take rest till they have brought their spec-
ulations into practice." [35] Political action was thus not a thing
indifferent: it might be a religious duty.

Cooperation with omnipotence was undoubtedly good for morale. "What coward would not fight when he is sure of victory?"
asked Sibbes.[36] "The godly being in league with God," explained
Thomas Gataker, "may have all his forces and armies for their help
and assistance, whensoever need shall be." Even when things seem
to be going badly, there is consolation in the thought that "the
enemies of God's church . . . shall never be able to root it out." [37]
Cromwell's account of his feelings before Naseby is the classic exposition of this philosophy in action: "I could not (riding alone
about my business) but smile out to God in praises in assurance of
victory, because God would, by things that are not, bring to naught
things that are. Of which I had great assurance; and God did it."

Yet "the providences of God are like a two-edged sword, which
may be used both ways," M.P.s said in 1656. "God in his providence
doth often permit of that which he doth not approve; and a thief
may make as good a title to every purse which he takes by the high-
ways. . . . If titles be measured by the sword, the Grand Turk may
make a better title than any Christian princes." [38] God spoke with

34. Sir H. Vane, *Speech in the House of Commons* (1641), pp. 8–9.
35. R. Hooker, *Of the Laws of Ecclesiastical Polity* (Everyman ed.), I,
139.
36. Sibbes, *Works*, I, 98; cf. John Downame, *A Guide to Godlynesse*
(1622), Book I, p. 52.
37. T. Gataker, *An Anniversarie Memoriall of Englands Delivery from
Spanish Invasion* (1626), pp. 10, 20.
38. *Burton's Diary*, I, xxx. The Great Turk often appeared in this context: see *Anglia Liberata*, p. 6.

different voices to different people, and problems of interpretation remained. At Putney, Lieutenant Colonel Goffe accused Cromwell of too freely and flatly declaring "that was not the mind of God" that someone had spoken. Cromwell defended himself by saying that mistakes of fact or of logic could not be from God, for "certainly God is not the author of contradictions." Some might be sure that God wanted to destroy kings and lords, but at least, "let them that are of that mind wait upon God for such a way where the thing may be done without sin and without scandal too." The Levellers were more sophisticated than Cromwell, but they were no less sure that God was with them. "God is not a God of irrationality and madness or tyranny. Therefore all his communications are reasonable and just, and what is so is of God." Tyranny is irrational and therefore ungodly.[39] Wildman appealed to the Army Council "to consider what is justice and what is mercy and what is good, and I cannot but conclude that that is of God. Otherwise I cannot think that anyone doth speak from God when he says that what he speaks is of God." [40] There is still room for discussion, and a way can be won through to arguments based on reason and humanitarianism; but only by postulating that these are in accordance with God's will. They cannot be justified in themselves.

Now it is clear that at any time in history the conviction that God is on your side in a struggle of cosmic dimensions is a powerful asset: the churches in all ages and all wars have tried to give men just that conviction. But there is a very real sense in which the Puritans were *right* in their conviction—more right than the many no less sincere churchmen who believed that God was on the other side in the Civil War. If for "God" we substitute some such phrase as "historical development" or "the logic of events," as the Puritans almost did, then there can be no doubt that powerful impersonal forces, beyond the control of any individual will, were working for Cromwell and his army. The evidence for this is not merely that Parliament won the Civil War: it is also the complete inability of the old government to rule in the old way which had been revealed in 1640, its financial and moral bankruptcy. John

39. R. Overton, *An Appeale* (1647), in Wolfe, *Leveller Manifestoes*, pp. 158–59.
40. *Clarke Papers*, I, 384.

Owen spoke in 1651 of "the constant appearing of God against every party that . . . have lifted up themselves for the reinforcement of things as in former days." [41] Not even 1660 brought back "things as in former days." The future lay with the causes supported by the Puritans and Parliamentarians. In that sense they were cooperating with history, with God. And this is true of the nobler as well as of the less noble aspects of the cause. When Milton wrote on Cromwell's behalf to the Landgrave of Hesse, advocating religious toleration on grounds of Christian charity, he concluded with a lofty confidence justified by the event: "With inculcating and persuading these things we shall never be wearied; beyond that there is nothing allowed to human force or counsels; God will accomplish his own work in his own time." God and the Cause would triumph in the end; but they would triumph the faster, and both God's glory and England's welfare would be the greater, the more convinced Christians fought the good fight here and now.

Sustained, then, by an outlook on life which helped them in the daily needs of economic existence; conscious of a bond of unity with others who shared their convictions; aware of themselves as an aristocracy of the spirit against which aristocracies of this world were as nought; fortified by the earthly victories which this morale helped to bring about: how should the hard core of convinced Puritans not have believed that God was with them and they with him? Believing this, how should they not have striven with all their might? "The greater the trust, the greater the account," Cromwell told Hammond; "there is not rejoicing simply in a low or high estate, in riches or poverty, but only in the Lord." In this sainthood of all believers the saints were perforce doers, not (for the best of them) in any calculation of reward for action, but simply because that was what being a saint meant. At Doomsday, Bunyan said, men will be asked not "Did you believe?" but "Were you doers, or talkers only?" [42] To be convinced that one was a soldier in God's army and to stand back from the fighting would have been a contradiction far less tolerable than that which philosophers have detected between individual freedom and divine pre-

41. J. Owen, Works, VIII, 336.
42. Bunyan, Works, III, 123.

destination. Previous theologians had explained the world: for Puritans the point was to change it.

Hence followed what appears the irrational conviction that God will look after the ends if we, according to our lights, attend to the means. "Duties are ours, events are the Lord's," said Samuel Rutherford.[43] This line of argument seems to have played no inconsiderable part in bringing about the moral conviction that Charles I must be executed; both Ireton and Cromwell used it in that context. Ireton in the Whitehall Debates of December 1648 declared that "men as men are corrupt and will be so." This, however, was not an argument for inaction (because the ungodly would pervert even good actions to evil ends) but for confidence that God will use our actions for his ends, provided we enter into them with integrity of heart. "We cannot limit God to this or that . . . but certainly if we take the most probable way according to the light we have, God gives those things" their success. It is therefore a duty to God far more than to ourselves to keep our powder dry and follow the sensible, prudent course. "Neglect not walls and bulwarks and fortifications for your own defence," wrote John Cotton about 1630; "but ever let the name of the Lord be your strong tower."[44] Oliver, writing to St. John, said of Sir Henry Vane, "I pray he make not too little, nor I too much, of outward dispensations. God preserve us all, that we, in the simplicity of our spirits, may patiently attend upon them. Let us all not be careful what use men will make of these actings. They shall, will they, nill they, fulfil the good pleasure of God, and we shall serve our generations."

To Hammond on November 25, 1648, Oliver wrote: "If thou wilt seek to know the mind of God in all that chain of providence whereby God brought thee thither and that person [Charles I] to thee; how, before and since, God has ordered him, and affairs concerning him; and then tell me whether there be not some glorious and high meaning in all this, above what thou hast yet attained? And, laying aside thy fleshly reason, seek of the Lord to teach thee what that is; and he will do it." Again, after a more

43. *Letters of Samuel Rutherford*, p. 238; cf. my *Puritanism and Revolution*, p. 265.
44. L. Ziff, *The Career of John Cotton* (Princeton, 1962), p. 62.

or less rational discussion of the nature of authority, Cromwell added: "But truly these kind of reasonings may be but fleshly, either with or against: only it is good to try what truth may be in them. And the Lord teach us. My dear friend, let us look into providences." "Reasonings" for Oliver clearly stand in the same relation to providences as theory to fact. ("We are very apt, all of us, to call that faith that perhaps may be but carnal imagination and carnal reasonings.") To Hammond, Cromwell concluded:

> Let us beware lest fleshy reasoning see more safety in making use of this principle [of suffering passively, Vane's principle] than in acting. . . . Our hearts are very deceitful, on the right and on the left. What think you of providence disposing the hearts of so many of God's people this way, especially in this poor Army? . . . The encountering difficulties therefore makes us not to tempt God, but acting before and without faith. . . . Ask we our hearts, whether we think that, after all, these dispensations, the like to which many generations cannot afford, should end in so corrupt reasonings of good men, and should so hit the designings of bad? Thinkest thou, in thy heart, that the glorious dispensations of God point but to this? Or to teach his people to trust in him and to wait for better things, when, it may be, better are sealed to many of their spirits? And, as a poor looker-on, I had rather live in the hope of that spirit, and take my share with them, expecting a good issue, than be led away with the other.[45]

The line of thought is identical in Ireton and Cromwell. Clement Walker—not always good evidence—fits into the general picture sufficiently well to be worth quoting here. "When it was first moved in the House of Commons to proceed capitally against the King, Cromwell stood up and told them 'that if any man moved this upon design, he should think him the greatest traitor in the world; but since providence and necessity had cast them upon it, he should pray God to bless their counsels, though he were not provided on the sudden to give them counsel.'" (Another report of the same speech has it "Since the providence of God hath cast this upon us, I cannot but submit to providence, though I am not yet provided

---

45. The whole letter deserves careful study as the *locus classicus* of the theory expounded by a man in the process of acting upon it to transform history.

to give you my advice.") Such arguments from such men on such
a subject at such a time deserve the closest attention: so they steeled
themselves to one of the boldest and most epoch-making gestures
in history—the public execution of a king by his subjects, for the
first time in modern Europe. The arguments were not invented
for the occasion: they were part of the normal apparatus of thought
of the fighting Puritans—of Oliver's beloved schoolmaster, Thomas
Beard, from whom he no doubt first learned them;[46] of Hugh
Peter, who wrote in 1646: "Our work will be only to look to the
duty which is ours, and leave events to God, which are his." [47]

For Oliver "waiting on providences" meant making absolutely
sure that the political situation was ripe before taking drastic action
—ensuring that the army and its leaders were with him, that the
City would acquiesce, etc., etc. One can see how all this to the
ungodly eye could look like waiting on events, waiting to see which
way the cat would jump—often indeed encouraging the cat to
jump in the desired direction at the proper time. Alternatively it
could be described retrospectively as making necessities in order
to plead them. ("Necessity, the tyrant's plea," his Secretary for
Foreign Languages was to call it.) The Royalist Joseph Beaumont
may have been referring obliquely to Cromwell in *Psyche* (1648):

> When this more than brutish General once
> In lawless gulfs himself had plunged, he
> Prints on his mad adventure's exigence
> The specious title of Necessity;
> To which he blushes not to count the law,
> Whether of earth or heaven, oblig'd to bow.

(Canto XI, stanza 32)

This suggestion roused Oliver to fury. To his first Parliament he
declared, "Feigned necessities, imaginary necessities, are the greatest cozenage that men can put upon the providence of God, and
make pretences to break down rules by. But it is as legal and as
carnal and as stupid to think that there are no necessities that are
manifest necessities because necessities may be abused and feigned."
"God knoweth," Oliver threatened, "what he will do with men

46. See Hill, *God's Englishman*, pp. 39–40.
47. H. Peter, *Gods Doings and Mans Duty* (1646), p. 6.

when they shall call his revolutions human designs, and so detract from his glory. . . . It is an honour to God to acknowledge the necessities to have been of God's imposing when truly they have been so. . . . It was, say some, the cunning of the Lord Protector; . . . it was the craft of such a man and his plot that hath brought it about. . . . Oh, what blasphemy is this! . . . Therefore, whatsoever you may judge men for, and say this man is cunning and politic and subtle, take heed, again I say, how you judge of his revolutions as the products of men's inventions!"

This relation between means and ends, the duty of keeping our powder dry until the time came to commit the Lord's forces, was a Puritan commonplace. It was indeed, it has been argued, a natural consequence of Ramus's logic so favored by the Puritans: none could know in advance how God would choose to work his effect in any particular case.[48] "The Lord is on our side," said a preacher at Paul's Cross in the year of the Armada; "but I beseech you to consider powder and shot for our great ordnance."[49] God "doth not always deliver his people by miracles," Oliver Cromwell's grandfather told the Huntingdonshire trained bands next year; "it behoveth us to reform ourselves."[50] The end of prayer and fasting, Richard Greenham told his congregation, is not "the neglect of the ordinary means, but the pulling away of our confidence in them; that we might rest in the only power and goodness of God."[51] Thomas Taylor perhaps expressed it most clearly: "Neglect of means ordained by God" is equivalent to presumption against God's power, leaving it to him to help us when we refuse to help ourselves. "For God, who hath not tied himself, hath tied us unto these [means], as these to his own ends." God can work his purpose a myriad ways, at any time: we have only the opportunities that offer themselves to us here and now. Those men sin

48. L. Howard, " 'The Invention' of Milton's 'Great Argument': A Study of the Logic of 'God's Ways to Man,' " *Huntington Library Quarterly*, IX (1946), 172.

49. M. Maclure, *The Paul's Cross Sermons* (Toronto University Press, 1958), p. 71.

50. W. M. Noble, *Huntingdonshire and the Spanish Armada* (1896), pp. 54–55.

51. R. Greenham, *Works* (1612), p. 212. Cf. John Preston, quoted in my *Puritanism and Revolution*, p. 265.

"that presume of his power to convert and save them, but reject and despise the means. It is a foolish presumption to say, God can preserve my life without meat and drink, and therefore I will not eat nor drink." [52] As an example of such foolish presumption and neglect of means we may cite the Scottish clergy, who in February 1649 were reported as proclaiming "that God is powerful enough of himself to punish the Independents, without requiring help from man." Perhaps Oliver and his regime erred in this way in the inadequacy of their preparations for the Western Design of 1655: "God has not brought us hither," Oliver told his council in July 1654, "but to consider the work that we may do in the world as well as at home."

Puritanism roused men from the passivity which, as Oliver shrewdly pointed out to Hammond, might be a cover for cowardice. "As if God should say, 'Up and be doing, and I will help you and stand by you,'" he wrote to the deputy lieutenants of Suffolk at the end of July 1643; "There is nothing to be feared but our own sin and sloth." Puritanism did not plunge men into fatalism. It taught courage, the victory of mind over matter, of reason over superstition: and trust in God was essential to this victory.

> Give me the man, that with a quaking arm
> Walks with a stedfast mind through greatest harm;
> And though his flesh doth tremble, makes it stand
> To execute what reason doth command. [53]

Wither's lines are entirely within the Puritan tradition. Freedom was action taken in conformity with the will of God.

On the other hand passivity, lack of personal initiative, might in some circumstances be evidence that a man or men was being used by God: that he was not self-seeking. [54] The Barebones Parliament was called by God (as well as by the Lord General) in consequence of "as wonderful providences as ever passed upon the sons of man in so short a time. . . . Neither directly nor indirectly did you seek to come hither." "I called not myself to this place," Oliver in his turn claimed of the Protectorate. "I should be false to the trust that

52. T. Taylor, *Works*, p. 101.
53. G. Wither, *Brittans Remembrancer* (Spencer Soc., 1880), I, 125. First published 1628.
54. See Hill, *God's Englishman*, pp. 137, 139, 143.

God hath placed upon me," he told his first Parliament, if he should consent to "the wilful throwing away of this government" which he had not sought. He would "sooner be willing to be rolled into my grave and buried with infamy." At the dissolution he added: if the cause "be of God, he will bear it up. If it be of man, it will tumble, as everything that hath been of man, since the world began, hath done." A major argument against accepting the crown in 1657 was that "at the best I should do it doubtingly. And certainly what is so done is not of faith," and consequently is "sin to him that doth it." [55]

In discussing the Puritan theory of providence, it is important to compare it with ideas and social attitudes prevalent before it, rather than with what came later. Puritanism overthrew the doctrine of passive obedience to divinely constituted authority. The Puritan theory appeals to human will power and to some degree to human reason; not to arbitrary divine intervention from outside. We are still dealing, we must always remember, with a pre-industrial age; an age when man's ability to control his environment was still undemonstrated, when only a Bacon dreamed that science might be "the instigator of man's domination of the universe," and thus "the conqueror of need"; when only a few like Bacon himself and George Hakewill were beginning to challenge the intellectual superiority of the ancient world, and the dogma of progressive cultural decay. In such an age confidence in man could be built up only slowly: activity on God's behalf was a necessary transitional concept between passivity in obedience to irresistible providence (tempered by magic) and activity for the relief of man's estate.

In this century man's age-old helplessness in the face of hostile nature was being broken down; ordinary men (as opposed to lords of serfs) could begin to envisage the possibility of controlling their environment, including their social environment. This is reflected in the growth of social contract theories, the new insistence on the rights of bourgeois communities.[56] Puritanism aided science by its

55. See my "Protestantism and the Rise of Capitalism," in *Essays in the Economic and Social History of Tudor and Stuart England, in Honour of R. H. Tawney,* pp. 15–39.
56. Cf. Perry Miller, *The New England Mind: the 17th Century* (New York, 1939), Chapter XIV.

abolition of mystery, its emphasis on law, its insistence on direct personal relationship to God and cooperation with him. For in order to cooperate with God's purposes one must first understand them: the more historical and scientific knowledge one possessed, the more capable one was of *active* cooperation. Science was for action, not contemplation: here Bacon, Hakewill, and Calvinist theologians were at one. The scientific approach to God's works in the universe was a way of getting to know him. The world glorifies God because of what it is: God himself pronounced it good. Hence the importance of studying it scientifically so as to read its lessons aright. But "Knowledge without practice is no knowledge," wrote the Puritan author of the marginal headings to Greenham's *Works*.[57] "The soul of religion is the practical part," Christian was still assuring Faithful a century later.[58]

The desire to grasp God's purposes drove the Puritan to science and to history; and the object of the new Ramean logic was described by a Puritan as being "to direct men to see the wisdom of God." These studies no less than divinity helped to build up that cosmic optimism and self-confidence which is the common faith of seventeenth-century Puritans and scientists. Their religion is of this world. A heavier emphasis on the consolations of the next world comes only after 1660, after the defeat of the radical Puritans.[59]

In this age of the accumulation of capital, then, little groups of men were very slowly pulling themselves up by their own bootstraps, intellectually and morally as well as economically. This is brought out very clearly in one of the Duchess of Newcastle's letters, in which she described a mock sermon preached at a Puritan service by an anti-Puritan. "There are some men," the pretended preacher is supposed to have said, "that believe they are or at least may be so pure in spirit by saving grace as to be sanctified, and to be so much filled with the Holy Ghost as to have spiritual visions, and ordinarily to have conversation with God, believing God to be a common companion to their idle imaginations. But this opinion proceeds from an extraordinary self-love, self-pride

57. R. Greenham, *Works*, p. 196; cf. p. 343.
58. Bunyan, *Works*, III, 122.
59. Perry Miller, *op. cit.*, pp. 160, 37–38; see also pp. 147–82 *passim*.

and self-ambition, as to believe they are the only fit companions for God himself and that not any of God's creatures are or were worthy to be favoured but they, much less to be made of God's privy council, as they believe they are—as to know his will and pleasure, his decrees and destinies, which indeed are not to be known, for the Creator is too mighty for a creature to comprehend him." [60] This is caricature, and our sympathies are with the caricaturist. Yet if there is any validity in the equation of God's purposes, in the Puritan's mind, with the historical process, then the last sentence is especially relevant, and provides food for thought.

The Duchess's preacher (like Hakewill's opponent, Bishop Goodman) is advocating the passivity, the acceptance of the *status quo,* which we know the Duke of Newcastle favored. The universe and its laws are incomprehensible: therefore neither scientific nor political action can change existing conditions. The "self-love, self-pride and self-ambition," unpleasant though they are, may have been the necessary price to pay for a Luther, destroying belief in magical religion, a Bacon, planning for the relief of man's estate, and a Cromwell, aspiring to carry out God's will on earth. We must set the theorists of passivity against their social background of economic stagnation, social inequality, and religious and political tyranny. Coleridge "could never read Bishop [Jeremy] Taylor's tract on *The Doctrine and Practice of Repentance* without being tempted to characterize High Calvinism as (comparatively) a lamb in wolf's skin, and strict Arminianism as approaching the reverse." [61]

The novelty lay in Puritanism's combination of a deep sense of God as law, of the universe as rational, with an equally deep sense of change, of God working through individuals to bring his purposes to perfection. "We do not imagine God to be lawless," Calvin had proclaimed. "He is a law to himself." [62] God's seeming arbitrariness (e.g., in his choice of the elect) is simply our

60. Margaret, Duchess of Newcastle, *CCXI Sociable Letters* (1664), p. 159. The great Puritan, John Preston, it was remarked by a bishop, "talked like one that was familiar with God Almighty" (T. Ball, *Life of the renowned Dr. Preston,* 1885, p. 159). Bunyan often wrote as though he enjoyed the confidence of God (e.g., *Works,* I, 524).
61. S. Coleridge, *The Friend* (1865), p. 289.
62. Calvin, *Institutes,* II, 227; cf. p. 577.

failure to comprehend. It is "from the feebleness of our intellect," Calvin explained, that "we cannot comprehend how, though after a different manner, he [God] wills and wills not the very same thing." [63] Part of God's covenant, Hakewill thought, is the orderly and perpetual working of the universe, the fact that "God alters no law of nature," as John Preston put it. Hakewill's (and Bacon's) starting point was human activity, man's endeavor to discover the world in order to change it.[64] This emphasis on the rationality and law-abidingness of the universe greatly expedited the long task of expelling magic from everyday life: miracles were driven back to the epoch of the primitive church. It prepared for the Newtonian conception of God the great watchmaker, and of a universe first set in motion by external compulsion but then going by its own momentum.

But Newton's conception, though it derives logically enough from Calvinism, is the static view of a post-revolutionary civilization. Hakewill's more agreeably active image is of "a great chessboard." [65] For the sixteenth-century Protestant and the early-seventeenth-century Puritan, liberty and necessity, predestination and free will, were still dialectically fused: and God is their point of union. In God "we see the highest contradictions reconciled," Bunyan believed.[66] God was needed to bring change into what would otherwise have been a static mechanical universe.[67] In the seventeenth century materialists were political conservatives: God was the principle of change. For the Puritan it was important to study history, no less than science, since it was the story of God in action. History, properly understood, was a rational process, revealing God's purposes. It had a meaning, and an ascertainable meaning. "Indeed there are [hi]stories that do . . . give you narratives of matters of fact," Cromwell told the Barebones Parlia-

63. *Ibid.*, I, 202; cf. pp. 187, 205, 254, 264. Cf. J. Owen, *Works*, XI, 140–204: *The Immutability of the Purposes of God.*
64. See my *Intellectual Origins of the English Revolution*, pp. 200, 268, 291; *Puritanism and Revolution*, p. 273.
65. G. Hakewill, *An Apologie or Declaration of the Power and Providence of God in the Government of the World* (3rd ed., 1635), Book V, p. 252.
66. Bunyan, *Works*, I, 431; cf. p. 434.
67. C. Caudwell, *The Crisis in Physics* (1949), *passim;* Perry Miller, *op. cit.*, pp. 227–31.

ment, but what mattered was "those things wherein the life and power of them lay; those strong windings and turnings of providence, those very great appearances of God in crossing and thwarting the purposes of men . . . by his using of the most improbable and the most contemptible and despicable means." There is no such thing as chance: what appears fortuitous to us does so only because we are ignorant of the grand design. The significance of this conception for the development of a more scientific approach to history needs no emphasis.[68]

The sense of sin, of guilt, is, I suppose, always especially intense in an age of economic and social revolution. Yet it may be true to suggest that it was more intense during our period than in any earlier or later crisis. This period sees the beginning of mankind's leap from the realm of magic to the realm of science. I am speaking now not of the advanced thinkers, but of the masses of the population. For them, throughout the Middle Ages and for countless centuries earlier, the real world had not been something external which men controlled: there was no subject-object relationship. One might influence external reality by magic (black or white, witchcraft or Catholicism), or one might fail to influence it; but there was no question of ordinary human beings understanding and mastering laws to which nature conformed. Traditional techniques and lore were learned by rote; but for ordinary men and women the goings-on of the universe were mysterious and undiscernible. When a natural catastrophe affected them, they had recourse to the intercession, by prayers and ceremonies, of the priest or the magician: the relationship was vicarious, secondhand. (Though in the sixteenth century the great magi, like Bruno or Dr. Faustus, hoped to attain a more direct and personal control.)

If we turn to the present day, the change is obvious. After two centuries of industrial civilization, most men and women accept the existence of scientific laws, even when they do not understand them. They expect uniformities: the surviving superstitions and magical practices are only semi-serious. How did mankind move from the one attitude to the other?

68. Cf. P. Miller and T. H. Johnson, *The Puritans* (New York, 1938), pp. 81–86, 362.

It moved, I believe, through Protestantism: through the direct relationship of the individual to God, the conception of God as law, order, and purpose, and of the duty of the individual to grasp and cooperate with these purposes. It was a terrible burden for the individual conscience to bear. Cut off from the social aids and supports of Catholicism (confession, absolution), as from the stable certainties of the medieval village, each individual had to make his own terms with the world and with God. We think of the Protestant bourgeois in the words of Tyndale's Bible which Professor Tawney made famous: "The Lord was with Joseph and he was a lucky fellow." [69] But it was very far from being as simple as that. Hundreds of Josephs were unlucky; but they had to wrestle on all through the night. Steady concentration, continuous trial and error, hopeless fighting in isolated corners—such was the lot of the protagonist of the new values as he slowly built up his certainties, and with them, accidentally, the scientific attitude. Things were always going wrong, but it was the duty of the godly to make them go right, to snatch impossible victory to the greater glory of God. It was *in defeat* that Milton set about justifying the ways of God to men. Both the sense of sin, and the feeling of justification, came, ultimately, from readiness to break with tradition, to obey the internal voice of God even when it revealed new tasks, suggested untraditional courses of action. Problems had to be solved within one's own conscience, in isolation from society. As the hymn puts it,

> Not the labours of my hands
> Can fulfil thy law's demands.

The metaphor is that of the small craftsman in his workshop, "for ever in my great Taskmaster's eye." It was impossible to fulfill the law, and yet one must continually strive for an elusive perfection, which from time to time suffuses one's whole being with a happiness and confidence more than human, and makes mere legal righteousness seem petty and irrelevant. Hence the tense effort, the self-confident elation when things were going well, the desperate feelings of guilt in defeat. (We recall Cromwell's early sense

69. R. II. Tawney, *Religion and the Rise of Capitalism* (Penguin ed.), p. 179.

of sin.) The nonconformist conscience as we know it today, the
deep sense of guilt, is the product of an epoch in which Joseph
has ceased to be a lucky fellow, and the Lord has ceased to inter-
vene on his behalf. For the world of scientific certainties has now
been built. The desperate search for God has ended by squeezing
him right out of the universe. And science is a collective activity:
knowledge is pooled. Man can again share his certainties with a
community, and he is now no longer passively at the mercy of a
hostile material and social environment: he can control them both,
within extensible limits. The individual need no longer bear the
sky on a single pair of shoulders. An approach to the world which
in our period produced a Luther, a Descartes, a Milton, a Bunyan,
today produces psychiatric cases.

God, then, is the principle of change, his will the justification of
action. Yet God works through individuals, and the success of a
virtuous human being is at once his victory and the victory of
divine grace working in him. The question whether one or other
of these, grace and the human will, may be the *causa causans* is
not one which would occur to the Puritan to ask. Joseph Caryl in
1643 preached before the Lord Mayor, aldermen, and City companies a sermon which the House of Commons ordered to be
printed. "When God makes a change in times," he told his auditors, "it becomes us to make a change also." [70] God makes the
change, and we cooperate: such is the historical process. In November 1640, Stephen Marshall had preached to the House of Commons on 2 Chronicles 15.2. "The Lord is with you while ye be with
him, and if ye seek him he will be found of you." They must be
up and doing if God is to continue to favor England.[71]

"God is beginning to stir in the world," Hanserd Knollys wrote
in 1641. "God uses the common people and the multitude to pro-
claim that the Lord God Omnipotent reigneth." "You that are of
meaner rank, common people, be not discouraged: for God intends
to make use of the common people in the great work of proclaiming the kingdom of his son." [72] That was to put the theory to

70. J. Caryl, *Davids Prayer for Solomon* (1643), p. 36.
71. E. Kirby, "Sermons before the Commons, 1640–2," in *American
Historical Review*, XLIV.
72. Woodhouse, *Puritanism and Liberty*, p. 234.

unorthodox uses, calling the lower classes into politics as God's agents: yet the theory is the same. God works through human agents: men cooperate with God, some consciously, some unconsciously ("will they, nill they," in Cromwell's words[73]). For those who consciously work with and for God, this is a two-way process. They, the elect, are free: the rest are God's pawns. God normally worked through kings, his lieutenants on earth, Thomas Scott wrote in 1623: but he might on exceptional occasions raise up a David to quicken Saul's zeal. "In the case of necessity, God himself dispenseth with his written law; because the law of nature, which he hath written in every man's heart, subjects him thereunto." Scott was going no further than to urge Prince Charles and Buckingham to oppose James I's foreign policy;[74] but twenty-six years later Milton used this traditional line of thought to answer those Royalists who argued that wicked kings should be left to God to punish. "Why may not the people's act of rejection be as well pleaded by the people as the act of God, and the most just reason to depose him?"[75]

God worked through men: human beings were the agents of God. Thus the cause was infinitely greater than the man, and criticism of the failings of individuals was beside the point. Cromwell wrote to Wharton, on January 1, 1650: "I do not condemn your reasonings; I doubt them. It's easy to object to the glorious actings of God, if we look too much upon instruments. I have had computation made of the members in Parliament—good kept out, most bad remaining; it has been so these nine years, yet what has God wrought! The greatest works last, and still is at work. . . . How hard a thing is it to reason ourselves up to the Lord's service, though it be so honourable, how easy to put ourselves out

73. See p. 203.
74. T. Scott, *Vox Dei* (1623), p. 16.
75. Milton, *The Tenure of Kings and Magistrates* (1649), in *Complete Prose Works* (Yale), III, 211. Milton refers to the orthodox Calvinist theory of the concurrence of first and second causes in the social contract, thus expressed by John Davenport: "In regular actings of the creature, God is the first agent; there are not two several and distinct actings, one of God, another of the people: but in one and the same action God, by the people's suffrages, makes such an one governor or magistrate, and not another" (J. Davenport, *A Sermon*, 1669, in *Publications of the Colonial Soc. of Massachusetts*, X, 6).

of it, when the flesh has so many advantages!" Three years later
Oliver himself made computations of members of Parliament, for
then God spoke with a different voice. But in either case, confidence in the Cause enabled him to transcend mere human reasonings. Such reasonings, where God is concerned, may miss the main
point.

A natural tendency of the theory of the cooperation of the elect
with God was to claim that worldly success was in itself evidence
of divine approbation. There is, of course, nothing specifically
Puritan in this attitude of mind. The doctrine that might is right
is at least as old as ordeal by battle, and corresponds to a primitive view of society in which each tribe has its own God. The
faithful reflection of such a stage of society in the Old Testament
helped to perpetuate the attitude of mind, and to justify the more
sophisticated version of the theory which the Puritans evolved.

The outbreak of actual fighting in the Civil War naturally
gave a great fillip to the argument from success. "Where is your
Roundheads' God now?" asked a triumphant Royalist in 1644.
"Hath he forsaken you Roundheads of Bolton now? Sure he is
turned Cavalier." [76] But soon the God of Battles revealed himself
consistently on the side of the New Model Army. After the second
Civil War, Cromwell explained to the Speaker the exception of
Poyer, Laugharne, and Powell from mercy in the terms for the
surrender of Pembroke on the ground that "they have sinned
against so much light, and against so many evidences of Divine
Providence going along with and prospering a righteous cause,
in the management of which themselves had a share." The fact of
military victories, "continued seven or eight years together" allowed a pamphleteer of 1648 to argue that: "In such cases successes
are to be looked upon as clear evidence of the truth, righteousness
and equity of our cause." [77] When the army decided to march on
London at the end of November in the same year, its generals

76. Ed. G. Ormerod, *Tracts relating to Military Proceedings in Lancashire during the Great Civil War* (Chetham Soc., II, 1849), p. 193. I
owe this reference to my former pupil, R. Allan.
77. (Anon.), *Salus Populi Solus Rex* (October 17, 1648), quoted by
Brailsford, *The Levellers and the English Revolution,* p. 346.

declared: "We are now drawing up with the Army to London, there to follow providence as God shall clear our way." [78] God cleared their way to the execution of the King, "a path," Milton thought, "not dark but bright, and by his guidance shown and opened to us." The justice of the sentence on Charles was confirmed by "the powerful and miraculous might of God's manifest arm." "The hand of God appeared so evidently on our side" that the disapproval of man was, for the poet, irrelevant. The ability to wield "the sword of God" came from heaven. If asked how he knew this, Milton replied that, on this occasion at least, the exceptional quality of the successful event carried its own stamp of divine approval. "Justice and victory," he added, are "the only warrants through all ages, next under immediate revelation, to exercise supreme power." [79]

I have already quoted many of Cromwell's references to "the providences of God in that which is falsely called the chances of war." [80] "How dangerous a thing it is . . . to appeal to God the righteous judge," he told the Scots in September 1648. "You have appealed to the judgment of heaven," he told the Dutch ambassadors in June 1653. "The Lord has declared against you." And in 1655, speaking to his first Parliament, Oliver generalized. "What are all our histories and other traditions of nations in former times but God manifesting himself that he hath shaken and tumbled down and trampled upon everything that he hath not planted? . . . Let men take heed and be twice advised, how they call his revolutions, the things of God and his working of things from one period to another, how, I say, they call them necessities of men's creations." Oliver had no doubts when he dissolved his last Parliament with the words: "Let God judge between you and me."

The argument from success proved convincing, or convenient, for many Royalists and Presbyterians when it came to accepting the Commonwealth. The plea that *de facto* power *ought* to be

78. Woodhouse, *Puritanism and Liberty*, p. 467.
79. Milton, *Complete Prose Works* (Yale), III, 191. The self-validating quality of remarkable events was of course a familiar argument to demonstrate the historical accuracy of the Bible.
80. See Hill, *God's Englishman*, pp. 137–38.

obeyed was used on behalf of the Commonwealth by Anthony
Ascham, John Dury, John Wilkins, and Marchamont Needham.
The success of the new regime helped to persuade Hobbes to
return to England from exile, even if he did not regard the
victories of the Parliamentary armies as providential. He claimed
that his *Leviathan* helped to persuade Royalists to submit to the
Protectorate.[81]

If success justified, did failure condemn? Richard Cromwell
decided in May 1659, logically, to acquiesce in "the late providences that have fallen out among us," and not to resist his overthrow.[82] The Restoration was, in Burnet's words, "an instance
much more extraordinary than any of those were upon which
they had built so much." [83] "The Lord had . . . spit in their faces,"
complained Fleetwood in December 1659. The Restoration forced
Puritans to rethink their whole position. Had they been wrong
in believing their cause to be the Lord's? Or had they pursued it
by the wrong means? The Scot Johnston of Warriston confided
to his *Diary* in January 1660: "And whereas I thought I was following the call of God's providence [in cooperating with Crom-
well] . . . the truth is I followed the call of providence when it
agreed with my humour . . . and seemed to tend to honour and
advantage; but if that same providence had called me to quit my
better places and take me to meaner places or none at all, I had
not so hastily and contentedly followed it." [84] Not all were as
honest as Warriston, who was to be executed three years after
writing those lines. Some, happy in the occasion of their death,
were able to preserve their faith because they did not realize the
completeness of their failure. Thus Major General Harrison,
taunted before his execution by "one telling him that he did not

81. T. Hobbes, *English Works,* ed. Sir W. Molesworth (1839–45), VII, 336.
82. D. Masson, *Life of John Milton,* V (1877), 450–51.
83. Burnet, *The Life and Death of Sir Matthew Hale* (1774), p. 26. It is perhaps worth recording that Burnet nevertheless still regarded it as "the safest rule for the conduct of one's life," which he "ever endeavoured to follow, . . . that from first to last it seemed to be carried on by a series of providences" (ed. H. C. Foxcroft, *A Supplement to Burnet's History of My Own Time,* [1902], p. 89).
84. *Diary of Sir Archibald Johnston of Warriston* (Scottish History Soc.), III, 167.

know how to understand the mind of God in such a dispensation as this," could still reply, "Wait upon the Lord, for you know not what the Lord is leading to, and what the end of the Lord will be." "Though we may suffer hard things," he proclaimed from the scaffold, "yet he hath a gracious end, and will make for his own glory and the good end of his people." [85]

But as the years rolled by it became clear that God's end was not that which the radicals had taken it to be. The problem of justifying the ways of God to men obsessed the more serious-minded among the Puritans. Most took the line of concluding that Christ's kingdom was not of this world, of accepting the Nonconformists' exclusion from politics, and turned their attention to business and quietist religion. In *Pilgrim's Progress* it was Mr. By-ends and Mr. Money-love who preached that worldly success justified.[86] In 1655 Milton had written on behalf of the people of England: "A cause is neither proved good by success, nor shown to be evil. We insist, not that our cause be judged by the outcome, but that the outcome be judged by the cause." [87] Nevertheless, the collapse of all his hopes, the rejection of all his sacrifices, forced him to wrestle with God as perhaps no man had wrestled before. The fruits of this anguish were *Paradise Lost, Paradise Regained,* and *Samson Agonistes.* But even in *Samson Agonistes,* Milton could envisage victory for his cause only by a divine miracle of destruction, something like that with which the Fifth Monarchists had consoled themselves after the defeat of the Levellers and Diggers in 1647–49.

The post-Restoration passivity of most Nonconformists was matched by a unanimity in deploring revolution, to which the ex-revolutionaries contributed loudly. Thus the historian of the Royal Society, eight years after his eulogistic poem upon the death of Oliver Cromwell, wrote that: "this wild amazing men's minds with prodigies and conceits of providences has been one of the most considerable causes of those spiritual distractions of which our country has long been the theatre." [88] In 1685 Sprat used the

85. *A Complete Collection of the Lives and Speeches of those persons lately executed,* pp. 6, 10.
86. Bunyan, *Works,* III, 134–35.
87. Milton, *Complete Prose Works* (Yale), IV, 652.
88. Sprat, *The History of the Royal Society of London,* p. 362.

providential argument on behalf of James II against the defeated
Whigs; after 1688 Ascham's "whatever is, is divine" was employed
to defend the new *de facto* regime of William III.[89] What had
been a revolutionary theory was transformed into a banal conservatism.

We can see perhaps a more significant outcome of the Restoration in theories of history. Charles II's return in 1660, so totally
unexpected until a few months before it actually happened, suggested once more the workings of an inscrutable providence,
bringing about results which no man had willed. Clarendon, one
of the few faithful old Cavaliers who had willed it, did more than
anyone to propagate this mystifying view, from which he no
doubt thought the monarchy would benefit. This could be part
of the explanation of the eclipse for a century of the dangerous
aspect of Harrington's theory of history, that changes in the
balance of property must lead to political change unless legislative action not in conflict with economic tendencies modified this
determinism. The aspect of Harringtonianism which was orthodox for the later seventeenth and eighteenth centuries was the
static conviction that property must rule. After 1688 property
became the *deus ex machina* inscrutably and ineluctably achieving its ends, whatever unpropertied men might will. Divine providence yielded place to the iron laws, not to be challenged until the
revival of political radicalism in the later eighteenth century.
God, who had been so close to Oliver Cromwell, withdrew into
the vast recesses of Newtonian space.

89. Sprat, *A True Account and Declaration of the Horrid Conspiracy
against the Late King* (2nd ed., 1685), p. 159; G. Straka, "The Final
Phase of Divine Right Theory in England, 1688–1702," *English Historical
Review*, LXXVII, 638–58.

D. H. PENNINGTON

Cromwell and the Historians

FEW CHARACTERS in British history are better known than Oliver Cromwell; and the verdict of the ordinary man today is not far different from that of most of the writers who have chosen their evidence and pronounced their judgments over the last three centuries. It is not true that Cromwell was universally reviled until Carlyle made a hero of him, nor that after this he was unanimously saluted as a founder of liberalism and nonconformity. The tendency of most of the many preconceptions from which the subject is approached is to end in a rather insipid mixture of approval and condemnation.

For contemporaries, of course, it was different. The opinions that got into print before the Restoration could seldom fail to be either black or white. Black won, even then. A few panegyrics (*The*

221

Portraiture of a Matchless Prince; Veni, vidi, vici) appeared; Milton produced verse and prose in his support, and Marchamont Needham some first-rate journalism. But the initiative was overwhelmingly on the side of the opposition. Denunciations of the murderer and the "Tyranipocrit," satires, comic allegories, evidently sold well, in spite of attempts at suppression; and the "vindications" that answer them are not likely to have aroused much enthusiasm. Narratives of traitorous and bloody plots against His Highness, from whatever source, had an excellent market. *Killing No Murder,* with its irresistible opening dedication to the intended victim, came out when assassination was already a favorite topic. It was all much more exciting than accounts of Oliver's imitation coronation.

But the Protector died in bed, of a "tertian ague." Few dogs barked at that; and the political atmosphere of the year that followed was not particularly favorable for the singing of his praises. Dryden, Marvell, and Edmund Waller, with some less respectable poets, soon had verses of a sort in circulation, and the journalists did their best for the funeral ceremonies. They had not much time for reprints. The Restoration brought the inevitable boom in vituperation: *Cromwell's Bloody Slaughterhouse*; *The English Devil*; *Hell's Higher Court of Justice*. A favorite theme, constantly plagiarized, was the discussions among the regicides in hell. More substantially, Walker's *History of Independency* and the abundant works of Prynne provided a mixture of wit and fact with which to lash the whole Cromwellian party.

In the popular market, the picture of Cromwell as the devil held its own for the next fifty years. The joys of reading of wickedness, for which the churches already catered well and to which Milton was now applying himself in a large way, were perhaps all the better for being up to date. James Heath's *Flagellum,* which Carlyle calls the "chief fountain of lies about Cromwell," achieved six editions under Charles II. A slightly less extravagant attack, *The Perfect Politician,* was aghast at the ambition and success as much as at the wickedness. The French reveled in it too. *La Tyrannie Heureuse* made his designs of usurpation begin in the 1630s, and as for religion *"il n'en eut jamais."* Some sort of miraculous portents were naturally desirable for mass consumption. The storm that heralded the Protector's passing was not much to work on.

His birth was occasionally made to coincide with the death of Elizabeth, or—another rather niggardly omen—with a fire at the Town Hall at Huntingdon. At the age of three—not having a bear to kill—he began to tear up pictures of Prince Charles, then aged two.

If the crude picture of the fiend incarnate remained the most general, it is surprising how soon and how widely it was modified or questioned. A concession often made by even the most irresponsible vituperators was that the Protectorate had made England respected abroad. When there was war with the Dutch again, Pepys remarked that "everybody do nowadays reflect upon Oliver and commend him." Baker's *Chronicle* in 1674, though it accepts the notion of a deep-laid design and hypocrisy, sets against it "generosity, courage, and resolution," and praises the discipline of the army as well as the "great renown" accruing to the nation.

At this stage, serious evidence about the man himself was not easy to obtain, even for those who wanted it. It was not until the end of the seventeenth century that the more cultured reader began to have access to reliable historical detail. Rushworth's *Collections* provided massive material for the political history of the war period that gave no support to extravagant Royalist views. Nalson's *State Papers,* equally impartial in the other direction, were only published as far as 1641. Well-founded histories of the Protectorate were hardly possible until Thurloe's correspondence appeared in 1742. By then several of the best eyewitnesses were in print to set beside the paper relics. Ludlow saw Cromwell only as the schemer who "sacrificed the public cause to the idol of his ambition." He "vehemently desired to be rid of Parliament" and to ascend the throne. Baxter, though bitterly critical of the army and the Independents, was determined to be just to Cromwell: "Never man was highlier extolled, and never man baselier reported of and vilified." His own conclusion is that "having been a prodigal youth and afterward changed to a zealous religiousness, he meant honestly in the main." But "general religious zeal gave way to the power of ambition." The one outstanding contemporary historian gave him no credit at all for religious zeal: "Though the greatest dissembler living, he always made his hypocrisy of singular use and benefit to him." The seeking of the Lord clearly nauseated Clarendon; the statesmanship evoked his repeated tributes, even though its ends had to be condemned. "Wickedness as great as his could never have accomplished those designs without the assistance of a great spirit, an admirable circumspection and sagacity, and a most magnanimous resolution." The awe in which Europe stood of England is described in highly exaggerated terms, and behind the denunciations there is constant shrewd appraisal of Cromwell's dilemmas and solutions. The master craftsman recognizes his equal.

By the end of the century, with Cromwell's opinion of the Stuarts to some extent vindicated, the standard formula of authors whose readers were deemed to be gentle, scholarly, and rational was to stress their superior impartiality compared with the prejudice of others. ("Some commending, some condemning him, both out of measure," says Burnet.) Nathaniel Crouch, alias Burton, advertised his policy of leaving every man to his own opinion. The biography by Kimber, himself a Nonconformist, after professing neither to lessen the bad nor to multiply the good deeds, in fact becomes a careful apologia. Ireton and the Levellers are blamed for the execution; Drogheda is excused, as later and more thorough massacres sometimes are, by the plea that in the long run it "saved much effusion of blood." There is no guilty admiration for successful villainy: he was "an enemy to vice and a lover of virtue." European readers were less eager for impartiality. Gregorio Leti, who became at first or second hand their chief authority, made him utterly and coldly devoted to tyranny, and to the destruction of everything that did not serve his ambition. He "refused a crown of gold to wear one of steel." English readers who wanted abuse could still find it, from both Whig and Tory writers. Lawrence Echard's standard history (1707) turns on full volume to create a Cromwell "lashed by his guilty conscience," and warms up the most scurrilous of the old titbits. Oldmixon, the enemy of both Echard and Clarendon (or his editors), was the center of an angry literary controversy about their inaccuracies and injustice to the Parliamentarians, but had nothing to say in favor of the Protector.

Not everyone now agreed that Cromwell was a particularly outstanding figure. Heath, having exhausted his invective, dismissed the events of the Protectorate in *England's Chronicle* as "too tedious to be inserted." Hume almost suggests that anyone could have done the same as Cromwell: once he had command of the army the rest was easy, and for the glorious foreign policy there is little but complaints. The seizure of power was "the effect of necessity as well as ambition." It is not clear how much reading Dr. Johnson had done before reaching the decision that "all that can be told of him is already in print." Historians have remained blind to this fact.

The American and French revolutions inevitably revived interest in the large issues, after a period when the minutiae and curiosities of Civil War history had been more in vogue. The "brave bad man" was now the "immortal rebel," arousing again closely allied feelings of admiration and horror. Alternatively, Charles Ashburton, in a work "carefully pruned of the errors of preceding historians," made the ingenious point that it was not Charles II but a republic that Cromwell deprived of power. "Of what therefore do the Royalist authors complain?" While the name of Cromwell was being used as a term of abuse against successive republican politicians, Napoleon Bonaparte copied down the observation that republicanism had yielded to the "devouring flame of his ambition." Thirty years later, labored comparisons between Cromwell and Napoleon were a favorite exercise for writers from Hallam down to the penny pamphleteers. It was from France that there came the first major work on Cromwell with a nineteenth-century background of faith in progress and liberty. Guizot, writing in 1826, claimed that neither the English Revolution nor the French originated anything, but only gave the nation "leaders who could direct it in its progress."

Meanwhile in England the obsession with revolution and republics had faded; and it was now possible to bring forward a Cromwell who had appeared only hesitantly before, and then among the bad rather than the good—the middle-class Protector. His family background had from the beginning been an obvious mine for the pamphleteers to dig in. Cromwell, they found, had been a brewer (a story firmly repeated by H. T. Buckle in 1857). The tones in which his social position was described by successive generations are in many ways more revealing than the ponderous assessments of his character. Clarendon described it as "private and obscure birth (though of good family)" and, with his usual penetration, noted the absence of "interest or estate, alliance or friendship" that would account for his rise. Sir Philip Warwick raised an eyebrow at the "plain cloth suit made by an ill country tailor" in which he appeared at Westminster; and, for eighteenth-century devotees of Polite Learning, Goldsmith introduced him as "an obscure and vulgar man." Very slowly the sentiment grew that this was a point on the credit side. William Harris's biography (1762)—a work that may well still hold the record for proportion of footnote to text—carries the "brewer" story, but stresses that "trade is no disgrace to a gentleman."

In a variety of ways the nineteenth century saw in him, as Macaulay put it, "the best qualities of the middling orders." And on the whole, the further down their ranks the historian addressed himself, the more he preached appropriate morals. Edmund Clarke, lecturing to members of the Manchester Mechanics' Institution in 1847, saw the period as "the first great effort of the middle classes of England in the assertion and vindication of their rights." Cromwell, though entirely free from the "revolutionary spirit," was a model of manly independence. If he dealt severely with the Irish, it had to be remembered that the Irish were almost as bad in the seventeenth century as in the nineteenth. And—as several of his earlier supporters had mentioned—he was the godfearing father of dutiful and affectionate children, very kind to his old mother, and sent into a decline by the death of his daughter.

The demand for Mr. Clarke's lectures had no doubt been stimulated, like many more, by the appearance two years earlier of Carlyle's edition of the *Letters and Speeches*. Carlyle's achievement was not any sudden reversal of an accepted view: it was to make Cromwell exciting again, but exciting as a man and part of a superman, not as a monster. In W. C. Abbott's words: "He danced and sang and shouted till the world came to see." [1] And behind the editorial asides, insertions, and amendments the Victorians saw Cromwell at first hand. No effort was needed to respond to his story: Carlyle did all the responding for them. He gave them the Englishman's ideal hero, one who can in quick succession be re-

---

1. Abbott's essay in *Conflicts with Oblivion* (1924) is the best short survey of the historians of Cromwell. His *Bibliography of Oliver Cromwell*, listing 3,500 items including over a hundred biographies, appeared in 1929.

vered, rebuked, and smiled at for his funny little ways. The work was reprinted in a score of editions, and began to be "edited" itself. But most of the "middling orders" knew it only indirectly through the heavy gilt-lettered volumes of knowledge that made their bookcases respectable.

They could still take their choice of sides. The subscribers to Cassell's *Illustrated History of England,* though discouraged from reading Carlyle, would learn that Cromwell was before his age, and became a "dictator" to establish a free and tolerant government; but those who joined Mrs. Valentine for *Half-Hours with English History* were back in the days of the tyrant giving up his guilty soul. *The Royal History of England* "embellished with engravings"—the first of which depicted the Queen in her most forbidding posture—also warned its readers against the fashion with "some writers" of praising Cromwell too highly. "His example is one which cannot be held up for unqualified approval." Presumably it would do them no harm to reflect on the pre-Raphaelite Cromwell of Ford Madox Brown, riding, Bible in hand, across his estate and observing an indeterminately symbolic bonfire.

Besides improving the adult mind, history now had to be mass-produced for the young; and it was hard to establish a uniform moral view of the Protectorate. The readers of Dickens' *Child's History of England* (1854) were left to discover for themselves the "real merits of Oliver Cromwell" by comparing England under him with England under Charles II—"than which were never more profligate times." Louisa Anthony's *Footsteps to History* (1852) consisted of an outline of each reign followed by a list of the "improvements" in it. Those under Cromwell were the beginning of banking and the Quakers. Edward Baldwin asked a less dangerous question than Dickens—"Which was the greater man, Cromwell or Milton?" The modern schoolboy, as far as he is expected to notice Cromwell at all, does not do so for his virtues or vices. He was, says one widely used book, "not a clear thinker but a practical man."

It is easy to make fun of the Victorians; but one of them remains the principal guide on whom the hordes of modern biographers rely. Gardiner's even flow of authoritative narration soothes one into the impression, if not that there is no more to say, at least that

there is little more to discover. His great work never reached the
end of the Protectorate; but his attitude to Cromwell was well
defined:

"The hesitations, the long postponements of action, are no less
characteristic than the swift, decisive hammer-strokes." The incon-
gruities are the essential thing: "every one of the interpreters has
something on which to base his conclusions." And it is the union
of apparently contradictory forces that made England what she is.
But Gardiner, contrary to the impression he sometimes gives, did
not ignore the failure of Cromwell's policies to survive him: if
anything he exaggerated it. And in a ponderous but salutary sentence, he remarked that individual policies do fail unless they are
"in accordance with the permanent tendencies of that portion of
the world affected by them." Why then was Cromwell "the greatest Englishman of all time"? Because, says Gardiner, he was "the
most typical." It is a sadly fatuous—and quotable—conclusion.

By Gardiner's time the approval of Cromwell's place in the triumph of middle-class virtues in a middle-class state was easily winning against condemnation of the rebel and tyrant. Theodore Roo-
sevelt's biography stated bluntly that it was the English upper
classes who spoke of him with horror, and claimed for America
the credit of following his constitutional ideas. But already a very
different kind of attack was beginning. Radicals throughout the
century had not failed to notice that whatever the Civil War had
achieved for the kind of men who sat in Parliament, "for the millions it did nothing." Marx himself proved disappointingly unen-
lightening about the place of the Protector in a predestined English history; but, by the time of the First World War, historians
and politicians were establishing the interest in the left-wing movements of the seventeenth century that has flourished ever since. In
this context Cromwell the "exploiting bourgeois" had to be seen,
not only as the enemy of Charles and "feudalism," but also as the
betrayer of the cause of Lilburne and Rainsborough. The Levellers,
however, could not do more than mark the point from which the
Revolution would have to retreat; and Cromwell's place at the
head of the victorious army led him straight to his new role in the
attempt to establish a bourgeois state with a King, or Protector, as
a "salaried servant." The Marxist interpretations have not so far

won widespread acceptance, even when watered down. But they have been the greatest single influence in changing the whole prevalent attitude of the academic historian. We are less concerned with the "character" of Cromwell than with defining the class he represented and its place in the structure of society—not with his personal motives, still less his morality, but with the conditions that brought such a man to such a career. In place of the hypocrite or the saint, the upstart murderer or liberal minister, is the epitome of the coldly analyzed "declining gentry."

But the fact remains that history cannot help being concerned with people, and that people as individuals are interesting, to writers as well as readers. So biographies of Cromwell multiply more prolifically than ever; and it is impossible to take more than random dips into the twentieth-century pile. Firth, the unchallenged heir to Gardiner, rejoiced in the military genius of Cromwell, and made the claim, which everyone now repeats, that Carlyle's evidence had dispelled all suspicion of hypocrisy. A generation later the popular biography by John Buchan summed him up as "the great improviser," "desperately trying expedient after expedient and finding every tool cracking in his hand." In the 1930s he acquired a new relevance: tentative parallels with Hitler and Mussolini were drawn, which turned out to flatter the modern dictators outrageously. The Second World War offered a better subject for comparison—and contrast—nearer home. Sir Winston Churchill, undoubtedly as good a Royalist as Parliamentarian, has some evident fellow feeling for Oliver, as Clarendon had in his time. The "reluctant and apologetic dictator" was "ever ready to share his power with others—provided, of course, that they agreed with him." The savage crimes, the misgivings in his "smoky soul," are duly assessed. But in the end "the repulsive features fade from the picture" and we see his passion for England, his respect for private property, his "place in the forward march of liberal ideas."

The biographers will, of course, continue to find what they look for. The last book before the tercentenary competition pulled heavily in the direction of religion, and credited Cromwell with showing the way ahead with a "practical experiment in a federal conception of the Catholic church." (J. R. Green, eighty years ago, was happier to find science and rationalism "spring into vivid life in their protest against the forced concentration of human thought on the single topic of religion.") But are we making any progress in the understanding of Cromwell—or any other historical character? Ever since the birth of scientific psychology, the historian who ignores it is inescapably naïve and unrealistic; and the historian who tries to talk its language is a glib and ignorant trespasser in a field that his colleagues may regard as a disreputable place. Was Cromwell a hypocrite? We cannot say because the word has lost all meaning. Perhaps by the fourth centenary a thoroughly established study of the mind will be firmly linked with the study of the past, and a shatteringly new biography will appear.

Bibliographical Note

W. C. ABBOTT, who edited *The Writings and Speeches of Oliver Cromwell* in four volumes (Cambridge, Mass., 1937–47), also compiled in 1929 a substantial *Bibliography of Oliver Cromwell* (Cambridge, Mass.). It may be supplemented by P. H. Hardacre's "Writings on Oliver Cromwell since 1929" in *Journal of Modern History*, XXXIII (Chicago, 1961), and, more generally, by G. Davies, *Bibliography of British History: Stuart Period 1603–1714* (Oxford, 1928; 2nd ed. by M. F. Keeler, 1970). The fullest narrative of Oliver's times is still S. R. Gardiner's monumental *History of England 1603–42*, 2nd ed., 10 vols. (London, 1883–4), and his *History of the Great Civil War 1642–9*, rev. ed., 4 vols. (London, 1893), continued in his *History of the Commonwealth and Protectorate 1649–56*, rev. ed., 4 vols. (London, 1903). C. H. Firth in *The Last Years of the Protectorate, 1656–58*, 2 vols. (London, 1909) and

G. Davies in *The Restoration of Charles II 1658–60* (San Marino and London, 1955) complete the work on the same scale. C. V. Wedgwood's *The King's Peace 1637–41* and *The King's War 1641–47* (London, 1955 and 1958 respectively) are the first volumes of a projected history of "The Great Rebellion." The Interregnum is also considered by I. Roots under the title *The Great Rebellion 1642–60* (London, 1966; 3 ed., 1972; published in the United States as *The Commonwealth and Protectorate,* New York, 1966), a study stressing the importance of the 1650's and attempting to place the Protectorate in the context of the conflicts—chiefly constitutional and political—of the period. Some indication of aspects of the period that attract the attention of specialists can be gotten from E. W. Ives, ed., *The English Revolution* (London, 1968); C. Russell, ed., *The Origins of the English Civil War* (London, 1973); R. H. Parry, ed., *The English Civil War and After* (London, 1970); G. E. Aylmer, ed., *The Interregnum: The Quest for Settlement 1646–1660* (London, 1972); and C. Hill, *Puritanism and Revolution* (London, 1958). *The Late Troubles in England* (Exeter, 1969) is a lecture by I. Roots which runs through some current interpretations of Oliver's times. Cromwell's role is intelligently assessed in D. Underdown's brilliant analysis of "the politics of the Puritan Revolution" entitled *Pride's Purge* (Oxford, 1971). Underdown's *Royalist Conspiracy in England 1649–1660* (New Haven, 1960) contains much that is relevant. Cromwell also figures prominently in C. V. Wedgwood, *The Trial of Charles I* (London, 1964; New York edition, 1964, *A Coffin for King Charles*).

There are numerous biographies of Oliver Cromwell; none is entirely satisfactory. The fullest is provided in the massive commentary by W. C. Abbott to his *The Writings and Speeches of Oliver Cromwell* (mentioned above), which has more or less superseded Thomas Carlyle's idiosyncratic *Oliver Cromwell's Letters and Speeches, with elucidations,* 2 vols. (London, 1845; best edition C. S. Lomas, 3 vols., 1904). Of briefer lives, perhaps the most balanced is that of C. H. Firth, *Oliver Cromwell and the Rule of the Puritans in England* (London and New York, 1900, frequently reprinted). M. P. Ashley has published three biographies, of which the best is *The Greatness of Oliver Cromwell* (London, 1957), but his earlier *Oliver Cromwell, the Conservative*

Dictator (London, 1937), though very much a product of its age, is suggestive. Ashley's *Oliver Cromwell and His World* (London, 1972) is notable for its illustrations. J. Buchan's temperate *Oliver Cromwell* (London, 1934) has been deservedly popular. *The Lord Protector* by R. S. Paul (London, 1955) concentrates on "religion and politics," while *Oliver Cromwell* by Brigadier Peter Young (London, 1962) understandably is more concerned with military matters. It is royalist in tone. The most recent popular biography of Cromwell, a long one, by Lady Antonia Fraser, appeared in London in 1973. R. W. Ramsey, besides his *Studies in Cromwell's Family Circle* (London and New York, 1930), wrote lives of *Richard Cromwell, Protector of England* (London, 1935), of *Henry Cromwell* (London, 1933), and of Oliver's able son-in-law *Henry Ireton* (London, 1949).

There are some—but not enough—lives of men closely associated with Cromwell at various times. M. P. Ashley's *Cromwell's Generals* (London, 1954) considers briefly, among others, Lambert, Fleetwood, and Desborough. On Lambert there is W. H. Dawson's rather flat *Cromwell's Understudy* (London, 1938). M. A. Gibb's *The Lord General* (London, 1938) tackles Fairfax, and J. Berry and S. G. Lee assess "the career of Colonel James Berry" under the title *A Cromwellian Major-General* (Oxford, 1938). There has been no biography of Major General Harrison since C. H. Simpkinson's brief but scholarly *Thomas Harrison, Regicide and Major-General* (London, 1905). Modern lives of value of such men as Nathaniel Fiennes, Edmund Ludlow, George Monck and Bulstrode Whitelocke are lacking, nor is there anything like a definitive biography of Charles I. *Sir Henry Vane the Younger* by V. Rowe (London, 1970) is a thoughtful but patchy "study in political and administrative history." There are two evocative evaluations of another remarkable man with whom Oliver pursued a "love-hate" relationship: John Lilburne. One by M. A. Gibb sees him as "a Christian democrat" (*John Lilburne the Leveller*, London, 1947); the other, by P. Gregg (*Freeborn John*, London, 1961), is equally scholarly and appreciative. Cromwell's relations with the Levellers can also be followed in H. N. Brailsford, *The Levellers and the English Revolution,* ed. C. Hill (London and Stanford, 1961) and in A. S. P. Woodhouse, *Puri-*

tanism and Liberty (London, 1938), which prints *inter alia* the text of "the Putney Debates," at which Cromwell was an able chairman.

There are numerous works in which the religious aspects of Cromwell's era can be traced. Among the best, happily as intelligent as they are argumentative, are M. Waltzer, *The Revolution of the Saints* (London and Cambridge, Mass., 1965); W. M. Lamont's *Godly Rule, Politics and Religion, 1603–1660* (London, 1969); and B. S. Capp, *The Fifth Monarchy Men* (London, 1972). Another of Cromwell's interests—law reform—is pursued in S. Prall, *The Agitation for Law Reform during the Puritan Revolution* (The Hague, 1966) and D. Veal, *The Popular Agitation for Law Reform, 1640–1660* (Oxford, 1970). D. Wormuth, *The Origins of Modern Constitutionalism* (New York, 1949) is helpful on "the Cromwellian constitutions." But the list is endless. Almost any serious work on the early seventeenth century, particularly in the years 1640–58, must refer directly or indirectly to Oliver Cromwell. Though frequently elusive as the lineaments of this Profile suggest, he remains always essential.

Contributors

Sir Ernest Barker (1874–1960) was a prolific writer and something of a polymath. He taught history, classics, and political science at Oxford (where he took a "triple first"), London, and Cambridge. A tireless tutor, he was a stanch advocate of interdisciplinary studies. The high value he placed upon "character" is revealed in his *Traditions of Civility* (1948), in the symposium he edited on *The Character of England* (1947), and in his autobiography—that of a European liberal—*Age and Youth* (1953).

John Roger Crabtree was Domus Scholar in Modern History at Balliol College from 1960 to 1965 and has since worked at the University of East Anglia on Cromwell's foreign policy. The essay printed in this Profile won a prize awarded by the Cromwell Association.

PAUL HOSWELL HARDACRE studied at Stanford and has taught history at Vanderbilt University since 1947. He has held Fulbright and Guggenheim fellowships. His "Writings on Oliver Cromwell since 1929" was included in *Changing Views on British History* (1966). With a former pupil, Professor P. J. Pinckney, he has compiled a valuable index of speakers in the debates reported in *The Parliamentary Diary of Thomas Burton* (ed. J. T. Rutt, 4 vols., 1828).

GEORGE D. HEATH III studied history and law at the University of Virginia and at Harvard. He has taught English history at Lafayette College since 1952. In 1960–1 he was visiting lecturer at University College, Cardiff. His prime interest is in the constitutional experiments of the Interregnum, and he has contributed an article, "Making the Instrument of Government," to the *Journal of British Studies,* Vol. 5 (1967).

JOHN EDWARD CHRISTOPHER HILL has been successively Scholar, Fellow, and (since 1965) Master of Balliol. He is particularly interested in radical and popular movements during the English Revolution. Among his numerous publications are *The Economic Problems of the Church* (1956), *Society and Puritanism in Pre-revolutionary England* (1964), and *The World Turned Upside Down* (1972). His Pelican edition of the works of Gerrard Winstanley was published in 1973.

HANNSJOACHIM WOLFGANG KOCH read history and American studies at Keele, and has taught history at the University of York since 1965. He is particularly interested in twentieth-century German history and has written on *The Origins of the First World War* (1972) and *Hitler Youth* (1972).

DONALD HENSHAW PENNINGTON was a history Scholar at Balliol College, where he has been a Fellow since 1965. Previously he was Reader in Modern History at the University of Manchester. He published *Members of the Long Parliament* (written in collaboration with D. Brunton) in 1954 and was co-editor with Ivan Roots of *The Committee at Stafford 1643–5* (1957). His stimulating textbook, *Seventeenth Century Europe,* appeared in 1970.

GEORGE DANIEL RAMSAY has been a Fellow and Tutor at St. Edmund Hall, Oxford, since 1937. He has specialized in Tudor and Stuart economic history. His publications include *The Wiltshire Woollen Industry in the 16th and 17th Centuries* (1948) and *English Overseas Trade during the Centuries of Emergence* (1957). He also contributed to the third volume of the *New Cambridge Modern History* (1968).

HUGH REDWALL TREVOR-ROPER has been Regius Professor of Modern History at Oxford since 1956. His first two books—*Archbishop Laud* (1940) and *The Last Days of Hitler* (1947)—point to two abiding interests: the early Stuarts and Nazi Germany. He has made substantial and controversial contributions to the debates over "the rise of the gentry" and "the general crisis of the seventeenth century." His major essays are collected in *Religion, the Reformation and Social Change* (1967).

AUSTIN HERBERT WOOLRYCH was educated at Oxford and has been Professor of History at the University of Lancaster since its inception in 1964. He has written extensively on aspects of the Interregnum, notably on Barebone's Parliament and the fall of the Republic. His publications include *Battles of the English Civil War* (1961), and a short life of Oliver Cromwell (1964).

Editors

Ivan Roots read modern history at Balliol College and lectured at University College, Cardiff, from 1946 to 1967. He was visiting professor at Lafayette College in 1960–1. In 1967 he was appointed Professor of History at Exeter University and since 1971 has held the title of Professor of Modern History. Professor Roots is interested in most aspects of seventeenth-century history but particularly in the Interregnum, including its local dimension. With D. H. Pennington he published in 1957 *The Committee at Stafford,* an edition of the Order Book from 1643–5 of the Staffordshire County Committee. His *The Great Rebellion 1642–60* appeared in 1966 (3rd ed. 1972). He edited *Conflicts in Tudor and Stuart England* (1968) and wrote the chapter on "Die Englische Revolution" for *Propylaën–Weltgeschichte* (1964). He has contributed articles to *The English Revolution,* ed. E. W. Ives (1968), *The English Civil War and After,* ed. R. H. Parry (1970), and (on Cromwell's Ordinances) to G. E. Aylmer's *The Interregnum 1646–60* (1972). He has published a lecture, *The Late Trouble in England* (1969), which assesses some current interpretations of Cromwell's times. He is currently working on the early Stuart volume of *English Historical Documents* and a textbook, *The Stuart Era.*

Aïda DiPace Donald holds degrees from Barnard and Columbia and a Ph.D. from the University of Rochester. A former member of the History Department at Columbia, Mrs. Donald has been a Fulbright Fellow at Oxford and the recipient of an A.A.U.W. fellowship. She has edited *John F. Kennedy and the New Frontier* and *Diary of Charles Francis Adams.*